The New York Times

Crossword Puzzle

OMNIBUS

Volume 2

Over 200 easy-to-hard puzzles
from The New York Times
to delight and challenge
the crossword fanatic

With a Foreword by
Will Weng

The New York Times

Crossword Puzzle Editor, Emeritus

Times
BOOKS

The puzzles that comprise this volume have been previously
published as *The New York Times Daily Crossword Puzzles, Vols. 4-8.*

SOLUTIONS TO THE PUZZLES ARE FOUND AT THE BACK OF THE BOOK.

Published by TIMES BOOKS, a division of Quadrangle/The New York Times
Book Co., Inc., Three Park Avenue, New York, N.Y. 10016

Published simultaneously in Canada by Fitzhenry & Whiteside, Ltd., Toronto

ISBN 0-8129-1018-4

Manufactured in the United States of America

10 9 8 7 6 5 4 3 2 1

FOREWORD

Assuming that you are one of those crossword solvers who like a bit of outside help on occasion, what sort of help is reasonable?

First, of course, it's handy to have a dictionary, preferably one on the collegiate level if you don't feel like going whole-hog with an unabridged one.

To supplement this, a crossword puzzle dictionary has its values. A moderately priced paperback edition will do. Basically one needs it for help on way-out short words such as the answer to "Killer whale" (orca), "Hindu pillar" (lat), "Two-toed sloth" (unau), and such. Finding such words this way really isn't cheating—it's more like taking a shortcut.

And finally a standard paperback almanac is helpful—such as the *World, Hammond, Information Please* or any other. It is a goldmine for finding such things as state flowers, birthstones, actors' names, astronauts, Nobel Prize winners and a host of other data.

The puzzles in this omnibus are all from the daily *New York Times* and should not require too much delving in reference works. They were designed for solving on buses and in offices. But even so there will be occasional unfamiliar short words. People who make the puzzles have problems, too.

One advantage here is that if all else fails, a quick peek at the answer in the back of the book may help. But only as a matter of last resort.

—Will Weng

1

ACROSS

1. North Atlantic fish
6. Spanish relatives
10. Swindles
14. Goddesses of the seasons
15. Heraldic band
16. Mohammedan priest
17. Semblance
18. Goad
19. Be "in"
20. Hawaiian island
22. Take it all back
24. Musical direction
26. Greek letter
27. Smear
30. Sitting in for
35. Roman spirit
36. __-frutti
38. Light craft
39. State
41. Pools
43. French dream
44. Verne character and others
46. Passover rite
48. Legal thing
49. "La __"
51. Lie close
53. Newt
54. Cup, in France
56. American novelist
60. Go over
64. Sharpen
65. Sinister glance
67. Overgrown, in a way
68. "__ the fence is out"
69. Fluid rock
70. Cape __ Islands
71. Gulls
72. Tarry
73. Eat, in Berlin

DOWN

1. Wedge of wood or metal
2. Lake or Perry
3. Russian range
4. Bangkok sight
5. Try to reach
6. Theme
7. Type of verb: Abbr.
8. African plant
9. Dignified
10. Type of staircase
11. Persian name
12. International org.
13. Diving duck
21. Collector's book
23. Soft mineral
25. Legal copy
27. Like a used pencil
28. Chewer
29. Albee's field
31. Mixed up, as type
32. Indolent
33. Unusual
34. Silly creatures
37. Exam
40. Birds, at times
42. One of five
45. Study, as clues
47. Fidgety
50. Bikini and Eniwetok
52. Answers a purpose
55. Adorn
56. Pronoun
57. Stopped a ship's motion, with "to"
58. Over again
59. Undiluted
61. Tunes
62. Give up
63. Garden
66. Girl's name

2

ACROSS

1. Without variations
8. Gasconader
15. Area in an arsenal
16. Raised on high
17. Arranges the pool balls
18. Examines
19. Inner: Prefix
20. "Origin of __"
22. Counterpart of ASCAP
23. Avoid
25. Committed a faux pas
26. Rack's partner
27. Arrangement
29. Poetic contraction
30. Glass slabs
31. Inhabitants of communes, ideally
33. City slickers
34. Zeros
35. W.W. I spy
36. Beverage
38. Rainy day scarcity
41. Economical one
42. Prohibit
43. "Dear Sir or __"
45. Infuriates
46. One of the Keys
48. "Zhivago" heroine
49. Disfigure
50. Letter
52. Brit. medical degrees
53. Draw a mental picture
55. Often-nice girls
57. Table vegetables
58. Cartilage
59. Rudimentary principle
60. Imposing

DOWN

1. Exit for Barnum
2. Puts down
3. Ill-mannered
4. __ of the covenant
5. Tweed, for one
6. Jeweler's glass
7. Monarchs
8. More occupied
9. Made a choice
10. Catch __
11. Sward
12. Defender of the people
13. Belligerents
14. Varnish ingredients
21. Louder, in music: Abbr.
24. Shades
26. Extremist
28. Monastery man
30. Jewish festival
32. Highest note
33. French spa
35. Wall decorations
36. Candy-counter item
37. Amount in excess
38. Nicotines' partners
39. Nudist
40. Item for a gymnast
41. Poetic device
42. Of the lowest kind
44. Former film actor Raymond
46. Fabric
47. Manifest
50. Imitator
51. Kazan
54. Sticky substance
56. Naval vessel: Abbr.

3

ACROSS

1. Social insect
5. Port of Spain
10. Where Tabriz is
14. Resound
15. Market place
16. Isinglass
17. Cupid
18. Diamond coup
20. Utensil ware
22. Councils in Europe
23. Hesitates
26. Recent: Prefix
27. Limber
29. Audience
31. Oxidizes
35. Hair style
36. Florida resort town
39. Pack
40. First __
41. Garden frame
43. Wonder
44. Boor
46. Customer
47. Exclamation
48. Lumberman
50. Ten rin
51. Awake
53. Tiny __
55. Unchanging
57. Thankful
61. Enhance
64. Playwriting
67. Post
68. Coin
69. Oakley
70. West Coast campus
71. Spots
72. Minimal
73. Passé dance

DOWN

1. Drip
2. Israeli port
3. Where the mannequins are
4. Kind of zone
5. Chaplain
6. In the past
7. Lady in a poem
8. Spheres
9. Art gallery
10. Profane
11. Vex
12. ". . . to skin __"
13. Some votes
19. Hardly __
21. Happening
24. Drives off
25. Quips
27. Disconcert
28. Duplicity
30. Yield
32. John Wayne oldie
33. Stand high
34. Fragrant
37. Curved line
38. Err
42. U.S. department
45. In good season
49. Latvian gulf
52. Acid indicator
54. Gold, for instance
56. Up till now
57. Race-track term
58. Cheese
59. Cloth
60. Sandhill
62. Threadlike structures
63. Ensign
65. Basic cell substance
66. U.S. troops

4

A crossword puzzle grid (partially filled in by hand) with the following clues:

ACROSS

1. Bird call
4. Prepares apples
9. Venus's island
13. Italian port on Adriatic
14. Wagnerian work
15. First letter: Abbr.
16. Thoroughfares: Abbr.
17. __ base
18. Siva's wife
19. Spots for statues
21. Avails oneself of
23. Birds, of a sort
25. Knowing
26. Fuel gas
31. Blood substances
36. Suppressed
37. Congers
38. Urban blight
40. Direction, in Paris
41. Indian maids
43. Eskimo's wherewithal
45. Ante
47. Washington
48. Condiment
54. Clearance, of a sort
58. Ancient city-state
59. Surrounded by
60. Kind of fund
62. Pigeon breeds
63. Occasion
64. San __, Calif.
65. Hill crest, in England
66. Laurel
67. "All wool and __ wide"
68. Word of agreement

DOWN

1. Find fault
2. Asian palm
3. Weak
4. Is made up of
5. W.W. II agency
6. Musical show
7. Muse
8. Like the ocean
9. Skirt
10. Girl's name
11. Like some TV
12. Early patriot
13. Judge's seat
20. "Iliad," for one
22. Vessels at Anzio landing
24. Earth scientists: Abbr.
27. Devious activity
28. Thine: Fr.
29. Goddess of destiny
30. Things to make meet
31. Harvest
32. Blood: Prefix
33. Custard pastry
34. Herb of grace
35. Fishing vessel
39. Careless
42. U-boats
44. ". . . a giant __ for mankind"
46. Transfusion material
49. Put to rest
50. Port opposite Gibraltar
51. Tidy the hedge
52. Lab items
53. File
54. Butter, oleo, etc.
55. Copy: Abbr.
56. Terza __
57. Anthony
61. Religious discourse: Abbr.

5

ACROSS

1. Detroit players
6. "__ small world"
10. Merry sound
14. Leading
15. Cruise
16. Bovines
17. Silly talk
18. Sooner
20. Mark in curling
21. Key Biscayne, for one
23. Poison for arrow tips
24. "And __ grow on"
25. Hot iron
26. Roman 1970
29. Have-nots
31. Egg-shaped
32. Capek of "R.U.R." fame
33. Pastured
36. Rare
40. Stain
41. Promenades
42. Egyptian singing girl
43. Voodoo
44. Cash keeper
46. Plods through mire
48. Scented
50. Deposit
51. Arctic canoe
52. Through: Prefix
55. Span
57. "Of thee __"
59. Tributary of Seine
60. Olympian goddess
61. Neighbor of Sverige
62. Asian weight
63. Large quantity
64. Sights in Holland

DOWN

1. Choir's place
2. Regarding
3. Western Indian
4. "__ as a Stranger"
5. Enigmatic one
6. Lady of Arthurian romance
7. Act like a champ
8. Muddy deposit
9. Term in cookery
10. Cheer
11. Logger
12. Got wind of
13. Bancroft
19. Obstacle
22. Latin 6
24. Word for a shoppe
25. Charqui
26. Humor
27. Rabbit
28. Small game for tabby
30. Discord goddess
32. Persian carpet
33. Coins of Iraq and Jordan
34. Madame Bovary
35. Wild game
37. Counterparts
38. Cheap platers
39. Pastry item
43. Small amount
44. Girl's nickname
45. Harsh
46. Narrow groove
47. Kind of change
49. Cash in Turin
50. Glengarry man
51. Layer of the iris
52. Dagger
53. American dramatist
54. Dark __
56. Electrical unit
58. Self, in France

6

ACROSS

1. Moonlighting group
5. Awry
10. Basic principles
14. Acknowledges
15. Stock, in cards
16. Child lacking manners
17. Authentic
18. Webfooted animal
19. Movie dog
20. Speech sound
22. Book of Bible
24. Girl's nickname
25. Replay medium
26. Primps
29. Quit
33. Ex-Yankee pitcher
34. Peg for Hillary
35. New Havenite
36. Mil. addresses
37. Guinevere
38. Short rail extension
39. Gumshoe
40. Bacharach and Lancaster
41. Scold
42. Sources of baseball bats
44. Do-__
45. Slacken
46. Coalition
47. Alive
50. More posh
54. Sustain
55. Hawkeye
57. Pale color
58. Villain of drama
59. Player of Chan role
60. Becloud
61. Animal sac
62. Eelworms
63. Ko-Ko's weapon

DOWN

1. Ibsen role
2. Frightens
3. Easy job
4. __ not (in all probability)
5. Ermines
6. Soigné
7. Word for Adenauer
8. Adversary
9. Irrationality
10. Marbles
11. Baloney!
12. Shelter
13. Yard
21. Rave's pal
23. Weave
25. French heads
26. S.A. river
27. Things to know
28. Period in history
29. Skips second helpings
30. Not so hot
31. Slip away from
32. More desperate
34. Soup
37. Wonder about
38. Horror movies
40. Light brown
41. Animal, for short
43. Drink-maker
44. Endocrines
46. Master, in Africa
47. "Odyssey," for one
48. Lab picture
49. Clothing
50. Enjoyed the surf
51. Image
52. Canal
53. __ of thumb
56. Cheer in Madrid

7

ACROSS

1. Mother of Isaac
6. Word for a young person
12. Famous shrine
13. Meandered
15. Tremble
16. Relinquish
17. Instrument: Suffix
18. Roman dictator
20. "___ one's life depended on it"
21. Soviet sea
22. Grafted, in heraldry
23. Feat of skill
24. Keep ___ on
25. You: Ger.
26. Football throw
27. Spanish queen
28. Expensive
29. Vivacious
30. Jargon
31. Members of blind trio
32. Goes for a spin
35. Yawn
36. Certain voter: Abbr.
39. Show
40. Irving's sleeper
41. Lustrous cloth
42. Like meshed fabric
43. Stun
44. Rara ___
45. Sandarac tree
46. Foreshadowed
47. Sleep uneasily
48. Form a passage
50. Excessively
52. Drew out
53. Dealer in hot goods
54. Recent
55. Honored

DOWN

1. Of a desert
2. "Arabian Nights" character
3. Becomes frayed
4. Soul: Fr.
5. Prudent judgment
6. Casino furniture
7. Sicilian city
8. Nigerian town
9. Debating side
10. Obliteration
11. Of part of the eye
13. Reuther or Scott
14. With dexterity
15. Roofing material
19. Eastern-rite Christian
23. Ingredient of a girl
26. Decamped
28. "Pride and Prejudice" hero
30. Kind of bridge
31. Corn color
32. Threat
33. Generally
34. Oberon's better half
35. Worked on a road
36. Reno specialty
37. Isolated
38. Having great bulk
41. Evident
43. Tractor-driven machine
46. Morsel
49. Illuminated
51. Churchill sign

8

ACROSS

1. Inky sea creature
6. Impossible dream
13. Treeless plain
15. Balloon rider
17. Food share
18. Revives
19. Freshen, as linens
20. __ fide
21. Poker round
22. Like a nervous stomach
24. Conduit
25. One-time editor's wear
26. Metric unit
27. Living-room sets
28. Beluga's gift to man
29. Electrical units
34. Stirs up
35. Hitchcock subject
36. Word with chicken or small
37. Regarding
38. Olympics contestant
44. __ majesty
45. Historic Utah rail site
46. Chemical endings
47. French milk
48. Grisly
49. Table wine
51. Martyred Armenian saint
52. Washington, Adams and Jefferson
53. Kind of pitch
54. Harden, as glue
55. British guns

DOWN

1. Rake with fire
2. Plover of Canada
3. Fallacious
4. Know-nothings
5. Farmer's fear
6. Taxi men
7. Water birds
8. Enraging
9. First name in Louvre
10. School course: Abbr.
11. Noted Russian
12. "__ of the Breakfast Table"
14. Aardvark
16. Walks off balance
23. Meets by arrangement: Abbr.
24. Disreputable place
26. Take it on the __
28. Pretentious fops
29. Dumbfounded
30. Husband of Helen of Troy
31. Sales tactic
32. Sea bird
33. Spoil
34. Kind of rubber
36. Remonstrate
38. Threesomes
39. Mounds
40. Difficulty
41. __ one's time
42. Up
43. U.S. painter and family
45. Cleveland suburb
47. Page
50. Explosive

9

ACROSS

1. One kind of race
6. Jenny Lind or Greta Garbo
11. Room in a harem
14. Part of a Virginia Woolf title
15. Grew ashen
16. Girl's nickname
17. Water activity
19. Language: Abbr.
20. Reward for a good horse
21. Distinction
22. Press agent's concern
24. Bowling alley
25. Hymn of praise
27. Have reference
30. Mineral suitable for jewelry
33. Incensed
34. Harass
35. Word with brass or banana
36. Tabletop décor
37. Gentleman of Acapulco
38. Emphatic negative
39. Superlative ending
40. Havelock
41. Let go
42. Light again
44. Conveyance of sorts
45. Wants
46. Vote count
47. Port of Brazil
49. Giants' old grounds
50. Certain G.I.
53. Nickname for a Greek
54. Having sway
58. Rubbing fluid: Abbr.
59. Fisherman
60. Nerve networks
61. Traveler's rider
62. Beans
63. Long

DOWN

1. Door fastener
2. Killer whale
3. Debacle
4. Sound of sorrow
5. Flow out
6. Malice
7. Beauty-parlor job
8. Hebrew priest
9. __ of thieves
10. Most nervous
11. Reciprocal pronoun
12. Rural oath
13. Heavenly creature: Fr.
18. "Thy will be __"
23. Launching pad for an acrobat
24. Recent
25. Mexican money
26. New World resident: Abbr.
27. Housatonic
28. Remove
29. Bringing up the rear
30. Aladdin's friend
31. Canonical hour
32. Lyric poem
34. Haberdashery items
37. Coasted
38. Not written
40. Ill-wishers
41. Convict population
43. Direction to a horse
44. __ in one
46. Presides at tea
47. Event for Cinderella
48. Canal finished in 1825
49. Legal action
50. Cordage fiber
51. "My __ Lady"
52. Social group
55. Prefix with classic or mycin
56. Texas leaguer
57. Launching pad on the links

10

ACROSS

1. Kind of hist.
4. Southern city
9. Savvy
12. Pastures
14. U.S.S.R. mountains
15. Put aside
16. Soaking
18. Unvaried
19. Great Lake
20. Safari redcaps
22. Signs
23. Pennsylvania city
24. __ de Boulogne
25. Sheep-counter's ailment
29. Arithmetic word
30. Favoring
31. "When day __"
33. Mild expletive
34. Bridge call
36. Roman dates
37. Remove by erosion
39. Religious group: Abbr.
40. North or South
41. Medicine injectors
43. Citrus fruit
44. Allot
45. Appetizer spread
46. Crusaders' foe
49. Shallow baking dish
52. Urge
53. Envelope contents
55. "__ Karenina"
56. Cordage fiber
57. Sediment
58. Jane __
59. Hebrew letter
60. Alphabet letter

DOWN

1. Likewise
2. Kind of sign
3. In a faultfinding way
4. North African city
5. Jason's ship
6. Cavernous opening
7. Military freshmen
8. Minor planets
9. __ a heart
10. Always
11. Submarine docks
13. Medina-Sidonia's fleet
15. Able to make lucky discoveries
17. Irritates
21. Objectives
24. Unshaped masses
25. Anger
26. Aristocrat
27. Of an antiseptic test
28. Anoint, old style
29. Snead's org.
30. Most attractive
32. Compass point
35. Suppliers of the ego
38. Started off a game
42. Kind of elbow
43. Varnish ingredients
45. Pulitzer novelist of 1918
46. Mining nail
47. Italian river
48. Certain ranger
49. Dressed
50. Prefix with meter and printer
51. Punta del __
54. Civil War initials

11

ACROSS

1. Large moth
5. Owns
8. Desert in northeast Sudan
14. Short saying
16. Lack of muscle coordination
17. Hemingway's "A __ Feast"
18. Tedious
19. Collection of items
20. Park features
22. Pieces of fuel turf
23. Hone
24. What a Manx lacks
26. __ escape
29. Inhabitants of southern Asia
33. Willow
34. Couch
35. Pol. party
36. Draw
37. Member of the electorate
38. Comet's head
39. Beverage
40. Dotted patterns, in heraldry
41. Weight unit
42. Chemical warfare weapon
44. Procession
45. Jai __
46. Chalcedony
47. Lewis Carroll animal
50. Artless
52. Dante's gal
55. City of Crete
57. Infant garments
59. William Waldorf and John Jacob
60. Civil War vessel
61. Word of appreciation
62. Feminine suffix
63. Deep cut

DOWN

1. Tibetan priest
2. Atop
3. Kind of star
4. Consumed
5. Mideast language
6. Shoelace tip
7. U.S. duck
8. Seize
9. Visionary
10. Just about
11. South African iris
12. Common contraction of sorts
13. Some horses
15. Egyptian goddess of mirth
21. Verses
23. Small bird
25. Winged
26. Man without a country
27. Sotto voce
28. Versifier: Var.
29. Small sums
30. Ancient assembly
31. Rover
32. Sudden outburst
34. Sphere of activity
37. Bright star
38. Droll fellow, familiarly
40. Original Robinson Crusoe
41. Course
43. Golf star of past
44. Roadbuilders
46. Fathers
47. Go away!
48. Old auto
49. Broadway group: Abbr.
51. Culmination
52. Part of an Eastern church
53. Epochs
54. Sholem __, novelist
56. Blockhead
58. Iron mold

12

ACROSS

1. Navy trials aboard ship
6. Sultan of __
10. Accepted: Abbr.
14. Honolulu greeting
15. Old ale jug
16. Past
17. Noted sculptor
18. Colonizer of Greenland
19. Directed
20. Coldstream men
22. Spartan king
24. Manual-training system
26. Slips
27. Old Spanish coins
30. Conveyance
31. Greek nickname
32. Library contents
34. Famed Swede
38. St. Andrews sport
40. Ice pinnacle
42. Hit it on the __
43. Organic compounds
45. Scandinavian wind god
47. Spanish article
48. Exclamation
50. Gargantuan
52. Ceramist
55. Brown print
56. Underwater apparatus
58. Latin gentlemen
62. Indonesian islands: Var.
63. Seaweed product
65. Soda adjunct
66. Camera part
67. Alaskan port
68. Extreme
69. Cattle feed
70. Waste allowance
71. Manchurian city

DOWN

1. Page edge: Abbr.
2. Matty of baseball
3. Scotch's companion
4. Craving
5. Ballfield of sorts
6. Sault __ Marie
7. October event
8. Name in long-run play
9. Famous Tiger
10. Dodger's Jackie
11. Sidestep
12. Kind of closet
13. Mini or midi
21. Arias
23. Certain word
25. Arab republic
27. Senate employee
28. Golf club
29. Missile housing
33. French river
35. Machete
36. Jacob's brother
37. Subtraction word
39. Dodgers' old home
41. Harvests
44. Queens landmark
46. Parches
49. Unmitigated
51. Mickey of the Yankees
52. Work of David
53. Botanical sheath
54. Changes color, as a leaf
57. Stravinsky
59. Straight: Prefix
60. __ avis
61. Graceful bird
64. Inactive: Abbr.

13

ACROSS

1. Prefix for physics
5. Small type
10. Spaniard's cloak
14. Encourage
15. Aromatic seeds
16. Elliptical
17. Bonbon
19. Dickens heroine
20. Whole
21. Consoles
23. Diameter parts
26. Franklin
27. Make a new judgment on
30. News hot off the press
34. Overlook
35. Adores
37. Army man: Abbr.
38. Relative, for short
39. Down-to-earth person
41. Stock-market quotation
42. Wing of a building
43. La Douce et al.
44. Hock
45. Equivalent of believing
47. Loams
50. Long __
51. Explode
52. Advance
56. Armed merchant ship
60. Melville hero
61. Colorful
64. S. A. country
65. Congo-Sudanese people
66. Abhor
67. Impertinence
68. Feminine suffixes
69. Greek god

DOWN

1. Spice
2. Black
3. Loose dress
4. ". . . loved not __ sight?"
5. Consent
6. Violin-string material
7. Friend, in France
8. Spanish uncles
9. Elevates
10. U.S. educator
11. With: Fr.
12. Enclosure
13. "__ well"
18. Periods
22. Minimal
24. Religion of East
25. Set apart
27. Flowers
28. Rousseau's fictional pupil
29. Two on the __
31. Chou __
32. Angry look
33. Localities
36. Shade
39. Starr
40. Argue logically
44. Covered vase
46. Metrical foot
48. Soups
49. Resorts
52. Soft foods
53. Big bird
54. Paddles
55. Common Latin verb
57. First word of a letter
58. Within: Prefix
59. U.S. 1 and others: Abbr.
62. Savings-bank word: Abbr.
63. Presidential initials

14

ACROSS

1. Cast out
6. Alps or Andes: Abbr.
10. Color
14. __ will (testate)
15. Paducah river
16. Piped
17. Auto rider's insurance
19. __-cake
20. Roulade
21. Shelter, in Soho
22. Lawful
23. Hoist
27. Slough
28. Performs
29. Daisy
31. Egg cells
32. Wash. agency
36. Physicist's concern
40. Superlative endings
41. Morsel
42. Perch
43. Native of Zanzibar
46. Sgt., e.g.
47. Hawk, so to speak
52. Wing-shaped
53. Wool: Prefix
54. Tennis score
55. Plant of pea family
56. Catcher's equipment
60. Hardwood
61. First-rate
62. Seething
63. Present-day netman
64. Hear ye!
65. Confab à la hippie

DOWN

1. Loop sights
2. Auto components
3. Shining
4. Office employee
5. Make lace
6. Capone, for one
7. Last stop
8. Naught
9. Inebriate
10. Garnish
11. Medicaster
12. Before
13. Playing marble
18. Couple, as oxen
22. __ Cruces
24. Indian of Canada
25. Hindu goddess
26. Subway, busses, etc.: Abbr.
27. European fish
30. Metallic elements: Abbr.
32. Tail: Prefix
33. Evergreen of Europe
34. Refuse to believe
35. Renowned Roman
37. Front seats in a theater
38. Algerian port
39. The Red
43. Furtive
44. Blasco-__, author of "Four Horsemen"
45. Auld __ syne
47. __ mañana
48. Agalloch
49. Indian leader
50. English admiral
51. Mecca shrine
56. __ Paulo
57. Heavy barge
58. Mideast initials
59. Road sign

15

ACROSS

1. Hawaiian gifts
5. Walk nervously
9. Ancient region of Asia Minor
14. Part of an auto
15. Blunders
16. Old Greek coins
17. River to the Colorado
18. Moderately priced
20. Thoroughly excellent
22. Ceremonies
23. Kind of nut
24. Bourbon St. feature
25. Oriental nurses
28. Servicing a dinner party
32. Levee sights of old
33. One past recovery
34. Tumultuous sound
35. Book holders
36. Raise livestock
37. Bristlelike part
38. Donkey, in France
39. Pointed instruments
40. Set in operation
41. Officious meddlers
43. Borders, in heraldry
44. Garden implement
45. Portico
47. One of a Tolstoi pair
49. TV divisions
53. Name in detective fiction
55. Courage
56. Kind of sanctum
57. Hunter's cry to hounds
58. Existence: Lat.
59. Exploits
60. Sweetsop
61. Nurture

DOWN

1. Falls behind
2. Stage direction
3. That, to Cicero
4. Explores
5. Jeopardy
6. Amphitheater
7. Jutting rock
8. Sigmoidal figure
9. Pine or spruce
10. Subtracter
11. Vestment
12. Misfortunes
13. Peer Gynt's mother
19. Made a formal speech
21. Minus-yardage in football
24. Certain candy shapes
25. Nautical word
26. Divine food
27. Northern tree
28. Some college students
29. Standard of perfection
30. Saltpeter
31. Annoying insects
33. British historian
36. Wall Street man
37. "__ in Paradise"
39. Surface mineral deposits
40. Promptly
42. Babbled
45. Portion
46. Armored vehicles
47. Yearn
48. Old slave
49. Talk, in a way
50. Gaelic
51. Mona __
52. Silver: Abbr.
53. Word with day or night
54. Rolled tea

16

ACROSS

1. Economize
7. After this, twilight
13. Eternally
14. Boone was one
16. Rival
17. King Arthur's mother
18. In medias __
19. Cuddled up
21. Open a barrel
22. Spatiate
24. Rumbullions
25. __ Raton
26. Be philanthropic
28. "__ Rheingold"
29. Handles, as a shrew
30. Jiggled
32. Up-to-the-minute
33. Skedaddled
34. Indian of Colombia
35. Declare
38. Withers
42. Baseball's hot corner
43. Companion of cry
44. Last straw
45. Participants in
24 Across
46. Met basso
48. Eldest: Fr.
49. Be beholden to
50. Tossed to and fro
52. Educ. group
53. Domestic
55. Giants or Jets
57. Territory on Adriatic
58. Surrounds
59. Pulled quickly
60. Out-of-studio TV
show

DOWN

1. Unidentified person
2. Zealot's enterprise
3. Electrical unit
4. Abdul the Bulbul's
rival
5. Gasman's reading
matter
6. Was chairman
7. Long-legged birds
8. Yens
9. Aromatic ointment
10. Saint-Tropez is one
11. Abstract
12. A-Q and K-J
13. Polecat's cousin
15. Meal
20. Natterjack
23. Carey and Shipton
25. City in New York
27. Mysterious
29. Language of Ceylon
31. Steep
32. Small ape
34. Tune-caller's creditor
35. Maximally
36. Raining off and on
37. Asian area
38. Brought to court
39. Noteworthy
40. Ancestry
41. Gets hot under the
collar
43. Insinuated
46. French toast
47. Old name for Ireland
50. Soak up sunshine
51. Campus building
54. City on 118 islands:
Abbr.
56. Spanish relative

17

ACROSS

1. Applaud
5. Moves
10. Thuringian city
14. Laugh
15. Sacred book
16. Assert
17. Caterpillar
20. Calif. time
21. Irish islands
22. Place of pleasant aromas
23. Disagreeable person: Slang
24. Broadway role
25. Abilities
28. Suffer from heat
31. Held and others
32. Swine
33. Pile
35. Pleasant
36. Nebs
37. Roman 1502
38. Overwhelm
39. Perry Mason's detective
40. Provide quarters
41. Gazing people
43. Made a breach in
44. Scarves
45. Byway
46. Expose
49. Saarinen
50. U.S. agency: Abbr.
53. Man who sees the dull side
56. "Pompeii" girl
57. Friction match
58. Spanish jar
59. Queries
60. Sumptuous meal
61. Slang for money

DOWN

1. Fellow
2. Moos
3. "There'll be __ time in . . ."
4. By: Sp.
5. Plays a bagpipe
6. Musical term
7. Persia, today
8. Brit. fliers
9. Shock absorbers
10. Book part
11. Bacchanal's cry
12. Close
13. Affected, in a way
18. Posts
19. Barriers
23. Frolic
24. Rouse
25. Mrs. Roosevelt
26. "Sees all, __ all"
27. Map addition
28. Penetrates, with "in"
29. Conclude
30. Lift
32. Trio of children's story
34. Jumbled, as type
36. Discontinue
37. Brood
39. Waste product
40. Asian capital
42. Degrades
43. Poet's traditional milieu
45. Laws: Lat.
46. Gov't. news agency
47. Army men: Abbr.
48. Fur
49. It, in Italy
50. Groundless
51. Amoeba
52. Suffix for demo or auto
54. Regret
55. Drink

18

ACROSS

1. Sphere of influence
7. Genus of African herb
13. In a wicked manner
14. Pop the question
16. Barren
17. Italian mush delicacy
18. Brother of Moses
19. Annual bank giveaway
20. Lily: Fr.
21. In the least
23. Fishing-fly barb
24. Syrian city, to French
26. Umpire's call
27. Oscar film of 1955
28. Mailer's "The __"
30. Declare verboten
31. Least interesting
32. Narcotics-squad man at times
35. O. T. book
36. Curse on an ocean cruise
38. Earthen pot
41. Basin
42. Swan or gainer
43. Run swiftly
44. Tear-sopping device
45. Fiber knot
46. Making use of
48. Good buy: Colloq.
50. Chanting
51. Feminine
53. Glut
54. Instanter
55. More hair-raising
56. Teased

DOWN

1. Gave chapter and verse
2. Supervisor
3. Spanish painter
4. Icelandic measure
5. Badly
6. U.S. humorist
7. Dismay
8. Fish, in a way
9. Part in a play
10. Munificent
11. Mull over
12. Suddenly
15. Betimes
16. Dieter's lunch
19. Part of a horseshoe
21. Embarrass
22. Biting
25. Borodin opera
27. Bit part in a play
29. Fast look
30. Recalcitrant
32. Downright
33. Natural elevation
34. Uncovered
36. Fine vase
37. Answer
38. Pursue
39. Small valley
40. City in New Jersey
41. Family-planning pioneer
44. Turning point
47. River of central Italy
48. Air-pollution factor
49. Pungent flavor
51. Civil or Crimean
52. Japanese river

19

ACROSS

1. Rotating machine part
4. Highway stops
10. Greek letters
14. Caucasian language
15. Turkish inn
16. "__ Britannia"
17. Excessive thirst
19. Initiate
20. Gay
21. Farming: Abbr.
22. Father: Prefix
23. Borscht topping
29. Gasket
30. Vistas
31. Restraint
32. Black: Prefix
33. Map lines: Abbr.
34. Misery
37. Pier, in architecture
41. Angers
42. Skyborne
47. Victim, of a sort
49. Button source
50. Porringers
51. Dutch __
52. Civil War soldier
53. Heathen
54. Issue
56. Portliness
61. Princess of India
62. Mosaic gold
63. Screw pines of Pacific
64. Restrained eating
65. Forest paths
66. Snake

DOWN

1. Trophy
2. Worship: Lat.
3. Home reserve
4. Snack time for some
5. Leave out
6. Faucet
7. Hesitant sounds
8. Garland
9. Depot: Abbr.
10. Usher's offering
11. Sherbet glass
12. __ de France
13. Japanese coin
18. Tales
21. Summit: Prefix
22. Warsaw's land: Abbr.
23. Undersized person
24. Breakfast dish
25. States of turmoil
26. Circular: Scot.
27. Swiss river
28. Future books: Abbr.
35. I hear, in Spain
36. Son of Zeus doomed to frustration
37. "The jawbone of an __"
38. Cpl. or sgt.
39. Resembling a bull
40. "Bon __!"
43. Kind of order
44. Pacific island area
45. Langford or Perkins
46. Vietnamese holiday
48. Decline
53. Influence
54. European shrew
55. French month
56. Camper's item
57. British peace Nobelist
58. British West Point: Abbr.
59. Oahu fare
60. Form of precognition: Abbr.

20

ACROSS

1. Oceanic tunicate
5. Bum __
8. Pointed tool
12. Hebrew month
13. Historic periods
15. City on the Seyhan
17. Returns
19. French sculptor
20. Okefenokee feature
21. Small cask
23. Plagiarize
24. Ad lib
27. Embrace
30. Menlo Park monogram
31. La __
32. Where the Shannon flows: Abbr.
33. Mild expletives
35. Soda __
38. Camping gear
40. Puts an end to
43. Mother of the Titans
44. Stripling
46. Spanish article
47. Oriental name
49. Weeks in the year: Lat.
50. With reference
51. Musician
55. Norse god
56. Ordinal ending
57. Castle or Dunne
60. Consternate
62. East African
65. Norwegian playwright
66. Formerly
67. Words for a bit more
68. Meeting: Abbr.
69. Back, in France
70. Does fancy work

DOWN

1. Bearish time
2. Star in Draco
3. Certain debris
4. Made raids on
5. Debater's second round
6. The Altar
7. Peddlers
8. Normal quality
9. Reveres
10. Seaport of Spain
11. Bolo, for one
14. Beehive
16. Hill dweller
18. Red or White
22. Certain party: Abbr.
25. Kind of bird
26. Oriental V.I.P.
27. White lie
28. Neighbor of Nev.
29. Mother of Helen of Troy
33. Factotum
34. Seafood
36. Poison ivy genus
37. English county
39. Gains
41. Employs
42. __ Paulo
45. Veteran
48. African hemp
50. ". . . things __ what they seem"
51. Aerosol devices
52. Edict
53. "Tell __ the marines"
54. Period
55. Chou En-__
58. Act of 1930s: Abbr.
59. "__ of Eden"
61. Letters
63. Army man: Abbr.
64. Some votes

ACROSS

1. Miss Marple
5. Never-lose lawyer
10. Family members
14. The __ Duke (Wellington)
15. Bone: Prefix
16. Broadway hero
17. Conrad's "__ Jim"
18. Twenty: Prefix
19. Civil wrong
20. Procrastinator's time
22. Sam Spade or Philo Vance
24. Horse color
25. Brew, in Munich
26. Comprehends
29. Urgent
33. Rajah's wife
34. Unrefined
35. Chaney
36. Retired
37. Move aside
38. Hindu deity
39. Luzon town
40. Stretches over
41. Type of berth
42. Old clerical scarf
44. Nuremberg events of 1945-6
45. Storm
46. Small talk
47. Spread open
50. Strangles: Var.
54. Nick Charles's wife
55. Battery part
57. Jot
58. Greek ruler of Syracuse
59. Extort from
60. Hebrew letters
61. Russian queen
62. Western park
63. Pâté de foie __

DOWN

1. Cast aside
2. Irish exclamation
3. Standard
4. Approved
5. Shearer and others
6. Type of sponge
7. Pack
8. Alphabet letters
9. Most raucous
10. Office stamps
11. __ ben Adhem
12. Soil
13. Thomas of clock fame
21. Cheap cigar
23. Minus
25. Seed coats
26. Galahad's quest
27. Amateur sleuth who slept late
28. Close by, in poems
29. Make concise
30. Ancient Spanish town
31. Out of the ordinary
32. Growls
34. Scabbard trim
37. Lost liquid
38. One kind of image
40. Boom
41. Mineral
43. Lizard
44. "Bad things come in __"
46. Put the bite on
47. Release
48. Short fiber
49. Amphibian
50. Foot ailment
51. Duty turn
52. Volcano
53. Talk back
56. Digits: Abbr.

ACROSS

1. Show
5. Pickpockets: Slang
9. Monopolized, with "up"
14. Nautical direction
15. "The very __!"
16. Famed fountain
17. Register
18. Dickens heroine
19. Free
20. Air-conditioning, so to speak
23. Sandwich, for short
24. __ Alamos
25. Floral leaf
27. Milieu for cop on the beat
32. List
35. Timetable abbreviation
36. Litigants
38. Shampoo cycle
39. One-time Turkish governors
41. Cheers
43. Swerve
44. Actress Stevens
46. Anaconda
48. Poet's word
49. Gender
51. Shakes
53. Stowed
55. Cover
56. One of D.D.E.'s titles
58. Impetuous
64. Peppery sound
66. Galway country
67. Noted marsupial
68. "__ evil . . ."
69. Mailbox part
70. Mine car
71. Annexed
72. Disseminates
73. Deal

DOWN

1. Tuileries Gardens, e.g.
2. Spread
3. Collation
4. Hawk
5. Alley Oop's mount
6. Common footnote
7. Lucre
8. Name for Shropshire
9. Speak haltingly
10. Sea bird
11. Killjoy
12. Corrupt
13. Regimen
21. Browbeats
22. Holzman or Grange
26. Monkshood
27. Developer of polio vaccine
28. Greek goddess
29. Killed from ambush
30. People born in July and August
31. Swedish coin
33. River in France
34. Delaware resort city
37. Dance extra
40. Bristle
42. Pans
45. California sight
47. Cause: Prefix
50. Pacific herb
52. Embraces
54. Gown
56. House, in Spain
57. Kind of tea
59. Wheeler-dealer of "Catch-22"
60. Edge of a hill
61. Dumb one
62. Equal: Fr.
63. Vault
65. Pronoun

23

ACROSS

1. Kashmir people
6. U.S. jurist
9. Feigns
13. On the other hand
14. Pronoun
16. Sound of thunder
17. Sublease
18. Hypocritical
20. Get new bearings
22. Ventilate
23. Soot
24. Modified
25. "Dear __"
28. Certain felons
30. Invent
32. Spanish hero
33. Printing style: Abbr.
36. Equivalent of a miss
37. Divinity degrees
38. Money: Slang
39. Carry on
40. Ruby or Sandra
41. Author of "Almayer's Folly"
42. Toothlike formation
45. Affirmative
46. New Netherland landholder
48. Mine car
50. African antelopes
51. Learned society of France
55. Other than indicated
57. Numbskull
58. Huntley
59. Maneuverable, as a ship
60. Tuscan city
61. Assuage
62. ". . . ring I thee __"
63. Rational faculty in Buddhism

DOWN

1. English lawyer: Abbr.
2. American author
3. French composer
4. Stadium sections
5. Hint
6. Cheap dives
7. Polly, to Tom Sawyer
8. Parts of cens.
9. Process of growth
10. High area of a cathedral: Var.
11. Item in a Paris bakery
12. Momentum
15. Alderfly
19. Meshed fabrics
21. River to the Seine
24. Black cuckoos
25. Cicatrix
26. Girl's name
27. Puts back
29. Music group
31. Take turns
34. Wings
35. Boys
37. Green or snap
38. Doctrine expounded by Leibnitz
40. Full of impurities
41. Girl's name
43. McKuen and Serling
44. Suffered from mosquito bites
46. Shilling components
47. Greeting
49. Press, radio, etc.
51. Farm unit
52. Carriage
53. Scottish island
54. Greek letters
56. Detroit-based union: Abbr.

24

A crossword grid with numbered cells (1-62).

ACROSS

1. North Dakota city
6. Normandy beach
10. Repose
14. Suppose
15. Have trust in
16. Perceive
17. Forks
19. Fratricide
20. Compass point
21. Transaction
22. Three in one
24. Ocean vessels: Abbr.
25. Auto-horn sound
26. Crowns
28. Radiant
32. Looked the place over
33. Leslie Caron role
34. __ account
35. Steel area
36. Brazilian dance
37. Rome's Censor
38. Sheltered, at sea
39. Equals
40. Church plate
41. Labyrinth monster
43. Mentions
44. Hodges and Blas
45. Be fatuous
46. Plow's trail
49. Paint medium
50. Common verb
53. Scope
54. Miner's disease
57. Speak falteringly
58. Uproar
59. Hunter of the sky
60. Arthritis aid
61. Very: Fr.
62. __ porridge

DOWN

1. Pendants
2. Sacred bull
3. Prevalent
4. African antelope
5. Unit of magnetic intensity
6. Russian great divide
7. Head: Fr.
8. Stout's relative
9. Emotional state
10. Give as good as one gets
11. Biblical brother
12. Gyrate
13. English river
18. U.A.W. output
23. Early auto
24. Three-D picture
25. Fall-planting items
26. Nobel physicist of 1945
27. Made of a wood
28. One taking a sight
29. Growing out
30. Ponies up
31. Ten o'clock scholar's hour
32. Last-minute study
33. Oedipus's father
36. True-blue
40. Pause in the Indy 500
42. Spanish relative
43. Mountain passes
45. Legislative assemblies
46. F.D.R.'s pet
47. __ acid
48. Remainder
49. Wind instrument
50. One of a world seven
51. Rivers: Sp.
52. Domestic slave
55. Title
56. Western state: Abbr.

25

ACROSS

1. Unit of magnetic induction
6. Iranian king
10. __ out (made do)
14. Concert hall
15. Renovate
16. Prefix meaning dry
17. Item on a spice rack
19. Acclaim
20. Event at the pass
21. Small compensation
23. Do a farm chore
25. Suitor
26. Mastodon feature
30. Secret nationalist org.
32. Blot
36. Word heard in the back room
37. Liquid container
39. Perplexed
40. Hospital employees
43. Certain potatoes
44. Enthusiastic
45. S-shaped molding
46. Author of "The Flies"
48. Pitiful
49. Information
50. O'Neill
52. Gillespie, for short
54. Hoarded
58. Of bodily motions
63. Musical instrument
64. Douglas fir
66. Grow hazy
67. Place
68. Obsolete
69. Understands
70. Lunar vehicles
71. Came into play

DOWN

1. Garment for a quaestor
2. Cheese
3. Balkan native
4. Whopper
5. Off the mark
6. Classmen: Abbr.
7. Jumbled mass
8. Comic's specialty
9. Cold remedy of yore
10. Total consumption
11. Shakespearean actor
12. Father of Leif
13. Disburse
18. Grade of meat
22. French smoker's item
24. Destruction
26. Hacks
27. U.N. agency
28. Part of a building
29. Pennsylvanians
31. Timber trees
33. American Indian
34. Breathe life into
35. Foundations
38. Work, as clay
41. Sharp spasm
42. Color
47. Sign up
51. Mountain stronghold
53. "The Prisoner of __"
54. Loads
55. Competent
56. Debauchee
57. Adjudge
59. Mast
60. European head of state
61. Feminine suffixes
62. Relinquish
65. Augie's other nickname

26

ACROSS

1. Maxwell
4. Rank above maj.
9. Guide
13. Stead
15. Redolence
16. Suffix with din or pal
17. Churchill's successor
18. Powers: Lat.
19. Fish
20. Denture bite, so to speak
23. __ good advantage
24. Fabulous bird
25. "__ down his throat"
28. Old English money
30. City south of Portland
34. Hams it up
36. "__ aboard!"
38. Mother of Pollux
39. Drag strip
42. Worn to __

43. Metric measure
44. Brand
45. Surveys
47. "__ were king"
49. Ermine
50. Approximate flight hour: Abbr.
52. Type of ink
54. Tokyo lifeguard, in a way
61. Smart one
62. Playwright Padraic
63. Prefix with space or naut
64. Four-handed exercise
65. Confuse
66. Tubers
67. Sovereigns: Abbr.
68. Wears
69. Sodium hydroxide

DOWN

1. Bar figure
2. Radames's beloved
3. Film part
4. "__ en Rose"
5. __ size (cut down)
6. Bare midriffs, in a way
7. Hebrew measure
8. Beam
9. Possible last words for "Life With Father"
10. Small case
11. __ extra cost
12. Dizzy
14. Turns for burlesque performers
21. Chemical compound
22. Mayday
25. Summary
26. Acid
27. Powerful person
29. Bar order

31. Release
32. Swelling disease
33. He took a bath
35. Main
37. Baseball positions: Abbr.
40. Numerical prefix
41. "__ the bag"
46. Penn, for one: Abbr.
48. Scurrility
51. Design transfer
53. Knights' wives
54. Weary
55. Styptic
56. Kind of show
57. Beverage
58. Type of ticket
59. Host
60. Pry

27

(Crossword grid with numbered cells)

ACROSS

1. Loyal
5. Vote to accept
10. Swimmers' milieu
14. Khayyám
15. Roman dictator
16. Jai __
17. Lizard
18. Cross as __
19. German nyet
20. Cede
22. Pea soup
24. H.H. Munro
26. Ago: Scot.
27. Ointment ingredient
31. Australian, for one
35. Of the ear
36. Actor Howard
39. __ Veneto
40. Common contraction
41. Part of a wedding gown
42. Part of S. A. R.
43. Direction: Abbr.
44. Undertake
45. Sheep
46. Meaning
48. Gulfweed
50. Macaws
53. Heat units: Abbr.
54. W.W. II propagandist
58. Present
62. Words of understanding
63. Collect
65. "__ But the Lonely Heart"
66. Biblical name
67. Like 45 Across
68. Sicilian peak
69. Without: Fr.
70. Present or past
71. Beloved

DOWN

1. Verne hero
2. Eastern prince
3. Spanish room
4. Negotiate
5. __ rule
6. Work by Joyce
7. Spread
8. Blueprints
9. Dilatory
10. Hide worker
11. Hebrew letter
12. Hawaiian tree
13. Honor card
21. Headwear
23. Formerly
25. Caber-tosser's wear
27. Morse and area
28. In agreement
29. Fabric
30. Namesakes of Isaac's son
32. Confesses
33. Grape products
34. Rope
37. Vegetables
38. Powerless
42. Experienced
44. Flying prefix
47. Writer Dorothy
49. Kind of string
51. Slang
52. Unravel
54. Spanish relatives
55. Greek peak
56. Sharp
57. German possessive
59. Show fondness
60. King Mongkut's teacher
61. Leap, for one
64. Wedding-account word

28

ACROSS

1. Behold: Lat
5. Baseball's Manny
9. Severe
14. Conversation
15. Cupid
16. Speak pompously
17. Covered with scales
19. Poem by Keats
20. Burning
21. Of the kidneys
23. Kind of verb: Abbr.
24. Two fins
26. "Call Me __"
28. Horse opera
30. Kind of street
34. German reformer
38. "Macbeth," for one
39. Spanish exclamation
40. Pours forth
42. Title
43. Tiniest
46. Drove recklessly
49. Money handler
51. Queen of Thebes
52. Bumpkin
55. Boring tool
58. Puts __ (delays)
61. Dried coconut
63. Cheer
64. Trees of a region
66. American writer
68. __ thief
69. Famous Knick
70. Sunder
71. Make rotten
72. Greek god
73. Squirrel's nest

DOWN

1. Fanfare
2. Rub
3. Williams play
4. Endless
5. __ de tête
6. Moslem leader
7. Animal image
8. Game place
9. City in Michigan
10. Constellation
11. Branches
12. Agitate
13. Learn
18. British courts
22. Fuss
25. Steeps
27. "La __"
29. In ecstasy
31. Trash
32. French friend
33. Measure
34. Foal
35. Away from the wind
36. Goddess: Lat.
37. Minnesota player
41. Cut
44. Roguish
45. British sweet
47. Bull, at times
48. French scholar and lover
50. Greek letter
53. Donizetti work
54. Gavel-wielder's word
56. Make amends
57. Indigent
58. Bones
59. Determine in court
60. Decamped
62. U.S. author
65. Lace
67. Newspaper items

ACROSS

1. Hindu title
4. Hardwood trees
9. All: Lat.
14. Haw's partner
15. Book of the Bible
16. Marine hazards
17. Itinerant Johnny
19. "What's It All About, __?"
20. Movie maker's light
21. Moderately slow, in music
23. Spat
25. Police officer: Abbr.
26. Abbreviation in a rental ad
29. Chose
31. Wedding-notice word
32. Digit
33. Manhattan garnishes
37. Game __ and seek
39. "You're pulling __"
40. Civil War initials
42. Was "in"
43. "Easy __"
45. Happily
47. Watercourse: Abbr.
48. Buchwald
50. Used credit
51. Religious group: Abbr.
52. Tarts
54. Bible book
58. Subjects of a discourse
61. Linen
62. "__ far, far better thing . . ."
64. Hand grenade
66. Impassive
67. Illusory paintings
68. Footlike part
69. Talking bird
70. Home, of sorts
71. Person

DOWN

1. Military cap
2. Answer
3. Bands of Kaffir warriors
4. Ty Cobb
5. Dawn goddess
6. Cruising
7. Wails
8. Darken
9. South African province
10. Relent
11. Egyptian queen
12. "__ Were King"
13. Direction: Abbr.
18. Belles __
22. Mars: Prefix
24. Early Tuileries resident
27. Seventh Ave. figure
28. Unkempt
30. Barrel
33. Naval officers: Abbr.
34. Head bone
35. Height
36. U.S. Indian
38. Style of car
41. Greek letter
44. Clip
46. Ram's mate
49. Dome of note
53. Stalk
55. Congo sight
56. Actress Terry
57. Della or Peewee
59. Chinese dynasty
60. "I never take __ after dinner"
62. Doctrine
63. Inter-office machine: Abbr.
65. Before, poetically

ACROSS

1. Whale's captive
6. Disengaged: Abbr.
9. Order to a dog
14. Funeral oration
15. Agency of U.N.
16. Hodge's other half
17. Automotive disaster
18. Never, in Bonn
19. Mongol, for one
20. Flattening with a hammer
22. Tantrum throwers
24. Hold back
25. Rough
26. ___ Paulo
27. Lamour wear
31. Guns or Scott
35. Moth family
38. Play
39. Canine sound
40. French eye
41. Braggart's quality
44. Stupid
45. Arctic ship
46. Farm sound
48. Roman poet
50. Woolly animal
54. Daydream
57. Obvious
59. Sweetheart: Sp.
60. Cuckoo
62. Pickling solution
63. Highest point
64. Remick
65. Gull
66. Dispatch
67. Sea call
68. Low-class Anglo-Saxons

DOWN

1. Vehicle
2. More mature
3. "Long time ___"
4. Insurance man
5. Athenian judge
6. Belfry sounds
7. Eastern collegian
8. "___ is human . . ."
9. Berlin prison
10. Subsequent
11. Adams
12. Seaweed substance
13. Ranges of perception
21. New Deal initials
23. Neighbor of Hung.
28. Greek theaters
29. River nymph
30. Sets
31. Spanish painter
32. Erie Canal city
33. Austen heroine
34. Arguer for the defense
36. Scrap
37. Sore losers
42. Change course
43. Limerick land
44. Up to
47. ___ to the good
49. Arrangements
51. Behind: Sp.
52. Stone marker
53. Oakley
54. Kind of worm
55. S.A. tree
56. Arteries: Abbr.
58. Scatters
61. Recent: Prefix

31

ACROSS

1. Elec. units
5. Tree with poisonous sap
9. James Truslow or John Couch
14. Flying turn
15. Hottentot tribesman
16. D.F.C., for one
17. French miss: Abbr.
18. "___ I didn't already know"
19. Previously, old style
20. Hit show
22. Stuck fast
24. Small: Suffix
25. Monster
27. Well-known Loch
28. Pierce
30. Certain bridge bids
32. Wild habitat
33. Bookkeeping abbr.
34. Belief in one God
38. Containing nitrogen: Prefix
39. Things to get hot under
41. Recent: Prefix
42. Size of type
44. Business: Suffix
45. Tunisian port
46. Corporal or sergeant
48. ___ spade a spade
49. Place for a coin
52. Years and years
53. Wing
54. National concern
56. Deducted
60. Counterpart
61. Test
63. Flexible shoot
64. Has a good standing
65. Muscle twitches
66. Prospector's quest
67. Exercise vigorously
68. "Touché" weapon
69. Son of Seth

DOWN

1. Gifts for the poor
2. Taupe
3. National concern
4. Schoolbook
5. Two-toed sloth
6. Beethoven symphony
7. "What a good boy ___"
8. Kenya outing
9. Eastern nurse
10. National concern
11. Love
12. Horses
13. Greenland vehicles
21. Poetic contraction
23. "___ Rides Again"
26. Old sailing ship
28. Biblical country
29. Axis follower
31. Querying sounds
33. Hat
35. National concern
36. Official stamp
37. Cauterizing material
39. Bill's partner
40. National concern
43. Whole number
45. Fit for marketing
47. Prairie wolf
48. Calloway
49. Pinnacle
50. Folklorist Alan
51. Egg-shaped
55. Part of R and R
57. Otherwise
58. Within: Prefix
59. Letters
62. Split

ACROSS

1. Pitcher part
6. Ad offering
10. Accessories
14. Anathema
15. Bible book: Abbr.
16. Nimbus
17. Forest of "As You Like It"
18. Arena
19. Believe, old style
20. Tear
21. Blues composer
22. Witty remarks
23. High note
24. Rib
25. Islands in North Atlantic
26. King of Morven
28. Meditative
30. Remove, in a way
31. Continent
32. Looked slyly
33. Historical records
38. Yorkshire river
41. Slag
42. Fairy-tale words
46. Average
47. Ranges
48. Radium discoverer
50. Supplement, with "out"
51. Join the poker game
52. Type of Greek column
53. U.S. Indians
54. Neighbor of Ky.
55. Of the ear
56. Assumed proposition
57. Old expletive
58. Sea eagle
59. Scarlett
60. Dunks
61. Droops
62. Lazy __

DOWN

1. Alarming, old style
2. Descendants through a single strain
3. Military weapons
4. Secondhand
5. Decade
6. Marsh birds
7. From within: Lat.
8. Two-seated carriages
9. Irritable
10. Robin's friend
11. Dawn goddess
12. F.D.R.'s prep school
13. Notching instrument
21. Hibernated
24. Like cheese
25. Betrothed
27. Needlefish
29. Noxious
34. React to a dull speech
35. Short songs
36. Old name for Parnassus
37. "Death of a __"
39. Island in Indian Ocean
40. Hardening
42. Harangues
43. Metaphysical word
44. Bit of shut-eye
45. Corrects
49. Prepares potatoes
52. Female animals
53. Hawaiian island
56. Two, in Spain

33

1	2	3	4	5		6	7	8	9		10	11	12	13
14						15					16			
17				18							19			
20				21						22				
		23	24					25	26					
27	28				29	30	31							
32			33		34						35	36	37	
38					39				40	41				
42			43	44				45						
		46					47		48					
49	50	51						52	53					
54					55	56	57				58	59	60	
61				62					63					
64				65				66						
67				68				69						

ACROSS

1. Stroll
6. Comedian Bert
10. Rascals
14. Marner
15. Understanding reply
16. __ contendere
17. River source
19. Yesterday: Fr.
20. Researcher's aid: Abbr.
21. In front
22. Unit of weight
23. Danny or Sammy
25. Gasoline Alley family
27. Pacific island
29. Leading
32. Exhausted
34. Indians
35. Possessive
38. Disinclined
39. Pharaoh, for one
40. Varnish ingredient
42. Kind of lot
43. Jockey Arcaro
45. Fives, nines or elevens
46. Owls
48. Aleutian island
49. Place of torment
52. Western hero
54. Type of race
55. Numbers
58. European fish
61. Mild oath
62. Shape of a chess piece
64. Verne character
65. Tops
66. City in Peru
67. Uniform
68. Mary and Catherine: Abbr.
69. Power source

DOWN

1. Tennis ace
2. Appearance
3. Blemish
4. Boy
5. Attempt
6. Money, in Milan
7. Sailing
8. Restaurant V.I.P.
9. Radiation unit
10. Divided
11. Fabric
12. Fold
13. Manners
18. Evergreen genus
22. Catchall home area
24. Relative
26. Drink
27. European capital
28. Like peas in __
30. All over
31. Ford
33. Speculation
35. Hat
36. Lazarus
37. Chance
41. Shakespearean character
44. Assume
46. Kind of collision
47. Withered
49. Dunne
50. Region of Israel
51. Sweetheart
53. Staff members: Abbr.
56. River of France
57. Functions
59. Famous U.S. editor
60. Kind of cheese
62. Possesses
63. Covering

34

ACROSS

1. Book reviewer, of a sort: Abbr.
5. Boatmen's river
10. Bator's partner
14. Specialty of Brockton, Mass.
16. Timber wolf
17. Native of the Volunteer State
18. Ages ago
19. Burr or brogue
20. __ personae
22. Sewing and others
23. "The Joys of Yiddish" author
24. Theodore White subj.
25. Kind of bridge
26. Undermines
30. Poetic contraction
31. Wherewithal
33. Proceeding
34. Oil-well equipment
35. Without a mate
36. G.I.'s garb
38. Technical study: Abbr.
39. Part of a fishline
41. Bowler's despair
43. Longfellow's contemporary
44. Early ascetic
46. Swoboda
47. __ ex machina
48. Quinnat and sockeye
50. Trite stuff
51. Journalist's milieu
54. Diet's cousin
56. Words of understanding
57. Boardwalk stroller
59. __ out of it
60. Price fixers, of a sort
61. That girl's
62. Ebbets Field name
63. Existence, in philosophy

DOWN

1. Movie canine
2. Harness parts
3. Doorkeepers, in France
4. Beliefs
5. Very spacious
6. Endorsements
7. Sprawl
8. Growls
9. Consanguineous
10. Vladimir Ilyich __ (Lenin)
11. Boodle
12. Hillside shelter
13. Certain votes
15. With 53 Down, clothing
21. Most paltry
23. Burma and others
24. Intrinsically
25. Held the reins
27. Posse's prey
28. Unexpected meetings
29. Hogs' housing
31. Hungarian playwright
32. Lawgiver
37. Sound of traffic
40. Suez Canal name
42. Do public relations work
45. Juliet, for one
47. Give
49. Code man
50. Meal for Caesar
51. Birthplace of Constantine
52. Old slave
53. See 15 Down
54. Dotted with stars, in heraldry
55. Gaelic
58. Prefix for deal or deed

ACROSS

1. Political group
5. Finns' neighbors
10. Tax
14. Mauna Loa coating
15. Frightening
16. Loyal
17. "__ There"
18. Figure of speech
19. Cinderella garb
20. Dovetailing piece
22. Lapse
24. Small insects
26. Kind of pudding
27. Wane
30. Henry VIII's sixth
31. Knack
32. Nullify
34. License-plate attachment
35. Thaws
39. Temporary
41. Hilltop fort
42. Assignment
43. Thing of beauty
44. Character in "Quo Vadis"
45. Running game
46. Welsh name
48. Plant
49. Customers
52. Implement for Rodin
54. Chokes
56. Thoreau outings
60. Theatrical award
61. Old district of Asia Minor
63. Not mad
64. Canal
65. Football kicks
66. Throw off
67. Musical instrument
68. Hide
69. Exclamation

DOWN

1. Design in Rorschach test
2. Bathe
3. Wall appliance
4. Pool shot
5. Tennis term
6. Radio message
7. Byword
8. Pan's creation
9. Prophet
10. Arrangement of parallel bands
11. Steep rocks
12. "You __ to be in pictures"
13. Snappish
21. Check sharply
23. Particle
25. Going out, in a way
27. Corrupt
28. Kind of china
29. Bridle parts
31. Moreover: Sp.
33. Leveled
36. Intimations
37. Spanish river
38. Arrange compactly
40. Cookout
41. Returns to the scene
43. Place of suffering
47. Fresh
49. Complete
50. Prop up
51. Man's nickname
52. Flat-headed nail
53. Beam
55. Upsets
57. Lhasa monk
58. Grow together
59. Matched groups
62. Certain Wednesday

ACROSS

1. Khan and others
5. Broadway flop
9. Fundamental
14. Busy one's self with
16. Pickling agent
17. Highly wrought
18. School course
19. Not sweet
20. Dance
22. Forward
23. Flocks of wildfowl
25. Brings into agreement
27. Norwegian poet
28. Asian country
30. Litigant
31. East or West __
32. Pronoun
35. Laugh, in a way
39. Representative: Abbr.
40. People apart
41. Bacteriologist's wire
42. Important range
43. "Come home; __ forgiven"
44. Reader of an almanac
47. Narrow headband
49. Fit to __
50. Suddenly
53. Kind of dance
55. Fruit parts
57. Chew on a sparerib
59. Take effect
60. Speech
61. Sight or touch
62. Crucifix
63. French river

DOWN

1. Festivals
2. Carl Sandburg's birthplace
3. Thing for timid people to take
4. Cry
5. Chemical element
6. Racetracks
7. Parcel out
8. __ Rabbit
9. Container: Abbr.
10. Asian peninsula
11. Squelch
12. Weak
13. Affords
15. __ Goodfellow
21. Propelled
24. Inspiring fear
26. Island in Aegean, to Italians
27. Russian hut
28. Dyeing vats
29. Harem rooms
31. Snow runner: Var.
32. Frameworks
33. Doubt
34. Regards
36. Ranger or wolf
37. Hindu god
38. Head, in England
42. Moslem princes
43. Church area
44. Watch parts
45. Make up for
46. Show again
47. Ipso __
48. Bothered
51. Incentive
52. European leader
54. Equal
56. Behold
58. Certain horse

37

ACROSS

1. Phone
5. Anita and Barbara
11. Erode
14. Busy as __
15. Waken
16. Asian deer
17. Dylan song
20. His: Fr
21. Ancient Asian
22. Rub out
23. Often-lent thing
24. Aide: Abbr.
25. Argot
28. Spring riser
30. Sea birds
34. Service charges
37. Kind of beer
38. Space
39. Red-yellow color
40. Dame Rumor
41. One opposed
42. Chorine's benefactor
44. Ship part
45. Weight
46. ". . . in someone __ arms"
47. Legal term
50. Chum
51. Light craft
53. Burn
55. Commercial degree
58. Gene Kelly film
61. Lodging place
62. "It's all the __ me"
63. Preposition
64. Cha
65. Escapes
66. Hammer part

DOWN

1. Hacks
2. Skilled
3. Certain people, zodiacally
4. Ayres of films
5. More stable
6. Dry
7. "__ but the brave . . ."
8. Word of contempt
9. Remains
10. Prognosticators
11. Greek goddess
12. Tops
13. Kennedy
18. Reflection
19. Victoria or Yosemite
23. Requiring
24. Tarzan
25. Former Belgian Premier
26. Actor Greene
27. Sharp ridge
28. Honor
29. Name for a discothèque
31. Anchorage areas
32. __ guerre
33. Props
35. Ethiopian title
36. Medit. island: Abbr.
43. "The Wreck of the Mary __"
48. Clamor
49. Of the kidneys
50. Hopi prayer sticks
51. Movies, in Roma
52. Held
53. Prune: Scot.
54. Feminine suffix
55. Thick hair
56. Mailman's hazard
57. In a while
58. Meet
59. Baking pit, in Hawaii
60. Irving character

38

ACROSS

1. City of Texas
5. U.S. research org.
8. Droplets
11. City of Spain
13. __ gras
14. Star in Cetus
15. Some platitudes
18. Title: Abbr.
19. Holly
20. Of yore
21. Negri of the silents
22. Livingstone's part of Africa
24. Constellation
27. Beldames
29. Musical instrument
30. Central state
31. Leg up
35. Within: Prefix
36. Principal force
37. Popular color
38. Famed couturier
39. Impersonates
40. Kind of practice
41. Set right
43. "Mack the Knife" creator
44. __ a sheet
47. Honor cards
49. Ancient Greek dialect
50. Found a line
51. Twice
54. Part of a "Keep Out" sign
58. Advantage
59. Pronoun
60. Smutch
61. Part of D.V.
62. Snoop
63. Latin "to be"

DOWN

1. Carry on
2. Class comprising the birds
3. French numeral
4. Corrida kudos
5. Nut: Fr.
6. Show __
7. Red or Black
8. Rectifier
9. Sea eagles
10. Common contraction
12. Musical direction
13. Sideshow attraction
14. Fountain items
16. The works
17. Sped
21. Disparaging
22. Below
23. Art course: Abbr.
24. Not up
25. Rajah's spouse
26. Preposition
28. One-sided wins
32. Prefix with valent
33. Quiet spell
34. Cloy
36. __ California
40. Cleans up
42. Numerical prefix
44. Toweled
45. Multitude
46. __ Jones, English architect
48. __ Magnon
50. Nimble
51. Arm, in France
52. "How sweet __!"
53. Auld lang __
55. Summit
56. Land mass: Abbr.
57. Juin, juillet et août

ACROSS

1. Adjective suffix
4. Immense
8. Location
12. Stake in a game
13. "__ by land . . ."
15. Asian range
16. __ on the map
17. Nellie Forbush's home
19. Comic strip character
20. Man's nickname
21. Integers: Abbr.
22. City on Rio Grande
27. Book of Bible: Abbr.
28. Boys
32. Terrapins' home
37. Cooker
38. Indian garment
39. Taxed
41. Dismounted
42. Substantiate
44. Superficial
46. Up in arms
47. Up: Prefix
48. Philadelphia attraction
55. Friend: Fr.
58. Forms in Greek philosophy
59. Calorie project
61. Home of Three Rivers Stadium
65. Doctrines
66. Space
67. Flower stalk
68. Hint
69. Grant's __
70. Genesis name
71. Region: Abbr.

DOWN

1. __ course
2. Kwajalein, e.g.
3. Abate
4. Book: Abbr.
5. Cuckoo
6. Attack
7. Sir, for example
8. California's Big __
9. Minnesota product
10. Mexican delicacy
11. Fraternal men
12. Indian mulberry
14. Bend
18. Tests
23. Some
24. Feature of Utah flats
25. Chicago airport
26. Underworld figure
29. "Whatever __ wants . . ."
30. Bad
31. Jet __
32. Trading center
33. In a line
34. Competitor
35. "Nothing doing!"
36. Coup __
38. Hot Springs, for one
40. Renounce
43. Indians
45. Commit a crime
49. Baby wear
50. Infer
51. Showed again
52. Decree
53. Thread
54. Nocturnal mammal
55. __ on the back
56. Spanish painter
57. Article
60. Part of Mao's name
62. Restaurant check
63. Mail center: Abbr.
64. "For __ a jolly good fellow"

40

ACROSS

1. Lend a hand
5. Hokum
9. About
14. Certain shape
15. Calhoun
16. Of a space
17. Western sight
18. Setting apart
20. Lures
22. Part of a golf club
23. Lose interest
24. Peer Gynt's mother
25. Drink
26. Serpent
29. Pinafore
31. German area
33. Prolong the coffee break
35. Pry
37. Newton
40. Accuse in a courtly way
42. Get feline revenge
44. Dress material
45. Cliff
47. Mother of Apollo
48. Kinds
50. Colors
52. Engage in seamy work
53. Iowa Indians
55. __ rule
57. First __
59. Noun form: Abbr.
60. Examines oneself
65. Clarify
67. Toward shelter
68. ". . . __ horse to . . ."
69. Scent
70. Trick
71. Lapse
72. Confines
73. Defeats at bridge

DOWN

1. Direct to a target
2. On the level
3. Foot model
4. Without frills
5. Stable-owner's concern
6. Soil
7. Overdue debts
8. Church songs
9. Gas' users
10. Annoy
11. Keeps on making a point
12. Hiawatha's craft
13. Writer of success stories
19. Sweetsop
21. Camper's gear
25. Kind of metabolism
26. Word of regret
27. Short-billed rail
28. Pernickety
30. Ages
32. Broadcast
34. Goes to the wall
36. Biblical brother
38. Deed, in France
39. Dog
41. Pen pal
43. Grooving tools
46. Parlor-game subject
49. Vanish: Scot.
51. Drink slowly
53. Heavy stake
54. Go, in France
56. Sharpen the razor
58. Darlings
60. River in Bavaria
61. Panay town
62. Hint
63. Tryout
64. Observes
66. Japanese herb

41

ACROSS

1. Barley beards
5. Word for some budgets
10. Clean the deck
14. Bar
15. Buffalo of India
16. Line-marking material
17. Acrobatic routine
19. Arthurian woman
20. Pad
21. Roman gods
23. Advice to Macduff
26. Appraise, with "up"
27. Rubbish
30. Free and clear
32. Certain compasses
35. Of the shoulder
36. Accompany
38. Shooter
39. Palm fiber
40. Tend, in a way
41. D.D.E.
42. Schubert's "__ könig"
43. Most wintry
44. Bowfin genus
45. Met again
47. Kind of cross
48. Scornful look
49. "Pardon me!"
51. Pay
53. Muckraking articles
56. Souls: Lat.
60. Sandarac tree
61. Recoil
64. Constituents of modern jam
65. Tea fare
66. Gardner
67. Mad, in Scotland
68. Audience reactions, sometimes
69. Beginning

DOWN

1. Helper: Abbr.
2. Stop!
3. Insensible
4. Brilliant
5. Savory
6. Dublin initials
7. Wildebeest
8. Word to a lifeguard
9. French heads
10. Flimsy
11. Season
12. Friend, in Lille
13. Garden areas
18. Sincere
22. Kind of light
24. "I'm not __ interested"
25. Time to start over
27. Horse opera
28. Warning device
29. Rivals the one-hoss shay
31. Thin paper
33. Former actor Jack
34. Promise
36. Cistern
37. Small bird
40. Stings
44. Resort near Nice
46. "Get __!"
48. Blab to the D.A.
50. In disarray
52. Horse features
53. "To __ his own"
54. Certain photo
55. Humane org.
57. Old gray one
58. Asian tree
59. Pieced out
62. Quarrel
63. Wayside, for one

42

ACROSS

1. Derrick part
5. Mild expletive
10. Mesozoic et al.
14. Stravinsky
15. Con __ (tenderly)
16. Honduran port
17. Isinglass
18. ID on stationery
20. Desk item of yore
22. Purse item
23. __ ease
24. Girl's name
25. Miami Beach features
27. Supports
31. __ nous
32. Disillusions
33. Mother's command
34. Site of Sugar Loaf
35. Husbands
36. Ripen
37. Cathedral: Ger.
38. British auto parts
39. Woman thief, in Rome
41. Shows contempt for
43. Summoned
44. Branch of medicine: Abbr.
45. Sans __
46. Musical direction
49. Rhythm
52. Comedian's forte
55. Brand
56. Restless desire
57. Kind of sale
58. First name in baseball lore
59. Sounds of discovery
60. Transfers
61. Anglo-Saxon slave

DOWN

1. Opera role
2. Once more, Western style
3. Saying popularized on TV
4. Vessel
5. Giant slain by Athena
6. Fish
7. Peppery
8. Craft
9. Early in the A.M.
10. Of a group
11. Emit vapor
12. Jai __
13. Marquis de __
19. Becomes angry
21. French pronoun
24. Adjusts
25. Flocks
26. Shish kebab ingredient
27. Desire wrongfully
28. Marquee names
29. Tidal flood
30. Stand in good __
32. Isaac's mother
35. Blood-pressure word
38. Nonsense
39. Honor
40. Gluck opera
42. Time periods
43. Moves on momentum
45. Location
46. Capital of Western Samoa
47. Famous Yankee
48. Early South American
50. Son of Adam
51. Gaelic
53. Chill
54. Reference work: Abbr.

ACROSS

1. Roentgen discovery
5. Coil: Prefix
10. Curves
14. Colleen's land
15. Morals man
16. Exchange fee
17. Harass
18. Thorny
20. French season
21. Life stories, for short
22. Missiles
23. Cheese bases
25. Cans
26. Measures: Abbr.
27. Like some birds
31. Proverb
34. Hamlet's objective
35. Eye part
36. Greek letters
37. School orgs.
38. Newspaper article
40. Mimics
41. Yankee Doodle took one
42. Anger
43. Intrigue
44. Oppressive
48. Breed of hog
50. Guthrie
51. Farm unit
52. Hatred of foreigners
54. Diminutive ending
55. Inner: Prefix
56. Jostle
57. Property claim
58. Shoal
59. O'Casey and others
60. Diet

DOWN

1. Medit. vessel
2. Lariat
3. Ram
4. In addition
5. Indian antelopes
6. Melons and squashes
7. Egyptian goddess
8. Nessen
9. Broadway events
10. Good-time Charlie
11. S-shaped curve
12. Gains
13. Drunkard
19. Burn
21. Plant stem
24. Describing some spirits
25. Not dissonant
27. Bristles
28. Heraldry word
29. Mark
30. Meeting: Abbr.
31. Syrian city, to French
32. Pedestal part
33. "It's __ to tell a lie"
34. Actor Conrad
36. Rolls
39. Deck
40. Mars: Prefix
42. Relatives
44. Constellation
45. Old port of Rome
46. Absolute
47. Ancient name for Aswan
48. Sand hill, in Britain
49. Wavy, in heraldry
50. Eban of Israel
52. Dry: Prefix
53. Bravo
54. Pixie

44

ACROSS

1. Gypsy
4. Roll logs
8. Father, in Spain
13. Nigerian people
14. Ancient theaters
15. Wartime menaces
17. Dogie phrase
19. Spreading out
20. Clermont
22. Celebrations
25. Passé
26. King, in drama
27. Former Chief Justice
30. Longing
34. Man's nickname
35. French waterway
36. New England city
37. Famed musicals
40. Having auricles
41. Idler
42. Poker word
43. Scanty
44. Plaintiffs
45. Breakwater
46. Space
47. Dice player
48. Alaska
55. Swapped
56. Le Roi Soleil
60. Horse
61. Moslem call to prayer
62. Ivy Leaguer
63. Dig
64. Gender: Abbr.
65. Small drink

DOWN

1. Outfit
2. Waistband
3. Quip
4. Soft mass
5. Lion
6. Let
7. Lake: It.
8. Go after
9. To the rear
10. Stupid one
11. Part of a fence
12. Latin abbr.
16. Cute
18. Distant
21. ___ news
22. Enamels
23. TV adjunct
24. Sidewise: Prefix
27. Who, in Italy
28. Bank capers
29. British victim in Revolution
30. Adjective ending
31. Surveyor's equipment
32. Louisianian
33. Miss Prynne
35. Postal initials
36. Grain: Fr.
38. Muffin
39. Dutch weight
44. Kind of shoe
45. Willie of baseball fame
46. Avidity
47. Lighter part
48. Aves
49. Son of Aphrodite
50. Twist
51. Spanish port
52. Pastry
53. Slime
54. Cookout on Oahu
57. Strange: Prefix
58. Sinkiang river
59. Big shot: Abbr.

45

ACROSS

1. Eastern-church title
5. Old Syrian fabric
9. Thing of value
14. Shades
15. Road, in Germany
16. Extreme
17. Former, old style
18. Height: Prefix
19. Kemal and others
20. Saver of a sort
23. Brit. fliers
24. Turkish weights
25. Home of el toro
28. Steelhead
30. Camp item
32. __ Nidre
33. Swan genus
35. French possessive
36. Tidal flood
37. Deck officer
39. Remove
41. Some mail addresses: Abbr.
42. Landon and others
43. Force, in old Rome
44. Austrian statesman
46. Labor org.
47. Hook
48. Banquet
51. Post-__
53. Burden
56. P.I. tree
57. Goatsuckers
60. Former Met pitcher Roger
62. Crooked
63. Music groups
64. Swiss city
65. Network
66. Peak
67. Man of many causes
68. Sandarac
69. Timetable, for short

DOWN

1. Have __
2. College figure
3. One way to stand
4. Wine city of Italy
5. Taken __
6. Hiding place
7. Poinsettia, for one
8. Soon
9. One seeking to escape reality
10. Electioneer
11. Uncomfortable time
12. One reaction to a mouse
13. Corp. officials
21. In __ (wholly)
22. Two fins
26. Gare du __
27. Pub drinks
29. Caucho trees
31. Dawn goddess
34. Make over
36. Scottish hill
37. Damage
38. Phone greeting, in Paris
40. Initials on a dismissal notice
45. "Win __, lose . . ."
47. __ counter
49. Famous dancer
50. Threw
52. Biblical possessive
54. Blood vessel
55. Beauty-parlor gear
58. S.A. rubber
59. Lupino and others
60. Firearm: Abbr.
61. Gov't. agency

46

ACROSS

1. African village
5. Pokes
9. Broadcast
14. Gully, in North Africa
15. Adjective ending
16. "__ là?" (Who goes there?)
17. W.W. II powers
18. Exactly right words
20. Reading aid
22. Lets up
23. Dear me!
24. Kittenish sound
25. Hussar's gear
28. Enraged
32. Residence
33. Sweetheart
34. Verb ending
35. Belgian city
36. Got along
37. __ au rhum
38. Sharp-cornered: Abbr.
39. Bombastic
40. Goof
41. Danger
43. Unseaworthy
44. Black
45. Pinza
47. Civvies
49. Sneaked away
53. Table wines
55. __ de Pinos
56. "Feed __, starve . . ."
57. Encourage
58. Winglike
59. Opens wide
60. Occupied
61. Taboo thing

DOWN

1. Exchange
2. Rainy-day cry
3. Tennis term
4. Certain bridge plays
5. Agra's river
6. African plants
7. Swiss coin
8. Older ones: Abbr.
9. Harsh
10. Struggle
11. Ceremonial
12. Nights before
13. Existed
19. Taunted
21. Robt. __
24. Colon and dinar
25. Hindu society
26. Have __ to pick
27. Small drum
28. Prolix
29. Moon goddess
30. Soviet republic
31. Arctic pioneer
33. Famed blues composer
36. Wooden cask
37. Crudely obtuse
39. Newspaper section
40. Radar reading
42. Trivial nonsense
45. Gardner et al.
46. Piquant
47. Transparent mineral
48. Running alone: Abbr.
49. Philippine port
50. Formerly Christiania
51. __ Bator
52. South Sea staple
53. Sharp turn
54. Small amount

47

ACROSS

1. Agreement
5. Billiard stroke
10. Prod
14. French composer
15. Mme. de __
16. Get under one's skin
17. Islands off Ireland
18. "__ Venice"
20. Desire eagerly
22. Inlet
23. Point in one's favor
24. Cuckoo
25. Rodents
28. Huntley and others
30. Egg: Prefix
31. Winter ailment
34. Certain neckline
36. Table syrups
38. Bikini, for one
39. Owns
40. Pronoun
41. Role in "Carmen"
43. Specialty for Schwarzkopf
44. "Ballad of the __ Cafe"
45. Fiber cluster
46. Poet Marianne
47. German composer
49. "Brother __"
52. Near
55. Indian weight
56. Musician Kaye
58. U.S. pianist of 1800s
61. Name in N.Y. theater
62. Math ratio words
63. Daises
64. It's often golden
65. Heyerdahl
66. Former Olympic star
67. Part of a Grieg title

DOWN

1. Old Spanish coin
2. Copland
3. Well-tempered item
4. A flat, for one
5. College degree
6. Sergeant __
7. Indian garments
8. Washington V.I.P.'s
9. Hebrew judge
10. Herbage
11. Artist's medium
12. Lily
13. Skillful
19. Some musical works
21. Gustav Holst symphonic work
26. Had a bite
27. Mother of mankind
29. Robust
31. Strauss opera
32. __ majesty
33. Addict
34. Containers
35. Portico, in Sparta
36. Partner of feather
37. Partner of Sonny
39. TV special for Bob
42. State: Abbr.
43. Chaney
46. Game fish
47. Instructor
48. Union general
50. Plentiful
51. Does an office job
52. Shake: Abbr.
53. Empty talk
54. Klemperer
57. Port on Guam
59. Navy man: Abbr.
60. Neighbor of Neb.

48

1	2	3	4	■	5	6	7	8	9	■	10	11	12	13
14				■	15					■	16			
17				■	18					■	19			
20				21	■	22				■	23			
■	■	■	24		25	■	26		27		■	■	■
28	29	30				31	■	32			33	34	35
36				■	37		38	■	39				
40			41		■	42			■	43			
44		45		■	46			■	47				
48				49	■	50		51					
■	■	52			53	■	54			■	■	■	■
55	56	57		■	58		59	■	60		61	62	63
64			■	65			66	■	67			
68			■	69				■	70			
71			■	72				■	73			

ACROSS

1. Turner
5. Candy
10. Circle of water
14. Animals
15. Banish
16. Time __ half
17. Linen fiber
18. Link
19. Designations for secret papers of 1790s
20. So-so
22. Gender
23. Makes friends
24. Audience
26. Slacken
28. Helped
32. __ yellow leaf (old age)
36. Crafty
37. Army V.I.P.
39. Doctor's instrument
40. Live
41. Ship wrecked off U.S. in 1928
43. Gardner
44. José's operatic victim
46. Ad __
47. Beaver skin
48. Lengths
50. Vexes
52. Mastodon features
54. Recent: Prefix
55. Historian's concerns
58. Querying words
60. Medit. ship
64. Resembling: Suffix
65. Seat
67. Defendant's plea
68. __-Coburg
69. Florida city
70. Corn lily
71. Tennyson lady
72. Garden flowers
73. Roman portico

DOWN

1. Attic
2. Shaft
3. Certain tide
4. Care
5. Commandment number
6. Cuts
7. Jack-of-all-trades
8. Melts
9. Kind of man
10. Brazilian dances
11. Cameo stone
12. Dressing tool
13. Russian agency
21. Grammar case: Abbr.
23. Queen of Scots et al.
25. Rulers
27. Wordbook
28. In front
29. Cleansing agent
30. Put into action
31. __ Plaines
33. Part of a Dickens title
34. Emphatic negation
35. Attracts
38. Indefinite degree
41. Planet
42. Plunder
45. Like household gas or water
47. Western capital
49. Draft
51. Lone Star nickname
53. Marine hazard
55. Eleanora of stage
56. King or Ladd
57. Urban vehicle
59. Kind of flight
61. Squarish
62. Yale men
63. Layer
65. Bribe
66. Negligent

49

ACROSS

1. Grizzly, for one
5. Uses the teeth
10. Tissue suspension
14. French pronoun
15. Have __ (watch out)
16. "I'm all __"
17. Parisian friends
18. Maugham novel
20. One on a fixed income
22. Morning event
23. Frightening
25. Large shark
26. "The Age of __"
28. River to Rio Grande
31. __-toe
34. Cry of disgust
36. Lizard
37. Two __ kind
38. Leave port
41. Bowling number
42. Kind of verb: Abbr.
44. Partner of dash
45. __ a bee
47. Lama land
49. Famous rider
51. "It's __ to tell a lie"
53. Tape again
57. Mishandled
60. Narrow
61. Redundant city
63. Hayworth
64. "__ Rhythm"
65. Bird sound
66. Steady
67. We: Fr.
68. Type of remark
69. Office item

DOWN

1. Scouts' founder
2. Gantry
3. Put in a row
4. Turn the key again
5. Type of lie
6. Mythological flier
7. Russian river
8. Asteroid
9. Antitoxin
10. Barrel of suds
11. Tourist mecca
12. Work units
13. Words of understanding
19. Bean or dragon
21. Concepts
24. Shift of a sort
27. Air group: Abbr.
29. Genus of trees
30. Without: Fr.
31. "Hop __!"
32. Moroccan area
33. Fonda film
35. One way to spend the winter
39. Craggy hill
40. Wigglers and spinners
43. End-of-game announcements
46. Fastened
48. River to the Danube
50. Type of threat
52. Salamanders
54. Drab color
55. Appraises
56. Bent the elbow
57. Victor's words
58. __ Maggiore
59. Day starter
62. Pacific neckpiece

ACROSS

1. Supervise
8. Buckingham and Crystal
15. Construction worker
16. Perk up
17. Air-signal devices
18. Non-blood relative
19. Noisy, in music
21. Source of formic acid
22. Gibbon
23. Stupefy
26. Aphrodite's prize
29. Pinnacle
30. Festivals
33. Cheers
34. Darling
36. Potato bud
37. Exclamation
38. "___ Sylphides"
39. Educ. group
40. Folk-lore heroine
43. Bare place on mountainside
44. Cathode's partner
45. Dotted cube
46. Keystone-cop event
47. Fortitude
49. Macaw
50. Anne or Marie: Abbr.
52. City near Albany
57. Crescent-shaped
60. Milk glass
61. Haliotis
62. Ancient district of Greece
63. Chopin composition
64. "Let's ___" (child's favorite)

DOWN

1. Spheres
2. ___ armis
3. Eternally
4. Abrogates
5. Asian plain
6. Weird
7. Formerly, of old
8. Footbridge
9. Bruckner or Chekhov
10. Position of golf ball
11. Current unit, for short
12. African port
13. Kind of jacket
14. Dispatched
20. Woodwind
24. Sounds of disgust
25. West
26. Palm
27. Deposit
28. Extraordinary
29. Well-known look-alike
31. Fields
32. Icy look
34. Lancelot or Galahad
35. Pekoe
37. Metrical units
41. Presidential initials
42. Property right
43. Small onion
46. Bring into existence
48. Drift
49. Turkish coin
50. Thick slice
51. Helicon
53. Castile
54. Wing: Fr.
55. Blue grape pigment
56. Perused
58. Wholly
59. ___ man

51

ACROSS

1 Mosquitoes, etc.
6 Kind of transit
11 Little, in Scotland
14 Stingy
15 Take out
16 Preserve
17 Pertinent New Year
   words
19 Decay
20 Actress Norma
   and others
21 Fasten
23 "As __ a bird"
25 Extremely violent
26 Attractor
30 Fastener
32 Lands
33 Legal order
35 Solomon island
39 Pack
40 Cunning
41 Mine car
42 Shrewd
43 Slangy negative
44 Welcome call by
   bridge partner
45 Up to one's __
47 Over there
48 Family members
51 Plants yielding tannin
54 Cores
56 Lineman's climbing
   aid
61 Medit. land
62 Perishables for Jan. 1
64 Started the fire
65 Mood: It.
66 Fountain of note
67 Western state: Abbr.
68 Slants
69 Meetings: Abbr.

DOWN

1 Hundredths: Abbr.
2 Querying sounds
3 Sprinkled, in heraldry
4 Mulberry bark
5 Plants with milky
   juices
6 Cook again
7 Shrub of Indian
8 Dalmatian island
9 Wife of Osiris
10 Hinders
11 Clean up
12 N.Z. native
13 Paid up
18 Do ushering
22 Rope-winding device
24 Backfield maneuver
26 Gender: Abbr.
27 Recorded
   proceedings
28 Seagoing drink
29 Happy day
31 Lawyer: Abbr.
33 Joint
34 Also-__
36 Sere
37 Mantel décor
38 Hebrew measure
40 Reo or Hudson
44 Famed Nile town
46 Puffed with conceit
47 Korean border river
48 Vance of whodunits
49 Gods led by Odin
50 Ex __
52 Naval direction
53 Play parts
55 Fractional prefix
57 Titles
58 Digits
59 Begrudge
60 Greek letters
63 Coin of Peru

52

ACROSS

1 Snooze
4 Western U.S. plant
9 "Yes, __"
13 Twittery
15 Independently
16 Can. province
17 Passable
18 Cretan sight
19 Pour __
20 Wall piers
22 Sanction
24 To __
26 Noon's follower
27 Center of attraction
30 Arranged in folds
34 Concerning
35 Urchins
37 Turkish leader
38 Greek letter
39 Elixir
41 Bench-warmer
42 Mathematical association
44 Marine bird
45 Italian town
46 Increased the pace
48 Bouncers
50 Muse
52 Latvian port
53 Message from Uncle Sam
56 In concealment
59 Relative of lieut.
60 Start
63 Similar
64 Twice 2055.5
65 Suspicious
66 Exactly suited
67 Fish sauce
68 Upbeat in music
69 Brit. award

DOWN

1 Space org.
2 Literary conflict
3 Price of a letter
4 Rotating machine part
5 Disposed
6 Certain business concerns
7 Tennyson's seaman
8 Put on
9 All-weather worker
10 High: Prefix
11 From __ (all the way)
12 Heavy hair
14 Facial feature
21 French possessive
23 Showery time
25 Famous last words
27 Port sights
28 Handy
29 Swiss river
31 Cancelled, in a way
32 Habituate: Var.
33 Substitute a voice on a soundtrack
36 Healthy in Spain
39 Tennis locale
40 Their, in France
43 Following the same course
45 Medit. sea arm
47 Compensation of a sort
49 Taste
51 Paint additive
53 Collegiate org.
54 Baleful sound
55 ". . . baked in __"
57 Buenos __ (good morning)
58 Biblical preposition
61 Biblical name
62 Cobb and others

53

Crossword grid with numbered cells.

ACROSS

1 Word with cow or slow
5 Eban
9 "A little __ Heaven . . ."
14 Gardner
15 Legal wrong
16 Fresh air
17 Make a fast dollar
19 Mae and wild
20 Pronoun
21 ". . . black sheep, have you __?"
23 Six dits and three dahs
24 Waterlogged
26 Friend of swimming bull
28 O.K. by radio
31 Turns out
34 Humane group: Abbr.
37 Suffix with arch or witch
38 Escape
39 Of an animal
41 Showing favoritism
42 Poppy product
43 Flow
44 __ hurry
45 Sex in grammar
46 "Why was __?"
48 Weight in gold
50 Type
54 Greek letter
56 Forty-niner since 1959
59 Gun group: Abbr.
60 "I've __"
62 Liqueur
64 Coeur d'__
65 Troubles
66 Blunt
67 Real gone birds
68 Prefix with phone or photo
69 Dies __

DOWN

1 __ Bill
2 Maine city
3 Bright light
4 Poet's adverb
5 Weigh __
6 Like some fish
7 Distillery's counterpart
8 "Here's looking __"
9 Flabbergast
10 Suffix with real or idol
11 Decide who pays
12 Undeceived
13 Parker of TV
18 Midwest clinic
22 Seasoning
25 Where the Alhambra is
27 Removing seeds
29 __ principles
30 Before
32 Sir in Singapore
33 French town
34 Toil
35 Le Moko
36 Matched
40 Repeats
41 British bar
43 Browned in deep fat
47 Talk turgidly
49 Implied
51 Lend __
52 Singing syllables
53 __ Cologne
54 African lake
55 Angelic headgear
57 Throw out, as type
58 Handle: Fr.
61 Daughter of Cadmus
63 Hitting record: Abbr.

ACROSS

1 TV comic Wilson
5 Women's __
8 Chapter of the Koran
12 Aspect
13 Crapshooter's gear
15 Son of Seth
16 Fun timepiece of the Nixon days
19 Having a will
20 Share
21 Alibi man
22 Principles
23 City on the Rhone
26 Invitation
27 Columnist Joseph
30 Pairs
31 Victory
32 Stow in a ship's hold
33 Member of U.S.N.
34 Narcotic
36 Pasture
37 "A __ grass is no less . . ."
39 "Drink of Englishmen"
40 Current water pollutant: Abbr.
41 Like __
42 Consumed
43 Fullness
44 Minute amounts
46 Bristle
47 Apparent
49 Baseball pitches
53 Rec room fixture
55 Feminine suffixes
56 Ritual ceremony: Var.
57 Approximately
58 Greek peak
59 Main and others: Abbr.
60 Hay and oats

DOWN

1 "Spartacus" author
2 Mexican Spitfire of films
3 Flag
4 Litigants
5 Partitioned-off area
6 Stopover spot
7 Honked
8 City on Puget Sound
9 Like young corn
10 Name for Alcatraz
11 Arthur of tennis
13 Moderate
14 Dive or song
17 Trees
18 Flower arrangement
22 Military headgear
23 Writer St. Johns
24 Spells
25 Sprawly city
26 Encore!
28 Manifest
29 Clingstone, for one
31 Member of U.S.A.F.
32 Compass reading
34 Some oratory
35 French land area
38 West Pacific island
40 ". . . wars begin in the __ men"
42 Infuriates
43 Event of the '40's
45 Division word
46 Edison's middle name
47 Shadow: Prefix
48 Periods of time
49 Spanish half dozen
50 Cork's land
51 __ of Sharon
52 Tidy, in Edinburgh
54 Opposite of hvy.

55

ACROSS

1 Hades V.I.P.
6 Poker moves
10 Fastener
14 Landscape
15 Lily plant
16 Latin 1201
17 ". . . a rather susceptible __"
19 Kind of rug
20 Musical note
21 Sturdy plant
22 Venomous snakes
24 Partner of quo
25 Dress length
26 Cleans
29 Formally permitted
33 "__ little maids from school"
34 Fred Astaire prop
35 Height
36 Tease repeatedly
37 Jokes
38 Central points
39 Sobeit
40 Raw materials
41 Fruit parts
42 Notation on an envelope
44 Deep red
45 Tidy
46 Lasted
47 What the captains and kings do
50 Fruit
51 Full of: Suffix
54 Norwegian king
55 When Captain Corcoran got seasick
58 Kind of seamen
59 Excited
60 Musical work
61 __-day service
62 Alaskan town
63 Cubs and Cards

DOWN

1 Army decorations
2 Nature's replay
3 Entrée order
4 Tavern
5 Have on the carpet
6 Packaged
7 French pronoun
8 __ late
9 Gross national product component
10 Well-known ship
11 Hurt
12 Certain tissue
13 Greedy ones
18 Goddess of discord
23 Food fish
24 ". . . ruler of the __"
25 Siberian sights
26 Word with black and boot
27 Steeple sound
28 System
29 Coat part
30 Contempt
31 Entertainment man
32 Certain believer
34 Jeweler's weight
37 David's friend
41 Behave foolishly
43 Poetic contraction
44 Kicker's objective
46 Pie cut
47 "__ I do"
48 Medit. island
49 Where the heart line is
50 College event
51 Baking equipment
52 Withered
53 Ages
56 Since
57 Roof ornament

ACROSS

1 Reveals
6 Fabled author
11 Marriageable
12 Milwaukee player
14 Sugar-cane residue
15 Lists of things
to be done
17 F.D.R. agency
18 Apparition
20 Seventh-century date
21 Research rooms
23 Byzantine image
24 Et __
25 Tending to: Suffix
27 Bard's nightfall
28 As regards
29 Stifle
31 Fleers
33 Unit of weight

34 Earthbound bird
35 Insults
39 Earhart et al.
43 TV's Mary Tyler
44 System
46 Old $10 coin
47 Son of Aphrodite
48 Where the girls are
50 What pigs do
51 Destroy by fire
52 Of the thigh
54 Greek letter
55 Hypodermic
feeder
57 Boise resident
59 Chef's specialties
60 Entire ranges
61 Girl's name
62 Auguries

DOWN

1 Imaginary terror
2 Camel's-hair fabric
3 Singer Stevens
4 Bovine name
5 More shabbily
dressed
6 Mother-of-pearl
mollusk
7 Work-heat measure
8 Perceived
9 Acknowledge
10 Pushcart salesman
11 Flame-thrower
adjunct
13 French dramatist
14 Pill for animals
16 Narrow openings
19 Turkish weight
22 Mill where gold
was discovered
24 Gaunt

26 Was eminent
28 Evangelist
McPherson
30 Boundary
32 Hebrew letter
35 Alpha and __
36 Discussion meetings
37 Highwayman
38 Chang and Eng
39 Vespucci
40 Luzon natives
41 Hawaiian greetings
42 U.S. nature writer
45 Impresario's
favorite sign
48 Wife of Menelaus
49 Word in a palindrome
52 Juan de __ Strait
53 Ineffectual
56 Parisian assent
58 Attila was one

57

ACROSS

1 The __ Kid
6 Unpretentious
12 French money
14 More unruffled
15 Star in Scorpio
16 Apprentice
17 Rural crossing
18 Pamphlet
20 Soul: Fr.
21 Instances
22 More unearthly
24 Pasha and Baba
25 Ski lift
26 European river
30 Performed
31 Rumanian city
32 Nature goddess
34 Call __ day
35 Comfort
37 Herb's predecessor
38 Rejected
40 __ even keel
41 Soprano Stignani
42 Field
43 Uniform
44 Hamper
45 River in Conn.
48 Greek island
49 College degrees
52 Manifest
53 City in Afghanistan
54 Ubiquitous
56 Raise
58 Hash house
59 Reprinted illegally
60 Specialist
61 Crossed out

DOWN

1 Small metric unit
2 Frighten
3 Becomes old-hat
4 Waxy finishes
5 Cockney residence
6 __ beaucoup
7 Speechify
8 Agnus __
9 Sicilian city
10 Appear
11 Bring to bay
12 Norma's big aria
13 Spanish Stephen
14 Belle or Ringo
19 Peruses
23 Plunder
25 Trampled
27 Slow down
28 Gave details
29 Banished
31 Red Baron,
    for one
32 Sib
33 Longing
36 Ballroom favorite
39 Cereal plant
43 Abrasive stuff
44 Entry at Longchamp
46 Hang suspended
47 Ward off
48 "I warned you!"
49 Zaharias
50 Man's nickname
51 Insult
55 __ and all
57 Cover

ACROSS

1 Mt. Rainier's range
8 Fired off-target
14 Ostensible
16 Maid of Astolat
17 Early period
18 Philippine island
19 Part for Theda Bara
20 Do lawn work
22 Branches
23 Old Siamese coin
24 Degraded
26 River called Ohre
   by Czechs
27 Enthusiast
29 Divisible by two
30 An Astaire
31 Fawn upon
33 Tissue
35 Take a bride
36 Aunt: Fr.
39 In the pink
41 Out in __
   (neglected)
43 Northern tree
46 Italian town
48 Robert __
49 Womanly weapon
50 Beethoven symphony
52 Hitler's wife
53 Old Irish fort
54 Winery refuse
55 American painter
57 Receiving visitors
59 Autonomous
61 Black eye
62 Shady businessman
63 Intricate
64 Fur-hunting area

DOWN

1 Winter melon: Var.
2 Gift
3 Frolicsome
4 "Mondo __"
5 Retiarius' milieu
6 Goddess: Lat.
7 Impress deeply
8 Apportioned
9 Pier union: Abbr.
10 Khachaturian piece
11 Fodder
12 Tooth part
13 Crave
15 Pester
21 City in Ohio
25 Climbing pepper
28 "Carmen" selection
30 Winglike parts
32 Imitator
34 Moral value
37 Put up with
38 Place for grain
40 Byron poem
41 Arm muscle
42 Clerical residence
43 Finally
44 Austro-Hungarian
   river
45 Enter abruptly
47 Trunk
50 Manicuring board
51 Town on the Tigris
56 Viva voce
58 Honey, in pharmacy
60 __ Dee,
   southern river

59

ACROSS

1 "__ Free"
5 Pit in a bone
10 W.W. II vessels
14 Space
15 Harangue
16 Atlantic fish
17 Dives
19 Ripped
20 Postulate
21 Mixed __
23 Back part often slipped
25 He or she: Abbr.
26 Family members
29 Lily part
32 Against property, in law
35 "Take __ from me"
36 One with a craving
38 Gershwin
39 Jot down
40 Midriff affliction
41 Pernicious
42 Ref. book
43 Look up to
44 Repast
45 Composer Franz
47 Relatives of mos.
48 Gets too much sun
49 Tighten tackle
51 Lofty
53 Irreproachable
57 Jumbles
61 Persian elf
62 Sloppily dressed
64 Awkward craft
65 Metrical stress
66 Low-lying land
67 Try
68 Baltic people
69 Israeli name

DOWN

1 __ California
2 Old Danish moneys
3 L.P.'s, for short
4 Desmond Morris subject
5 Type assortments
6 Mouth: Prefix
7 Keep
8 Restrain
9 Fabulist
10 Liquid cosmetic
11 Locale of an anthology
12 Mountain lake
13 "__ the sweetheart of . . ."
18 Malay dagger
22 Third: Prefix
24 Army assignment
26 Section
27 Expiate
28 Farm implements
30 Name in psychiatry
31 Assimilate mentally
33 Of a geologic time
34 Shopping centers
36 College degrees
37 Portland output: Abbr.
41 Of a photo-developing fluid
43 Pertaining to an epoch
46 Atelier man
48 Small blister
50 Lever
52 Collect
53 Young oyster
54 Father, in Nice
55 Beget
56 Sibilant sound
58 Generous piece of bread
59 Miss Logan
60 Noted
63 Successful show

1	2	3	4	▓	5	6	7	8	9	▓	10	11	12	13
14				▓	15					▓	16			
17			18							▓	19			
20								▓	21	22				
▓	▓	▓	23			▓	24				▓	▓	▓	▓
25	26	27			▓	28		29			▓	30	31	32
33			▓	34			▓	▓	35			
36			▓	37			38	▓	39			

ACROSS

1 Abandoned
5 Show biz chap
10 Relative of O.K.
14 Hebrew lyre
15 Author of *On the Beach*
16 Wild goat
17 Made up
19 Alaskan port
20 March 17 wear
21 Conflicts
23 Garden bloomer
24 Calendar abbr.
25 Feel pain
28 Key
30 Grammar case: Abbr.
33 Type-metal space
34 Try
35 Road-sign word
36 Tongue of Pakistan
37 Borage and tansy

39 Leap or light
40 City of Syria, to French
41 With, in Arles
42 Tear down
43 Draft initials
44 Turkish city
46 Soft drinks
47 __ Passos
48 Servicewoman of Britain
50 Alaskan port
54 Settle
58 Something to grind
59 Appoggiaturas
61 Girl of song
62 Pieces
63 Some Coloradans
64 Dele's opposite
65 Playing cards
66 Average

DOWN

1 Girl
2 Man of Tallinn
3 __ song (cheaply)
4 Fabricated
5 Surprise
6 Meat cuts
7 Ottoman
8 Inhabitant: Suffix
9 Indian
10 Hoodoo
11 Arabian name
12 Band leader
13 Former spouses
18 Dernier __
22 Midwest state: Abbr.
24 " 'Twas brillig" etc.
25 Greenish blues
26 Ringlets
27 Where the Styx flows

29 Insect stage
30 On top
31 Temporary thing
32 Processes, as meat
35 Unjustly severe
38 Unblemished
44 Nabokov novel
45 Zero
49 Long time
50 Traffic woes
51 Basic thing
52 Moniker
53 Turnpike sign
54 Sugar source
55 Give __ (berate)
56 Letters
57 He, in Turin
60 Capek's play

61

ACROSS

1 __-pie
5 Follows a bearish market trend
10 Shoo!
14 Sheik, for one
15 Self-esteem
16 Small jug
17 Partner of tattered
18 __ bell
19 Western world: Abbr.
20 Adds to a poker pot
22 Small knob of land
24 Lady Jane
25 Edible mushroom
26 Chrysalises
29 Exhibitionism
33 Makes happy
35 Tempters
36 Sulfur: Prefix
37 Salt tree
38 Houston player
40 Of brain tissue
41 Scream, in Nice
42 Time-bomb mechanism
43 Meander
45 Carpentry sound
48 Tendencies
49 Becomes tiring
50 Med. course
52 Mortar and __
54 Lack of appetite
58 Encourage
59 Tropical fruit
61 Divide
62 Posture
63 Exeunt __
64 "I'm __ hurry"
65 Communal insects
66 Urban problem
67 Fling

DOWN

1 __ pajamas
2 Lined up
3 Reduce
4 Relinquish
5 Carousal
6 One of the Furies
7 Mythical unicorns
8 Ahead: Abbr.
9 Nautical nations
10 Plant part
11 Finish
12 Biblical brother
13 City of purple
21 Up a __
23 Eye part
25 Act
26 Fruit
27 Extreme
28 Reworked parchment
30 Ship launcher of legend
31 Commandment word
32 Window parts
34 Popular flavor
39 Egyptian goddess
40 Past tense in grammar
42 Stumbled
44 Beam of a certain shape
46 Dull finishes
47 River of India
51 Gear for a horse thief
52 Family member
53 Black
54 Years, for Caesar
55 Alien: Prefix
56 Hostelries
57 Bustles
60 Common Latin verb

ACROSS

1 Tiger star of old
5 Actor Henry
10 Numerical prefix
14 Atmosphere
15 Bandleader Lester
16 Come into view
17 Cliff
18 Upright
19 Olden days
20 Name for old
Brooklyn team
22 Moscow sight
24 "__ live and breathe'
25 Parking-lot mishap
26 Chestnuts
30 Does a baseball job
34 Wild ox
35 Deity: Ger.
37 Disdain
38 Fairy: Sp.

39 Canadian area: Abbr.
40 Rattan
41 Improve
43 Music-box joint: Var.
45 Chinese dynasty
46 "Fidelio" heroine
48 Denied
50 Iranian ruler
51 Bill time: Abbr.
52 Northwest range
55 Talks testily
59 Chorus part
60 Habituate
62 Shakespearean villain
63 Save, with "away"
64 Indian lute
65 Golf tourney
66 Nautical speed unit
67 Skater Carol
68 Snoopy

DOWN

1 Fishing maneuver
2 Sound of pain
3 Scottish hillside
4 Big name on ice
5 Skater Peggy
6 Racing-shell needs
7 Compass direction
8 Famed figure skater
9 Bone cavity
10 Title for 4, 5, 8 and
29 Down and
67 Across
11 Collected
12 Anchor rings
13 Sign
21 G.I.'s friend
23 Sovereigns: Abbr.
26 Taj __
27 "What's in __?"
28 Western event

29 Ice queen
31 Friars Club event
32 Pyle
33 Golfing great
36 Brace
42 Capital of Qatar
44 Professional
mourners
47 Relish-tray vegetable
49 Gazelle of Tibet
52 "The __ of
Amontillado"
53 TV's King
54 W.W. II battle site
55 Spanish ladies: Abbr.
56 Soap, in old Rome
57 Iron and Stone
58 B'way award
61 Make use of,
in prescriptions

63

ACROSS

1 Division
7 Squanders
13 Part of an ode
14 Gluck opera
16 High spirits
17 On the bias
18 Ham's click
19 Become a pest
21 Duster
22 Mischa Elman's teacher
24 Yes-man
25 Hurling or curling
26 Hackneyed
28 Cruise port
29 Electronic device
30 Lamb and Bacon products
32 Residents
34 Horner's prize
36 Ingenuous
37 Flowed
41 Earth pigments
45 Androcles' extraction
46 The __ Affair in 1797
48 Celebes squall
49 Roma was one
50 "__ bolt from . . ."
52 Collapsed
53 Third-rate mark
54 College lecturers
56 Episcopacy
57 Max Baer's predecessor
59 Prone to anger, old style
61 Footstool
62 Holding rights
63 Companion of silks
64 Car accessory

DOWN

1 Gateway city
2 Rings on the moon
3 Faucet word
4 Philippine tree
5 Piglet
6 Wise counselor
7 Clean thoroughly
8 Brass, for one
9 Read meter
10 Sawbuck
11 Dais
12 Certain clam
13 Composed
15 Lawn tools
20 Moslem official
23 Farm machines
25 Links luggage
27 Poet Thomas
29 Gain altitude
31 "Cogito, ergo __"
33 __ de vie
35 Citizens of Guadalajara
37 Fine plaster
38 Warnings
39 Kern musical
40 Levee: Var.
42 Effacement
43 Glutton
44 Chargers
47 Highest point
50 Navigator's aid
51 Up __ (stumped)
54 Half: Prefix
55 Capital of Yemen
58 Paar's "I Kid You __"
60 Director's command

64

ACROSS

1 Police operation
5 Arrayed
9 Gambling casino word
14 Miss Baxter
15 Angel's I.D.
16 Eastern nurses
17 With 25, 39, 53 and 63 Across, quote by Alfred de Musset
20 Annoying roommate
21 Kind of talk
22 Consumed
23 Word on a bill, with "please"
25 See 17 Across
27 Marry
29 Philippine trees
30 Baba
31 Eur. country
33 Woman's age, for one
37 Bobby Orr's milieu
39 See 17 Across
41 "My Name Is __"
42 Strike-and-spare man
45 Boy's pistol fodder
48 Uris protagonist
49 Buffalo's relative
51 Threw a coin
53 See 17 Across
56 Atlantic island group
57 French pronoun
58 Castor's mother
60 Graphs
63 See 17 Across
66 Gorge
67 Kind of guard
68 Sicilian city
69 Nothing to marry in
70 Controversial planes
71 Breathing: Abbr.

DOWN

1 Cheers
2 Familiar author: Abbr.
3 __ order (usable)
4 B.A. or Ph.D.
5 Showgirl
6 Roman household god
7 Et __
8 Thingumajig
9 Established
10 French friend
11 Brazilian port
12 Vouchers
13 Bone: Prefix
18 Flop
19 Arm bones
24 Hebrew letter
26 Large land mass
27 Twain
28 "I cannot tell __"
32 Ad __
34 One source of info
35 Horse
36 Surrounded by
38 Secret order
40 Wave: Scot.
43 Kindle: Var.
44 City on the Seine
46 Deposits containing gold
47 Sweetener
50 Northern trees
52 Songwriter Cole
53 Slider
54 Relative of adieu
55 Russian huts
59 Campers' aids
61 Long times
62 Cinch
64 Superlative ending
65 Siamese, for one

65

ACROSS

1 Tittle
5 Stanza
10 Seaweed
14 Amonasro's daughter
15 Rose-colored dye
16 Bulrush
17 Aerial menaces
19 Moslem ruler
20 Loki's daughter
21 Dolls' companions
22 Ill-tempered
24 Monk parrot
25 Pickle
26 Insipid
29 Speculated
32 Winglike
33 "Anitra's __"
34 Shake
35 Blue or green shade
36 Join together
37 Senate figure
38 Timber tree
39 Adds spirits
40 Ilia's neighbors
41 Catherine et al.
43 More dismal
44 Penurious
45 Church fixture
46 Port on Gulf of Salerno
48 Baseball maneuver
49 Kimono accessory
52 Overindulge
53 Tar
56 Baker
57 Jargon
58 Templeton or Waugh
59 Nuisance
60 Opposite of broadside
61 Slat

DOWN

1 Coat thinly
2 Tramp
3 Pastoral poem
4 __ Mahal
5 Make fast
6 Asian capital
7 Enzyme suffixes
8 Latin man
9 Settle snugly
10 Military command
11 Woodsman
12 Voluble
13 Penthouse
18 Anguish
23 Boorish
24 Bait
25 Psalms
26 Bodice trimming
27 Howe
28 Coxcomb
29 Merchandise
30 Tidal flow
31 Cheerless
33 Waste away
36 Lower jaw
37 Role
39 Gladly
40 Annual V.I.P.
42 Yield
43 Castle's inner tower
45 Tierra del __
46 Over
47 Migrate
48 German league
49 Neighbor of Ark.
50 Vegetable
51 "The Seven Year __"
54 Yutang
55 Presidential nickname

66

ACROSS

1 Andean land
5 Wheezy plane
10 Cheese-eaters
14 Valhalla man
15 Dams
16 Gumbo
17 Gives the glad eye
19 Some votes
20 Astrologers
21 Math abbr.
22 Pounds and marks
23 Diminutive suffix
25 Every 60 minutes
27 Type of owl
31 Governments
35 Exclamation
36 Part of a hearth
38 Sum, in Naples
39 Hearty guffawing

43 Pressed
44 Stray
45 Relative of the cassowary
46 Submitting
48 Meantime
51 Khayyam and Sharif
53 Dunk
54 Young salmon
57 Kind of meal
59 Not so good
63 Author of "Topaz"
64 Roar with merriment
66 Adam, for one
67 Stained
68 Giant of myth
69 Retired
70 Onagers
71 Contrary one

DOWN

1 __ asinorum
2 Miss Adams
3 Food staple
4 Like Munchausen tales
5 Weight unit: Abbr.
6 Old coin of Spain
7 Alphabet letter
8 Vibration
9 Feminine suffix
10 Colossal structure
11 Image
12 American Indian
13 __ does it
18 Alderney, for one
22 Guildhall statue
24 Spiny anteater
26 Election news
27 Indian sir
28 Task
29 Novarro

30 Hic, haec, __
32 __ dolorosa
33 Resin
34 Cheese residue
37 Wheat: Fr.
40 Approved
41 French cathedral city
42 Onassis
47 Stadium sounds
49 Junior city
50 Name giver
52 Pillages
54 Cougar
55 Bedouin
56 Vex
58 "Of __ I sing"
60 Thailand king
61 Agitate
62 Spooky
64 U.S. spy org.
65 Parts of the psyche

67

ACROSS

1 Antiles resort island
6 __ to the good
9 Kind of wind
14 Lawyers' concerns
15 Scottish river
16 Ship
17 Flood stage
18 Periodical, for short
19 __ acid
20 Italian poet
21 Overwhelms
23 Galleys
25 Ski lift
28 Withers
29 Actual being
33 Turndown
35 District on the Thames
37 One at __
38 Rulers
39 Thatched

42 Part of R.O.T.C.
44 Noted
45 Relative of applejack
47 Bright light
48 Exceed
50 Early church language
54 Arizona Indians
58 Tony or Oscar
59 Cost of borrowing: Abbr.
60 Informed
61 Phileas Fogg's creator
62 __ out
63 Basis for a Scout badge
64 Viper
65 Ukraine, for one, Abbr.
66 Squeeze

DOWN

1 Statement: Abbr.
2 __ avis
3 Takes advantage of
4 Lady from Independence
5 U.S. capitalist
6 Nelson or Nimitz
7 Inclined
8 Vegetables
9 Witches'-brew ingredients
10 Terza __
11 Dismounted
12 Sand hill, in England
13 Greek god
22 Oriole's home
24 "__ body kiss a body . . ."
25 Volcanic rock
26 Actress Davis

27 Light __ under
29 Mamie
30 Trap
31 Power brake
32 German city
34 Do tailoring
36 Cockney's headgear
40 S.A. country: Abbr.
41 Short songs
42 Go back onstage
43 Period
46 Milk and water
48 More mature
49 No. 1 athlete
50 Mauna Loa output
51 Inspired
52 Late, in Paris
53 Sea bird
55 Reduce
56 Rainbow
57 New-math units

68

ACROSS

1 Menu item
6 Italian town
10 Street urchin
14 Home __
15 River to the Caspian
16 __ contendere
17 __ in the bucket
18 Military offense
20 Manta
22 Tipsy: Colloq.
23 Period
24 Aphrodite's son
25 Bird of legend
26 Mindanao native
27 Descendants of Esau
32 Flat
35 On the briny
36 Southern specialty
37 Particular ones

39 Put in order
41 Give __ steer to
42 Solar disc
44 Brain passages
45 Insanity
47 Diamonds, to Lorelei
48 Educators' org.
49 Garment
51 W.W. II initials
54 Types
57 Boob
59 Minions
61 Moslem religion
62 Winged
63 Tilt
64 Wrap
65 Depend on
66 Hardy heroine
67 Used a strop

DOWN

1 Black card
2 Tree
3 Grub
4 Thine: Fr.
5 Empties
6 TV part
7 Locks
8 Impetuous
9 __ de France
10 Expect
11 Vex
12 Lily plant
13 Fleming man
19 Space
21 Lippo Lippi, for one
25 Jungle sound
26 Nourishing
28 Martin
29 Character
30 Art process: Abbr.

31 Understands
32 Surveyor's nail
33 Lab item
34 Calla lily
35 __ spumante
38 "So-long!"
40 Pilaf, for one
43 Like some corn plants
46 Mare's __
47 __ Saud
50 Ejects
51 Fabric
52 U.S. painter
53 Ready for action
54 Cliff
55 Shield border
56 __ estate
57 Cheese
58 This: Sp.
60 Last: Abbr.

69

ACROSS

1 Small missile
5 Future tulip
9 Logmen's contest
14 Field for Cicero
15 Mime
16 Lend __
17 Radius' companion
18 Dial __
19 Special treat
20 Trapped
23 Miss Dallas
24 Gun
25 Like
28 Lifted
32 Some jewelry
36 Fruit
38 Jot
39 Move slowly
40 Ticket man
41 Trucks
42 Do afternoon honors
43 Is obligated
44 Malay state
45 Win over
47 Have it made
49 __ homo
51 Moors
56 Time
61 Havelock
62 Chew
63 "Von Stroheim: The man you love to __"
64 Tropical vine
65 Solo
66 City of U.S.S.R.
67 Men's sizes
68 Depend
69 Partition

DOWN

1 Fingerpaints
2 Shoelace tip
3 French income
4 Fishing net
5 Flat-bottomed river craft
6 In the know
7 Forty weekdays
8 Beverages
9 Triangular topsail
10 Twenty percent
11 King of drama
12 Let up
13 Scraps
21 Or __
22 Distinct
26 Chela
27 Boy Scout, sometimes
29 Amphibian
30 Sight from Taormina
31 Track event
32 Corncob
33 Shortly
34 Move before the wind
35 Kind of circus
37 Plateau
40 Flambeau
44 Sharp
46 Represents
48 Pave __ for
50 Cayce or Poe
52 Put on __ of force
53 Coronet
54 Arthur Hailey subject
55 Fishing leader
56 Cut down
57 Hodgepodge
58 __ Bator
59 As to
60 Post

ACROSS

1 Do a slow burn
7 Smart
11 Traffic component
14 Total
15 Island off Scotland
16 Uris hero
17 Ersatz-brain study
19 Encore!
20 Cottonwood
21 Finally
23 Gator's cousin
26 Sediment
28 Fisherman
29 Oriental nanas
31 Eleven or nine
33 Healthy: Sp.
34 Restraining rope
36 Bevel
38 Specifies
40 Jimmy
44 Fountain orders
46 Addison's friend
47 Event, in Spain
50 Saratoga et al.
52 Musical key
53 Uneasy headwear
55 Bede
57 U.S. inventor
58 Minted
60 Sad
62 Hooter
63 Milk proteins
68 Arikara
69 Secret group
70 Restless
71 Insecticide
72 __ up (completes)
73 Hassles

DOWN

1 Western Indian
2 English cathedral city
3 Jujube shrub
4 Fair distribution
5 Toss
6 Spirit lamps
7 Old dulcimers
8 __ polloi
9 "Child of the sun"
10 Social division
11 Occult doctrine
12 Not down
13 Café
18 Discharge
22 Part of Kipling's plea
23 Against: Prefix
24 Gypsy men
25 Grain
27 Chalky mineral
30 Utah flower
32 Red planet
35 Boxing periods: Abbr.
37 Mark: Lat.
39 Grape juice
41 Zone
42 Jai __
43 Soaks, as flax
45 Depresses
47 Agreement
48 Boasted
49 Grooming process
51 Loose garment
54 Capes
56 Waiters' offerings
59 Valley
61 Excellent
64 ". . . ere I __ Elba"
65 Consume
66 Naval initials
67 Part of CBS: Abbr.

71

ACROSS

1 Two-wheeled carriage
5 Of a chemical compound
9 Swiss cottage
11 Los __
13 Hawthorne character
14 Trampler, in Scotland
15 Electrical unit
16 One who gasps
17 Mouths
18 Type of cartridge
20 __ Moines
22 Fay Wray's King
24 Monte Carlo colors
25 Versifier
26 Old-womanish
28 Way: Abbr.
29 Area of a ship's bow
30 Service branch: Abbr.
31 Possess
32 Measure in Europe
34 Cuba libre base
37 Asian palm
40 U.S. tennis man
41 Detection device
43 __ to a turn
44 Presidential nickname
45 Cockney's 'eadgear 'olders
47 W.W. II area
48 Dominion
50 Weather-map line
52 Alarm clock, for one
53 ". . . all __ created equal"
54 Certain poem
55 Writer __-Beuve
56 Thumbs down, Russian style
57 Fasten

DOWN

1 Astronauts' host in 1969
2 File
3 Fix over
4 Look, in a way
5 Church fixtures
6 River near Paris
7 "__ my wits' end"
8 Return, astronaut style
9 River Styx V.I.P.
10 Vibration
11 Yearn
12 Binges
17 Turkish weight
19 Felicitous
21 Sault __ Marie
23 Look daggers at
25 Handled rudely
27 "All About __"
29 Fireplace area
32 French month
33 Glacial ridges
34 Fulton or Lee
35 One, in Italy
36 Proverbs
38 Access
39 Zodiac sign
41 Sesame, for one
42 Close again
45 River to the Oise
46 Russian girl's name
49 Underweight
51 Prohibits

ACROSS

1 Decides
5 Port near Hong Kong
10 Obscenity
14 __-ran
15 Get away from
16 Attention
17 Duck
18 Transform
19 Work units
20 Set
22 Scents
24 Flowering shrub
26 Kind of dance
27 Caused
30 Cato and others
34 Vetch
35 Severe
37 Maid or butler part, usually
38 Wife of Geraint
39 Obstruct
40 Parisian's dream
41 Poetic word
42 Wrist motion
44 Consumer
45 Polar hazard
48 Reading stand
50 Heed
51 Hanger-on
52 Setback
56 Snitch
60 Native of Yemen
61 Reduce
63 Indian tribe
64 Fox's pride
65 Tree mammal
66 Asian garment
67 Old-time slave
68 Feelings of ardor
69 Petitioned

DOWN

1 Swearing-in formality
2 Not guilty, for one
3 Peter or Nicholas
4 Repaired, in a way
5 Wander
6 The works
7 Like one's own baby
8 Drinks
9 Magnetic unit
10 Emotional outbursts
11 Connelly
12 Press
13 Girl's nickname
21 Leather
23 Age
25 Nonpoisonous
27 Czech town on Elbe
28 Alarm
29 Revolt
30 Inner or dress
31 Plump
32 Hudson, for one
33 Grim
36 Merry: Fr.
40 Cruel
42 Bargain sign
43 Legal-size fish for anglers
46 Lacking force
47 Malay gibbon
49 Third-century date
51 Children's zoo favorite
52 Price
53 Time periods
54 Conceited
55 Adam's son
57 German wife
58 Galway's land
59 Ogden of N.Y.
62 Cask

73

ACROSS

1 Hied
5 San Luis and Grand Coulee
9 Evidence of anger
14 U.S. inventor
15 Miscellany
16 Kind of yell
17 Hebrew letter
18 Kind of carpet
20 Isolate
22 Partner of Jones
23 Family __
24 Stage direction
27 Beginnings
29 Buddy
32 Shoe parts
34 Member of the family
35 Andy's sidekick
37 In the know
38 Colosseum, for one
41 Admirable precept
44 Violinist Isaac
45 Summer coatings
46 W.W. II battle site
47 Digits: Abbr.
48 Clung to
50 Uncle __
51 Moosehead, for some
54 Rapiers
56 Nissen __
57 Roy
59 Sylphs
63 Cast out
67 Exam
68 Object of exorcism
69 Herb
70 Gangster's money
71 Mountain ridge
72 Walked
73 Viewed

DOWN

1 Cover of a kind
2 Negri
3 Pitcher
4 Crusoe's creator
5 Where the activity is
6 __ bonne heure
7 Opposite of civ.
8 Real estate sign
9 Adult
10 Actor Cody
11 Tax deductions
12 Got the fire going again
13 French pronouns
19 Extremely
21 Light-switch positions
25 Charles and George
26 Clarify
28 Out of __
29 Mishandles
30 Common Latin verb
31 Be efficient
33 Mended
36 Barber's need
39 Piano piece
40 Tiny portion
42 Cherish
43 Mounted
49 Map explanation
51 Bara
52 Nicholas, for one
53 Hither's partner
55 Pollution factor
58 Fiber
60 Importune
61 Nathan
62 Vehicle
64 Bon __
65 Feather holder of a sort
66 Something to bolster

74

ACROSS

1 Food fish
5 Ending for gab
9 Meager
14 Sharpen
15 Table spread
16 Musical group
17 Three to a side
18 Cheat, in a way
20 Ran a meeting
22 "__ land of the free . . ."
23 Cocktail
24 Pain
25 Parched
26 Vocal trio
30 Light-bulb word
32 Type of salesman
34 Heavyweight name
35 Features of clown's feet
36 Place for notes: Abbr.
37 Performances
39 Comply
40 Photography plate
41 Say one's thank-__
43 Snow field
44 Abandon
47 Money in coin
50 Embark
51 Cassini's field
53 Theater org.
54 Sluggish
55 Penmanship
56 Retain
57 Plaster of Paris
58 Automotive name
59 Being: Lat.

DOWN

1 Boutiques
2 Beautiful woman
3 Preceding in time
4 Menu item
5 Nutritionist's concerns
6 Young eel
7 Sesame product
8 High crag
9 Lively movements
10 Mapped
11 Artery: Prefix
12 Almost
13 Ash, for one
19 V.I.P.-treatment aids
21 Here, in Paris
24 Wading bird
26 From head __
27 Churchyard sights
28 Ripped
29 Unbridled action
30 Alert
31 Sheltered
33 Pointed arch
35 Start eating, as an apple
38 Rockettes, for instance
39 Discarded film
42 __ Gang
44 Position
45 Stringed instruments
46 Storehouse
47 Gulp
48 Corn bread
49 Scottish friends
50 Waterproof
52 "__ can it be?"

75

ACROSS

1 Semitic deity
5 Outcast
10 Shakespeare
14 Singer Eames
15 Remove
16 Gov't. agency
17 Give off
18 Something for
the mill
19 Face
20 Merlin, for one
22 Delight
24 Listen
25 Cork locale
26 Give the speaker
a hard time
29 One of seven
in Rome
33 Bitter drug
34 Alla __
35 Zodiac animal
36 Calla or tiger
37 Sierra __

38 Bathe
39 Exclamation
40 Kind of common
denominator
41 Approach midnight
42 Respite
44 Go __ (deteriorate)
45 Engrossed
46 Sometimes it's dim
47 Diet food
50 Current time period
54 Melody
55 Frome
57 Patron saint
of sailors
58 Mail
59 Nautical call
60 Where 59 Across
is heard
61 Italian town
62 Classifies
63 Tear

DOWN

1 Busy creatures
2 Munitions
3 Moslem prince
4 Door-opener
5 Stowe's villain
6 Strayed
7 Set
8 Letter
9 Do a hunting dog's job
10 It's usually tight
11 Home for two billion
or so
12 Coin of Iran
13 Carnegie
21 They're slippery
23 Sea bird
25 Happening
26 Moon phenomena
27 Root
28 Red or green
29 Came up

30 Incensed
31 "The Queen's __"
32 Edit
34 Jungle dweller
37 1976 or 1980
38 Recent time period
40 King of Elizabethan
drama
41 Deductible item
43 Invent
44 Defiles
46 Aspect
47 Superman's garb
48 Cupid
49 Shopper's guide
50 "Is __ so?"
51 Otherwise
52 __ corner
53 Highway
56 Power-project initials

ACROSS

1 Having a glossy finish
8 Given to jesting
15 Howl like a wolf
16 Gourmet
17 Impala
18 Modern
19 Anger
20 Call __ (be in charge)
22 Furnace tender: Abbr.
23 Ocean vessel: Abbr.
24 Number
25 Waikiki's island
26 Part of Mao's name
27 Made fun
30 Papal name
31 Zest
32 Counterfeit
33 Relative of karate
36 Mourn

38 Empty
39 Miss Vague and others
40 Smarten, with "up"
41 Certain pitch
43 V.I.P.'s for elopers
46 Roman date
47 Beverage
48 Norse god
49 Character in "Oklahoma!"
50 Bland deception
54 Education org.
55 Indigestion source
57 El __, W.W. II battle site
59 Faded out
60 Differing
61 Antarctic penguins
62 Thoroughfares

DOWN

1 Expert in law
2 Puts on the qui vive
3 Cause shame: Lat.
4 Priest's robe
5 Seagoing: Abbr.
6 Implant firmly
7 Frat man
8 Insipid
9 Started
10 Refer to
11 Fiddler-crab genus
12 Companions of jibs and spinnakers
13 Small orchid
14 Gave another hosing-down
21 Dorothy's dog
25 Gems
27 Burlap fiber
28 Road curve
29 Actor Erwin

31 Odd people: Slang
32 Dread
33 Panama hat
34 Not developed
35 Figure in Mormon belief
36 Nourished
37 Before
39 Mountain climber's reward
41 River of S.C.
42 Big name in London
43 Port of Alaska
44 Full, in France
45 Viewpoints
50 Betel
51 Coffee, informally
52 King of Norway
53 Expose
56 Wilmington's state: Abbr.
58 Marie Dressler role

ACROSS

1 Bugle call
5 Personification of man
9 Fastener
14 Parisian friend
15 Lounging spot
16 Relative of largo
17 William, for one
19 Moldings
20 Cabbage dish, for short
21 Initials on handbags
23 Elusive fellow
25 Bulgarian coin
26 Gaelic
27 "Faerie Queene" poet
31 Sooner than
33 Military abbr.
34 Chef d'__
37 Affectionate name
40 Infrequently
43 Lilliputian
44 City on the Rio Grande
45 Unusual person
46 Leyden, for one
47 Search into
49 Chicken-out word
52 Indistinct
55 Nobleman in France
56 Mariner's aid
59 "Oh, how __ to get up . . ."
63 Choleric
64 Roman province in Gaul
66 Religious plate
67 Abner's friend and others
68 Sgts., etc.
69 Sitka vehicles
70 Barks
71 Unit of force

DOWN

1 Sailing maneuver
2 Cupid
3 Fine cloth
4 Gin-player's holding
5 "Peer Gynt" character
6 Frat house section
7 "__ and his money . . ."
8 River of W.W. I
9 Kind of slipper
10 Symbol of cruelty
11 Close, to poets
12 Arrests
13 Hoss-thief chasers
18 Indians of West
22 Doting
24 Bernstein and others
27 Unwieldy craft
28 Maine symbol
29 Noun ending
30 Kind of admiral
32 Caddoan Indian
35 Rubber tree
36 Cousin of veni
37 Kind of skirt
38 Biblical measure
39 Not more than
41 Waterfront group: Abbr.
42 __ go (precarious)
46 Made a memo
48 Stop
49 Tiny bits
50 Of a time interval
51 Harangue
53 Land of the Apennines
54 Chilean shrub for wine-making
57 Excitable ones
58 Fragmented governing group
60 Noun suffix
61 Action suffix
62 Lighten
65 Philatelist's concern: Abbr.

ACROSS

1 Spiked staff
5 Elevate the spirits
10 Prepare for finals
14 Woeful cry
15 Gaseous element
16 Golfing unit
17 Campus mil. group
18 Night alley sounds
20 Car parts
22 Arteries
23 Sophia
24 Long __
25 Timid
26 Bragged
28 Belief
30 Oriental, for one
31 Author Frances Parkinson
33 New Mexico flower
37 Small carrying case
39 Greek island
41 South African Dutch
42 Puppy
44 King of Crete
46 "__ for the show"
47 Asian locale
49 Class of enzymes
51 Restaurant bill
54 Scottish name
55 Having musical quality
56 Oil
58 Becoming passé
61 Strewers
63 Concerning
64 Ripped
65 Part of a coop
66 Penpoints
67 Book holders
68 Lilies of the West
69 Step

DOWN

1 Planet
2 "Little things mean __"
3 Librarian's list
4 Legal deposit
5 Surpassed
6 Discover
7 Insects
8 __ the mark
9 Incense
10 Burn
11 Expels
12 God of Islam
13 Sloppy
19 Hayes or Allen
21 Journey
24 Certain crime
26 Shell occupants
27 Naomi's helpmate
28 "As You Like It" girl
29 In and __
32 Arabian country
34 Spanish region
35 Cornfield sounds
36 Lily
38 Kind
40 Performers
43 __ with pride
45 __ Fein
48 Estimators
50 Part of a bellhop's job
51 Savor
52 Elbow
53 Meals
55 Statuary piece
57 Natives: Suffix
58 School subject: Abbr.
59 __ et orbi
60 Trial
62 Fish eggs

ACROSS

1 Solicits
5 Wild: Lat.
9 Hose
14 Radar-screen image
15 Of an acid: Prefix
16 Commune in Iowa
17 Church division
19 Nightingale-like call
20 Small openings
21 Went wrong
23 Not the clergy
25 Concoct
26 Long-termers
29 Without a middle
33 Aroma
34 Degrees: It.
35 One __ million
36 Gehrig's position
38 Some drs.
39 Inactive gas
41 Child

42 Cheeses
44 Where Lima is
45 Little Corporal's last abode
47 Kind of baby or neck
49 Slackening in tempo: Abbr.
50 Opera
52 Scottish emblem
55 Grade-A movie
59 Consecrated bread and wine
60 Sergeant's chant
62 Barrymore
63 Spread
64 Mountain: Prefix
65 French measure
66 Relative of drat
67 High __

DOWN

1 Skilled
2 Kill
3 Franklin device
4 Ones who let out the beans
5 Loud consonant
6 Live
7 Hairpiece
8 Hebrew letter
9 Italy, poetically
10 Breakfast item
11 Wagon-maker
12 Cypress feature
13 Ibn-__
18 Close
22 Retired
24 Railroad worker
26 High golf shots
27 Fool
28 Honest

30 Sinclair Lewis character
31 Boiled __
32 Boat
34 U.S. agent
37 Poe's heart
40 Kind of pool game
43 Retired valley
46 Less constricting
47 Certain Frenchman
48 Gen. Bradley
51 Bid
52 Pronoun
53 Detest
54 Reichenbach's electrical force
56 __-Finnic
57 Electrical prefix
58 Collar
61 Highest note

80

ACROSS

1 Place for mint
6 Classmen: Abbr.
9 Assets for no-trump
13 Soap plants
15 Asian holiday
16 __ nostrum
17 Illusory thing
18 Calif. menu items
20 Grows, as one's savings account
22 Agenda, for short
23 Algerian soldier
24 "__ fool"
27 Take out
28 Old wound
29 White wines
33 Hall, in Paris
34 Snakes
35 Wall, for one
36 Familiar name in prizes
37 No longer modish
39 Folk singer
40 Madrid figure
42 Atmosphere: Prefix
43 Heavy paper
44 River of Hungary
48 Display
51 __ basis (firm)
53 Infancy
54 Frenchman's name
55 Town in Nigeria
56 In this place
57 Spanish home
58 Ribbed material
59 __ as a beet

DOWN

1 "Home, __"
2 Eskimo craft
3 Actor Peter
4 Large antelope
5 Tent adjuncts
6 Output of Phidias
7 Work on the fudge again
8 Feel a craving, with "for"
9 Andy's pal
10 Hymns of praise
11 Before
12 French possessive
14 Dogs trained to catch game
19 Shelter
21 Piano player's standby
25 Certain people
26 Mountain spur
27 "__ M for . . ."
28 F.D.R.'s mother
29 Violent desire
30 Superior to
31 Working dogs
32 Scottish uncles
33 French town
35 Moolah
37 Like a prune
38 Smorgasbord items
40 __-made
41 Burning
43 After JKL
44 Takes top billing
45 Legal act of help
46 Pleasing, to a Parisian
47 Upright
49 Bewildered
50 Locale
51 Grampus
52 Educ. group

81

ACROSS

1 Extinct birds
6 Mulberry cloth
10 Brief attempt
14 Public
15 Added frosting
16 Church book
17 African animal
18 External: Prefix
19 Pedestal part
20 Attract
22 Extraordinary person
24 Levels of achievement
26 Time abbreviation
27 Cranberries' home
30 Went wrong
31 Mineo
33 Sound to gain attention
35 Bushy clump
36 Italian sculptor
39 "Tragedy tomorrow, comedy __"
41 Conveyer

42 Cooking wine
43 Cry from the fold
44 Atmosphere
45 Kind of bread
46 Authoritative statements
48 Reflux
49 King's predecessor
51 Abalone
54 Desk item
56 Skiing event
60 Tel __
61 Steam chamber
63 Polish province
64 Extent
65 Three-pointer in football
66 Trace
67 Harold of old comics
68 Remnants
69 Kind of preview

DOWN

1 Catnap
2 Kiln
3 National burden
4 Fragrant rootstock
5 Spice used by early Jews
6 Ten to ten
7 Kind of interest
8 Variety of firecracker
9 Be fond of
10 Kind of fountain
11 Lowell Thomas forte
12 __ Ababa
13 Sound praises for
21 Unrefined
23 Palm of Brazil
25 Horse race
27 Baseball equipment
28 Exclamation
29 Leave out details

32 Old coin of India
34 Like slush
36 Orange boxes
37 Action word
38 Bedouin
40 Verdant
41 Composer
43 Interpret incorrectly
46 Constellation
47 Distributes
49 "With __ of thousands" (movie ad)
50 "C'est __"
52 Saying
53 Coat fur
55 Unruffled
57 Unfrequented
58 Russian girl's name
59 Long-suffering
62 Author's monogram

82

ACROSS

1 Table scraps
5 Isaac's mother
10 Troy campus: Abbr.
13 Incubator sound
14 Certain small planes
17 Abundant in
shade trees
18 Typewriter part
19 Never: Ger.
20 Call's partner
21 Pointed arch
22 Venetian painter
26 Village on the Arno
27 Pungent vegetable
28 Nobleman
30 Photo developer's
abbr.
31 Numerical prefix
32 "Sierra Madre" star
34 Door opener

35 Michigan city
36 Hindu reign
39 Bigwigs of industry
40 Catawba, for one
41 Certain artist: Abbr.
44 Concrete piece
45 S.A. capital
46 Man's name
48 Cause irritation
51 Athenian of drama
53 Not one
54 Commit a holdup
55 Nonsense
58 Nail or secret
59 All over the place
60 Acclaim
61 Scottish
waterfall
62 Does a bank job
63 Anecdote collections

DOWN

1 Something fully
known
2 Attitude of trust
3 Undue boldness
4 Cooper character
5 Abstemious
6 Have __ in the hole
7 Complete
irresponsibility
8 Invite
9 "For __ a jolly
good . . ."
10 Perform, in a way
11 Musician Andre
12 "Life __! life is
earnest!"
15 G.I. mailing address
16 Puts out a base
runner
20 Rule out
23 Stadium shout
24 Cicero's tongue
25 Fetters

29 Coat's inside: Abbr.
32 Selassie
33 Remove from impost
lists
35 Mil. officers
36 Situated by water
37 Asian part of
Turkey
38 Wicked women
40 Trojan or Crimean
41 Quantity, as of soup
42 Svengali's girl
43 Stay
45 Rocket expert Willy
47 Between M and R
49 Spanish toast
50 Part of the media
52 South Bend
campus: Abbr.
56 Linseed product
57 Native of: Suffix
58 Gov't agency

83

ACROSS

1 July 4 sight
5 Ceylon sandstone
9 Ford
14 Rinse
15 Writer Gardner
16 Bridge call
17 Past
18 Noisy bird
20 ". . . were __ enow"
22 Moslem nobleman
23 Memo
24 Decorate
25 Mississippi name
28 Appreciative
32 Scoundrel
33 Vainglory
34 Literary scraps
35 News piece
36 Shade of gray
37 Pleased look
38 Neighbor of U.S.
39 English novelist
40 "__ Train"
41 Theater-lobby sign
43 Kind of writing
44 Flunky of old
45 Grit
47 Interval
49 Steel-refining
   process
53 Mickey Mouse films
55 Ibsen heroine
56 Coat piece
57 Gypsy __ Lee
58 Leprechaun land
59 Copycats
60 Encourage
61 Marsh growth

DOWN

1 Dud
2 Pelée product
3 Declare
4 Flowerpot favorite
5 European plover
6 Cropped up
7 Tonic herb
8 Buttons or
  Holzman
9 Religious recluse
10 Flower cluster
11 U.S. missile
12 Bohemian river
13 Poetic word
19 Promenade
21 Completed
24 Corny
25 Moment
26 Wagnerian god
27 G-man
28 A or B-plus
29 Wells __
30 __ Pacific
31 Singer Ross
33 Finish second at
   Yonkers
36 Theatrical
   trumpet call
37 Mary's occupation
39 Scamps
40 Triumphs
42 Finishing tool
45 Wisdom
46 Thing of value
47 Break suddenly
48 Smoker's item
49 Simpleton
50 Additional
51 Indian
52 Famous fan dancer
53 Wing
54 Gershwin

84

ACROSS

1 Early motor man
5 Actress Virna
9 Summarize
14 1912 Peace Nobelist
15 Angered
16 Ooze
17 B'way producer's concern
19 Airport runway
20 Obstructs
21 Conceal
23 Line of movement
24 Common choice in an exam
25 Former pitcher Dave __
28 Talmudic commentary
32 Scottish alder
33 Stylish
37 Apollo's birthplace
38 Connie of baseball fame
40 See 14 Across
42 Uses a straw
43 With the switch on "off"
45 Steak
47 Drone
48 Docks, as a ship
50 Emulator of a well-known marquis
52 D.S.C. winner
54 Elfin creature
55 Loose-fitting shirts
58 Draw to
62 Modify
63 Whole-hog
65 Euripides tragedy
66 __ Van Kull
67 Find fault pettily
68 Certain kind of council
69 Vaulted area
70 Ancient port of Phoenicia

DOWN

1 Spheres
2 Swag
3 Ism
4 Heavy-footed dances
5 "Three-score years and ten"
6 Swift's nationality
7 Short time, for short
8 I.e., in full
9 Did a favor for Pauline
10 Utmost lengths
11 Preserve
12 Passage
13 Spanish nickname
18 Edicts
22 Work unit
25 Entire range
26 Native of Isfahan
27 Toby of "Tristram Shandy"
29 Excuse
30 Riatas
31 Auditor's entry
34 Height: Abbr.
35 Eve, originally
36 Tai people
39 Capital of Moldavia
41 Disarrange
44 Weld
46 Planet with one satellite
49 Anterior to: Prefix
51 Manage
53 Japanese fair city
54 Becomes wearisome
55 Bivouac
56 U.S.A., Mex., etc.
57 Middle: Prefix
59 "__ in a manger..."
60 Creator of Gideon Fell
61 Roman or boldface
64 Rim of a pitcher

85

ACROSS

1 River fish
5 Sew
10 A, b, etc.: Abbr.
14 Invigorating
15 Kind of committee
16 Like __ potato
17 Times of day
19 Hindu sacred writings
20 Something easy
21 Mean one
22 Stage drapery
24 Lawn wrecker
25 Deer
26 Recently
29 Millinery items
32 Cinder
33 Lake
34 Greek letter
35 Travel agent's
   suggestion
40 S.A. country
41 Imparted
42 Origin
43 L.I. Sound resort
45 Group of French
   students
47 Antiquated
48 Mansard
49 Richard's need
51 Major __
52 Sternward
55 Defeat
56 Dec. 31 need
59 Choir voice
60 Opened
61 Desert lizard
62 German highway
63 Spring bloomer
64 However

DOWN

1 Exchange
2 Stereo set
3 Stake
4 Color
5 Bracelet
6 Worship
7 Brogan
8 Weight
9 Rapturous
10 Ceremonial basin
11 Decade
12 Took a cab
13 Headliner
18 Take hold
23 Live coal
24 Crèche figures
25 Farm unit
26 Famed statuette
27 Gaudy
28 Bass variety
29 Moor
30 Relaxes
31 Leather
36 Consecrate
37 Like scrambled
   eggs
38 Ref. work
39 Flying initials
44 Actor Richard
45 Stage fare
46 Place for woof
48 Varnish
   ingredient
49 Bedouin
50 Señor's greeting
51 Caper
52 Related
53 Chop down
54 Waiter's gear
57 Pronoun
58 Long __

ACROSS

1 Stinker
5 Fellows
10 Soup ingredient
14 She, in Paris
15 Antagonist
16 Beverage
17 Lynne's direction
18 Finnish lake
19 Ooze
20 Parts of the street scene
23 Corolla segment
24 Famed U.N. name
25 Youth org.
28 Plainclothesman: Abbr.
29 Vagrant
33 Pacific parrots
35 Record
36 Scarlett's manse
37 Jackets
38 Morose
39 Basement reading matter
40 Rat-__
41 Brim
42 Gnawing mammal
43 Cuernavaca's state
45 Bridge term
46 Holy __
47 Defunct car
48 Surfeits
50 Reputed Crimean stage prop of 1700's
57 Word of regret
58 Javelin
59 Forearm bone
60 Breach
61 Habitual way
62 Pole or Czech
63 G.I.'s of Seoul
64 Prods
65 Loathe

DOWN

1 "Copperfield" character
2 Ardor
3 Other than
4 Ease off
5 Produces
6 Indicate
7 Advantage
8 Paris area
9 Malamute, for one
10 Committed to
11 Ship part
12 Authentic
13 Vessels
21 Early Asians
22 L.A. athlete
25 Sparkle
26 __ voce
27 Noisy
29 Sleepy-head's land
30 Appointments
31 "Goodnight" girl
32 __ blanche
34 Concerns
35 Once-around
38 Family member
39 Modern hospice
41 Researches
42 Leaves the scene
44 Moon module
45 Uncivilized
48 Kind of thief
49 Some funds
50 Young salmon
51 Table item
52 Oil receptacle
53 __ facto
54 __ breve
55 Picnic pest
56 Roof part

87

ACROSS

1 Clashing
5 Beer or ale
9 Plum varieties
14 Occur, as a thought
16 Poplar
17 With 24 and 53 Across, quote by 40 Across
18 Badger's relative
19 Atlantic cape
20 Letters
21 Clothes
22 Suffix for cash
23 Move slowly
24 See 17 Across
30 Achieve entry
31 Skirt panels
32 Apprehend
34 Composition
35 Dragged forcibly
36 Sharpen
37 Tiny one
38 Flower bract
39 Miss Stevens
40 See 17 Across
43 Musical sounds
44 Scotsman's so
45 Mountain spurs
47 Ski-slope equipment
49 State: Abbr.
52 Low point
53 See 17 Across
55 What some actors do
56 __ occasion (cope)
57 Regaled, in a way
58 Organic compound
59 Merchandise

DOWN

1 Recorded proceedings
2 Doe
3 Prayer word
4 Civil War figure
5 Jacket
6 Hamlet, for one
7 Adam's grandson
8 Soaked
9 Jewelry stones
10 Iranian town
11 Drive
12 Robt. __
13 Musical offerings: Abbr.
15 Pub
21 Went wrong
22 "Tell it like __"
23 Breakfast fare
24 "__ Rhythm"
25 Color
26 Came across
27 African natives
28 Figure in Jewish folklore
29 Actor Conrad
33 European capital
35 Merry sounds
36 Common noun ending
38 Decorator's color
39 Getting nowhere
41 Emu or ostrich
42 Girl's name
45 Over
46 Branches
47 Like unsafe ice
48 Kiss, in Cádiz
49 Can. province
50 Glass oven
51 To __
53 After uno and due
54 Kind of ground or blow

ACROSS

1 Hearty dish
5 Northern European
9 Servicewomen
14 Opera solo
15 Pianist Peter
16 Neckwear
17 Harpo
18 Teen-__
19 Sonora Indian
20 Observer
23 Alpine sled
24 Mountain: Prefix
25 Ill-wishers
27 __ dig
30 Meager
31 Cozy places
32 Stubborn
33 Helmsman's course
36 Vehicles
37 Stall
38 Do damage
39 Word for a ship
40 Good-humored
41 Demands
42 In truth
44 Trainee
45 Uniformly
47 Brothers
49 Actor Alfred
50 California river
55 Twiners
57 Poise
58 52 Down's rival
59 Stage fare
60 Pitch
61 Cupid
62 Deli fare
63 Is done
64 Posse

DOWN

1 Duplicate
2 Server
3 Where the Shannon flows
4 Mme. Tussaud's place
5 Growing out
6 Musical sign
7 Abele or teil
8 Roughhouse
9 Give tongue
10 O.T. book
11 Agreed
12 __ et noir
13 Eye ailments
21 Cleo's attendant
22 Sinuous
26 Noun ending
27 Business abbrs.
28 Webster
29 Omen
30 Girl of song
32 Complain
34 Requested
35 Of yore, of yore
37 Good-looking gals
38 Puffer-fish dish
40 Punch
41 Athletic org.
43 Trenchermen
45 Jostle
46 Quechuan calculator
47 Inlet
48 Bakery items
51 Certain word
52 West Point
53 Look __
54 Ointment
56 Calendar abbr.

89

ACROSS

1 Region around Athens
7 Portions: Abbr.
10 Ship pole
14 With 21, 26, 54 and 64 Across, quote by a famous American
15 Korean soldier
16 Band instrument
17 Kind of play
18 Unoriginal one
20 Customer
21 See 14 Across
23 Smooth consonants
25 Nears midnight
26 See 14 Across
30 Bow
33 Theater box
34 Fasten
36 Peanuts, for one
38 Kind of salad
41 Word before deep or high
42 Shakespearean villain
43 Dry, as wine
44 Source of the quote
49 Nickels and dimes
50 Ataturk
54 See 14 Across
58 Archeologist's find
59 Gets even
60 Separated, in Madrid
62 Construction piece
63 N.Y.C. subway
64 See 14 Across
65 Enclosures
66 His: Fr.
67 Duplex feature

DOWN

1 Entangled
2 Nervous
3 Relative of twixt
4 Turkish inn
5 Medical prefix
6 Flower: Prefix
7 G.I.
8 "The Iceman __"
9 Pares, as leather
10 __ stripes
11 Golf stroke
12 __ ben Adhem
13 Infrequent
19 Color
22 Straighten
24 Aria
27 Bid for
28 Ancient temple
29 Dreadful
30 __ emma (A.M. in England)
31 Resounded
32 Sculling group
35 Kind of current: Abbr.
37 Kind of pet
38 Union concern
39 Insurance man: Abbr.
40 Appearance
42 Swallows
45 Climb, in a way
46 Scottish dish
47 Belong
48 State
51 __ Gras
52 Flower
53 Certain looks
54 LSD user's experience
55 Youth goddess
56 Welsh name
57 Keep __ on (watch)
61 Poe's pendulum choice

ACROSS

1 Fixes the piano
6 Name in long-run show
10 Like some trains
14 Separated
15 Colt
16 Miss Claire and others
17 Natives of Addis Ababa
19 Burden
20 Mauna __
21 Shopping place
22 Native
24 Shrew of musical
25 Part of A.D.
26 Arab, for one
29 Species of buttercup
33 Salty deposit in lake basins
34 Evening: Fr.
35 Brazilian palm
36 Wagner series
37 Analyze, in a way
38 Hagen and others
39 Prefix for morph or plasm
40 Opposite the wind
41 Peaceful places
42 Customer of an inn
44 Bead of carnelian
45 Outfits
46 God of Memphis
47 South Pacific island
50 Rests
51 Scottish negative
54 Irish islands
55 With 10 Down, words for Haile Selassie
58 Opposite of plu.
59 Stead
60 French income
61 Lip
62 German river
63 Riser

DOWN

1 Chinese weight
2 Until
3 City of Okinawa
4 Silkworm
5 Leaf openings
6 Burning
7 Gravy holder
8 Fleming
9 Home of Hamlet
10 See 55 Across
11 O'Neill's Christie
12 Strained
13 Being: Lat.
18 Spread
23 Wind direction
24 Epithet for Christ
25 Get up
26 Scatter
27 Heath genus
28 British W.W. II general, to friends
29 Kitchen utensil
30 Of a grain
31 Zoo animal, for short
32 Italian poet
34 White or fire events
37 Small bit
41 Blackboard needs
43 River island
44 Aleutian island
46 Wounded vanity
47 Russian agency
48 Concert selection
49 Dutch skater's name
50 Rebuke, in Scotland
51 Vessel of 1492
52 No-voter
53 German river
56 Salad topping
57 Soak, as flax

ACROSS

1 Breathe heavily
5 Pacific sight
10 Anarchist Goldman
14 Excessive
15 Stop
16 Close
17 Raced
18 Nobelist in medicine, 1958
19 Branches
20 Stuck-up
22 Made a speech
24 Isolated
25 Easy job
26 Arithmetic chore
29 Tosses, as chicken feed
33 Solution
34 Forest opening
35 Myrna
36 Extended
37 Sudden outburst
38 Pan, for one
39 Hitler's love
40 Urbane
41 Part of a poem
42 Recount at length
44 Did a floor job
45 "__ well"
46 Dead Sea feature
47 Hi-fi gear
50 Cartoonist
54 Mountain lake
55 Up to
57 Truck, for short
58 Cap-__
59 Hollow stone
60 Eye part
61 Papyrus, for one
62 U.S. painter
63 Pay up

DOWN

1 Utensils
2 English river
3 Roman violinist
4 Multiplying, in a way
5 Temporary
6 Taunt
7 Sworn statement
8 Baton Rouge campus
9 Picnic drink
10 Transported
11 Gist
12 Lansbury role
13 Dry
21 Prepare for a test, with "up"
23 Scold
25 Kind of crow
26 More capable
27 Herd
28 Shore
29 Aesop, for one
30 Antelope
31 A.A.A. map marking
32 Council
34 Tumbler
37 Leave
38 Disney film
40 Store-ad subject
41 Peaceful
43 Deserved
44 Masted ship
46 Nasty
47 Regulus or Polaris
48 Recording
49 Pennsylvania city
50 Power source
51 Sea bird
52 Leave out
53 Slope
56 Recent: Prefix

ACROSS

1 Army off.
4 African tribesman
9 Discordant
13 Marco
14 French passion
15 Fictional gumshoe
16 Greenland settlement
17 Granite center
18 Attention-getter
19 "__ comes marching . . ."
21 Genetic initials
22 Follower of boo
23 Mauna __
24 Lamech's wife
26 Britishers
32 Bedeck
33 Herb genus
34 __ volente
35 "The __ thickens"
36 Soap substitute
37 Card round
38 Express
39 Anoint
40 Feather
41 Predecessor of R.M. Nixon
43 Global area
44 Harem chamber
45 Timetable abbr.
46 Pronoun
47 Sherwood Forest man
54 Succeeds
55 Worship
56 Obsolescent wedding word
57 Public houses
58 Dawdler
59 Flaw
60 Duchess of Alva painter
61 Glorified
62 Man's nickname

DOWN

1 __ eaten (shabby)
2 Wings
3 Declaration signer
4 Hindu mister
5 Eastern nurse
6 Norse goddess of fate
7 Vaudeville act
8 Nobel chemist
9 Tinder
10 Priscilla and spouse
11 __ hearty meal
12 Gypsy man
13 Right church, wrong __
20 Saint or Prester
23 Wts.
24 Unrehearsed
25 Stage __
26 Bandit brothers
27 Convex molding
28 Hokinson or Hayes
29 Wind direction
30 Inclined, in London
31 East Indian herb
32 Be __ to a boy
36 Harding of films
37 Certain kind of letter
39 Triumphant cry
40 Marquette
42 Black Sea port
45 Brisk
46 Of an Asian race: Prefix
47 Dear one
48 Joss
49 Drink heavily
50 Very, in Versailles
51 Musical instrument
52 Arrested
53 American humorist
54 British court wear

ACROSS

1 Fall flat, as a show
5 Cavalry weapon
10 Part of a doorway
14 Culture medium
15 Alpaca's relative
16 Lamb
17 First word in Vergil work
18 Painter's need
19 __ in the saddle
20 Dark-room event
22 Physical irritability
24 Sheltered nook
26 Snarl: Scot.
27 New voting age
31 N.Y. lake
35 Wherewithal
36 Correct
38 Pronoun
39 Claire and others
40 Cold winds of Europe
41 __ in one
42 Rifle range: Fr.
43 Hymn of praise
44 African language
45 Stipend
47 Proximity
49 Tops of aprons
51 Explorer Hedin
52 Master chef's customers
56 Newsroom man
60 Aleutian island
61 Cowboy
63 Mother Hubbard's lack
64 Traffic sign
65 Dinner course
66 U.S. budget outlay
67 Wine
68 Belgian battle site
69 Old English court

DOWN

1 Barnyard sounds
2 Fearsome one
3 Doll's word
4 Subdivisions
5 Part of a jacket
6 Winglike part
7 Groundwork
8 Corundum
9 Sir Walter and others
10 Beverly Hillbillies man
11 Jai __
12 Wire measures
13 Healing agency
21 French president
23 Allowance for waste
25 Strange
27 Issues
28 Old Greek region
29 Knot in wood
30 Jewish month
32 River of France
33 Young sows
34 Ostrich-like birds
37 Factors in heredity
40 Popular candle scent
41 Famous crosser of the Alps
43 Neat
44 Engendered
46 Hasty
48 Wards off
50 Bend down
52 Sound of surprise
53 Financier Kahn
54 Use: Lat.
55 Mineral
57 Rent
58 "This one's __"
59 Relaxation
62 Direction

ACROSS

1 Foolish
5 Not ruddy
9 Union general at Shiloh
14 Paris' field
15 Terrible or Great
16 Final stanza of a ballade
17 Mythomaniac
18 Attend to
20 Take, as a plea
21 Apple section
22 Everlasting, long ago
23 Minstrel performer
25 Teasdale and others
27 Wild __
28 Big W.W. I guns
32 Tropical Asian tree
34 Selected
36 __-way street
37 Mineral deposits
38 Secreted
39 Alloy of lead and tin
41 Follower of fa
42 Instant
44 More unusual
45 Dreamy
47 Desert-like
48 Informal taboos
50 Showy plants
53 Noisy-eating sounds
56 Unit of illumination
58 House part
59 Six-sided solid
61 Metalware
62 Mountain ridge
63 Palm product
64 Golden or slide
65 Flat sides
66 Hurricane areas
67 Danube tributary

DOWN

1 Music direction
2 Talking horse of Greek myth
3 Nonsense
4 Norse war god
5 Mountain-climbing gear
6 Caucasian language
7 Finger and Great
8 Direction
9 Scram
10 Disquiet
11 "Thanks __ so much"
12 Diving bird
13 Prison sentence
19 Roman goddess
21 Utter disasters
24 Render
26 Habitation
29 Dreadful
30 __ of Cleves
31 Al Capp's Old Man Mose
32 __-ran
33 Quickly
34 Marx brother
35 This: Lat.
40 __ a reputation
43 Henna, for one
46 Prisoner
47 Tea cakes
49 Cut-flower display
51 Amazon slain by Hercules
52 Insulting expression
53 Fellow
54 Wife of Zeus
55 Bovines
57 French innkeeper
60 D-Day leader
61 Prefix for angle

95

ACROSS

1 Academic lowly
6 Papal cape
11 Taxi
14 Capone contemporary
15 Spring flower
16 Part of H.M.S.
17 Mercurochrome and others
19 Common verb
20 Fuel
21 German admiral
22 Mystic cards
24 Spanish uncles
25 Guru's relative
27 Crowns
30 Jews living outside Israel
33 __-arm
34 Gene or Grace
35 Waiter's expectancy
36 Bore
37 Seasonal song
38 Weather abbr.
39 Noun suffix
40 Hook features
41 Cheese shape
42 Scantily
44 Frame for candles
45 Approaches
46 French port
47 Edsel, for one
49 Food fish
50 __-relief
53 Mary Todd's husband
54 Self-reliant
58 Dash's partner
59 Fanatic, in France
60 Like an egg
61 Firm up
62 Epic writer
63 Multiplication word

DOWN

1 Banner
2 Rockfish: Var.
3 Chooses
4 Specialized strip of wood
5 Mercenary
6 Wine pitchers
7 Formal act
8 Baba
9 Fond du __
10 Overpowering bliss
11 Ben Hur, for instance
12 Prefix for gram or naut
13 Harte
18 Certain poetry
23 Elec. unit
24 Edge
25 Missile sites
26 Berlin sight
27 River of China
28 Castle or Dunne
29 Resort near tip of L.I.
30 Epsom Downs event
31 Frosts
32 Strudel component
34 Marx and others
37 Vikki
38 Conjunction
40 Like the market at times
41 Jesus' words to widow
43 Exclamation
44 March animal
46 Prank
47 Young ones
48 Instrument
49 Give in
50 Radiate
51 Stake
52 Jean d'Arc et al.
55 Recent: Prefix
56 Kind of wit
57 Roman 506

ACROSS

1 Scrooge's word
4 Stay
8 Weight units
14 Service club
15 Oahu dance
16 _ cracker
17 Item for Perry Mason
19 Calder art form
20 Amo, veni, ubi, etc.
21 Many times
23 _-given
24 Land measures
26 Scoreboard trio
27 _ of guns
28 Brilliant
30 Sets in motion
33 Street peddler
35 Salamander
36 Posts
40 Imposing
44 Move quietly
45 Direction
46 Italian island
47 Described
51 Timetable abbr.
52 Limits
55 Bustle
56 Garage worker: Abbr.
58 Wine: Prefix
59 Stigma
61 Light cigar
64 Get hold of
66 Stood
68 Danish port
69 Bridge bid
70 Arabic letter
71 Could tell, in a way
72 Lawman of West
73 Campus org.

DOWN

1 Singer Ives
2 Confused
3 After "chili today," in weather joke
4 Excels
5 Wine measure
6 Spread
7 About as expected
8 Dramatic bits
9 Later
10 Umbrella part
11 Friend
12 Claw
13 Go-devils
18 Strain
22 Drink, as of rum
25 British gun
27 Card
28 Channels
29 Part of Q.E.D.
31 Mat. time
32 Desert lizard of the U.S.
34 Grass unit
37 What the devil finds work for
38 Law degrees
39 Hot or driver's
41 Area in the Seine
42 Insect study: Abbr.
43 Look
48 Cloyed
49 Witness-box response
50 Depart in haste
52 Texas river
53 Battery pole
54 Italian star
57 Roman 151
59 Objective, for one
60 Poet Walter _ Mare
62 Interpret
63 Tote-board data
65 Hosp. people
67 After Feb.

97

ACROSS

1 Cleans floors
5 Burst of energy
9 Prepares gifts
14 "Will you have __ of tea?"
15 Asian sea
16 Emulator
17 Question closely
19 Express an idea
20 Wonderland girl
21 Identified
23 Newspaper item
25 Hosiery mishaps
26 Prefixes meaning inner
28 Reaches
32 Discover by diligence
37 Warehouse
38 Australian native, for short
39 Jackrabbits
41 Onassis
42 __ up (appears)
45 Determines exactly
48 Adds up
50 Girl's toy
51 __ Peak
54 Converse, in a way
58 Was nosy
62 Famed Finnish runner
63 Bizarre
64 Makes tentative inquiries
66 Chemical compound
67 Major or minor
68 First word of Mass. motto
69 Ballistic missiles
70 __ out (supplements)
71 Rural highway hazard

DOWN

1 Parrot
2 Florida city
3 Deposit
4 Phantom
5 Word before humbug
6 Like the Gobi
7 Hitler and others
8 Gather
9 Maligned
10 Counterstroke
11 Girl's name
12 Breaded: Fr.
13 Coaster
18 Stop
22 One-liner
24 "The lady __ protest too much"
27 Soft __
29 Bridge
30 Wrongful act
31 U.S. inventor
32 Truth
33 Spanish river
34 Fountainhead
35 Swiss canton
36 Watch over
40 Sully
43 Decorator
44 Baseball pitches
46 Warner of Chan films
47 Treated unjustly
49 __ lift
52 Result
53 Wading bird
55 Danish coin
56 Charm
57 Strength of a solution
58 Sandburg
59 Carry the football
60 Give __ (scold)
61 English river
65 Pensacola site: Abbr.

ACROSS

1 German pistol
6 Today in Turin
10 Humorous poet
14 Together
15 Fur bearer, for short
16 Indian of Peru
17 Mrs. Fitzgerald
18 Thanks __
19 Equable
20 Teaching degree
21 Dental fixture
24 Marine science center
26 Cecil or Agnes de __
27 Supply's partner
29 Heavens: Prefix
31 Unchanged
32 Marble
33 Merry, in Marseilles
36 Electrical power
39 Old alloy
41 Southern gentleman's word
42 Lorna
44 Wings
45 De la Roche book
46 Miss Hawn
48 Name in Erie Railroad lore
50 Certain student
52 California
54 Gallic soul
57 Irish
58 "What __?"
59 Port of Brazil
61 Sailing
62 Dull
63 Paradises
64 Mass. city
65 Marital discards
66 Asian country

DOWN

1 Be idle
2 Handled
3 Cellini, for one
4 Finish
5 Ronald of California
6 City near Silver Springs
7 Insect of mystery tale
8 Err
9 Close
10 Ornamental alloy
11 Famed chorus
12 Location
13 Kind of nail
22 __ hat
23 Like a careworn face
25 Bridge hand
27 Grackles' relatives
28 Pottage buyer
30 Lightly cooked
32 Age
33 Arizona name
34 Turkish troops
35 __ fixe
37 Allan-__
38 Valuable certificate
40 Festival
43 Kindergarten period
45 Of a Biblical land
46 Obtain
47 Long Russian river
48 Like furze
49 Norse name
51 Scolds
52 Of the earth
53 Tunisian port
55 Horsehair
56 Lanchester
60 Fuss

ACROSS

1 Sailor's saint
5 Paper size
9 __ system
14 N.Y.S.E. trader
15 Slangy suffix
16 Part of Hispaniola
17 Storm omen
19 Of an element
20 Decorative brass
21 Individual
23 Residence, in Soho
24 Base-hit
27 Farm animal
30 Descartes
31 Olympian
32 As a friend: Fr.
34 Recipe abbr.
36 Deadlocked
39 Flamboyance
41 Port of Italy
43 Pother
44 Sale condition
46 Tête-__
47 Chaotic, as type
49 Pinches
51 French possessive
52 Constitutional right
56 __-de-sac
57 Skirt style
58 Devastate
62 Cast
64 Pictured as flawless
66 __ space
67 Seek to find out
68 __ swath
69 Nostradamus et al.
70 Gaelic tongue
71 Mine car

DOWN

1 River of Spain
2 Regan's father
3 Cripple
4 Whether __
5 Ritzy
6 Leading man, in Soho
7 Desserts
8 Alpine air
9 Ram's-horn trumpet
10 Western group: Abbr.
11 Vehicles to airports
12 One at __
13 Kitchen item
18 Abbé, for one
22 Minimal
25 Feeds the kitty
26 Reach effectively
27 Capitol Hill men: Abbr.
28 Art course: Abbr.
29 Handle
33 Tallchief
35 Affirm
37 Diminutive ending
38 Executes
40 Mecca pilgrim
42 Scapegrace
45 One in the know
48 Rice and Fudd
50 Buccaneer
52 Narcissus' admirer and others
53 Evidence of S.R.O.
54 Join
55 Throw out
59 Côte d' __
60 Japanese clogs
61 Dutch export
63 Poetry: Abbr.
65 Letter

ACROSS

1 Brown ore
5 Tooth
10 Genesis name
14 "Now __ me down to sleep"
15 Rope fiber
16 Role in a play
17 Lose out
19 Neglect
20 Useful receptacle
21 City near Brisbane
23 Audience
24 Dyes
25 Kind of telephone hookup
29 Gulled
32 __ of Court
33 __ alai
34 Breeze
35 Mae West role
36 Byron work
38 Time period
39 Dough
41 Low-key lie
42 Stern
43 Hairnet
44 Partridge locales
46 Ladder-like
48 Surface measure
49 Special pitcher
51 Tornado
55 Tip
56 Stereo devotee
58 Nautical term
59 Belief
60 To __ (everyone)
61 Tidy up, in Scotland
62 Cut
63 Make right

DOWN

1 Cotton fabric
2 Muhammad and others
3 Till contents
4 Seafood
5 High Hindu
6 Mind
7 Testing place
8 Keenness
9 Mexican dance
10 Exposed
11 New World, for one
12 Explorer
13 Closet menace
18 Kind of door
22 __ with (favored)
24 More formal
25 Movies
26 Pungent bulb
27 Set free
28 Fled
30 Mountain nest
31 Small amounts
34 Tropical tree
36 Term of address
37 Small inlet
40 Found
42 British economist who coined a law
44 Set of jewelry
45 Junket
47 Percolate
49 Scorch
50 Miff
51 Non-waiter
52 See 51 Down
53 Vitality
54 Tear
57 Moisture

101

ACROSS

1 Catch one's breath
5 Relative of Tubby
10 Critical remark
14 Skill, in Italy
15 Rule needing no proof
16 Adams
17 Author linked with 49 Across
18 Sauce
20 Quiche __
22 Type of bug
23 Those: Scot.
24 Same: Fr.
25 Ferryman
28 Supplying food
32 Orphant Annie's creator
33 Two-__ suit
34 Partner of neither
35 Unicorn fish
36 French maidservant
37 House for señors
38 Metric weights: Abbr.
39 __ powder
40 Realty sign
41 Bookie
43 Irish port
44 Decorator of sorts
45 Charges
46 Evangeline's home
49 Subject of famous dissertation
53 Alphabet purée, literally
55 And others: Lat.
56 London gallery
57 Medicine: Prefix
58 Incarnation of Vishnu
59 Hebrew lyre
60 Be
61 Kind of roe

DOWN

1 Celt
2 Guthrie
3 Culinary direction
4 Partridge habitat
5 Politically cautious
6 Nerve-cell process
7 Weary
8 Earth
9 Menu item
10 Kitchen tool
11 Mine entrance
12 Companion of shine
13 Rarebit ingredient
19 Treats the lawn
21 Sea call
24 Spiritual food
25 Small bit
26 Door holder
27 Canting, as a ship
28 Chair repairer
29 Totally
30 "Long time __"
31 Culinary direction
33 Card game
36 Prepare dessert
37 Sleds
39 Silent
40 Word used with "chic"
42 More in order
43 Tempest locale
45 Petits __
46 Movie dog
47 Auditors: Abbr.
48 Choir voice
49 French menu word
50 Egyptian god
51 "__ Camera"
52 Pleased
54 Musical instrument

ACROSS

1 Nimble
6 Oodles
11 Go back on one's word
13 Vote
14 Forecast
17 Fixed a squeaky wheel
18 Cape
19 Cather
20 Constellation
21 Chases birds
23 Electrified particle
24 Work unit
25 TV choice
27 Knowledge source: Abbr.
28 Wife of Henry VIII
30 Envoy's residence
32 Hostelry
33 Scottish name
34 Developing sprouts
38 Odd
42 Land measure
43 Waxes
45 Sea bird
46 Italian number
47 Swiss town
48 Soak flax
49 Conveyances
52 Wire: Abbr.
53 Tennis star
55 Unaccountableness
58 D.A.'s concerns
59 Briny
60 Bear
61 Gratified

DOWN

1 Behind, in France
2 Rock study
3 Playwright
4 __ a hand
5 Freudian word
6 Indian tribe
7 Type of hammer
8 Prefix with meter or tude
9 Relatives of place mats
10 Slender branches
12 Lesion
13 Advice to bridge player with a fair hand
14 North and South
15 E. Indian tree
16 French city
21 Gave a wide berth
22 Mideasterners
25 Geometric section
26 Structural beams
29 Copying machine: Abbr.
31 Collection of facts
34 __ Casazza of opera
35 Wandering ones
36 Make another effort
37 On the house
38 Roman robes
39 Soothing
40 Acted as a host
41 Ingress
44 With, in Paris
50 African plant
51 Cross over
53 Girl's name
54 Got off
56 Legal degree
57 __-relief

103

ACROSS

1 Trouble's partner
5 Snowy and barn
9 Guatemalan Indian
14 Voice
15 Relative of groovy
16 Set straight
17 Tells whoppers
18 Maxwell
19 Changes habits
20 Double-take words
23 Aunt or uncle: Abbr.
24 Vox populi, vox __
25 Place for a certain light
30 Fish hawk
35 __ Gatos
36 Lithe
38 Firm
39 Entrance
41 Sewing packets

43 "Thin Man" dog
44 "As I __"
46 Oozes
48 Hindu weight
49 Entranceway
51 Slobberers
53 Born, in France
55 __ spree
56 Words of a grammatical skeptic
65 Chronicler of Poker Flat
66 Pull a boner
67 Dress part
68 Asian V.I.P.
69 Poker term
70 Vent
71 Softens
72 Use the library
73 Dakota Indians

DOWN

1 Soft mineral
2 Conglomeration
3 Collector's __
4 Traditional weepers
5 Martini ingredient
6 Shoe part
7 Whip
8 Sober
9 Sentimental
10 Table item
11 Late chanteuse
12 Years, for Caesar
13 Kind of egg
21 Fictional girl
22 __-Nazi
25 Hug
26 Western show
27 Willow
28 N.Y. five
29 Pasted
31 Kentucky grass

32 Charlotte __
33 Compound
34 Time periods
37 Row
40 Small bird
42 Pampered
45 Vessels
47 "__ of India"
50 Welcoming wreath
52 Perry Mason, for one
54 First name in U.S. fiction
56 Comic-strip sound
57 Harness unit
58 Russian city
59 Printing word
60 Finished
61 Greek letter
62 Kind of plate
63 Dust Bowl migrant
64 N.Y. nine

104

ACROSS

1 Certain households
7 Chess pieces
14 Hanger-on
15 Arthurian abode
16 Farm assets
17 Cat
18 Empty
19 Heating vessels
21 Move with care
22 Be situated
23 Slippery one
24 Inside info
25 Directed
27 Indignation
29 Field of snow
30 Candidate's plea
32 Pupil's need
34 "Thereby hangs a __"
35 Plant disease
36 Queer chap
39 Dixie river
42 Black
43 Ancient city
45 Miss Turner
47 Seize
48 Mass process: Abbr.
49 Umbrella part
50 Power source: Abbr.
52 Hinder
54 __ clocks
55 Sun porches
57 Insignificant
59 Handbag décor
60 Rival
61 What a chef does
62 Earth goddess

DOWN

1 More versatile
2 Early home of D.D.E.
3 Congealed dew
4 Greek letter
5 Farm animal
6 Roman coin
7 Igneous rock
8 Egyptian goddess
9 Post: Abbr.
10 Payne subject
11 Acid salts
12 Inert
13 More excessive
14 Acclaims
20 Adroit
26 Wyoming range
27 Whip marks
28 Virile guy
29 African area
31 Tai tribesman
33 Abrade
35 Europeans
36 Beginning
37 Calif. seafood
38 Flowering plant
39 Mine passage
40 Nautical, old style
41 Vivacious
44 Goals
46 White poplar
51 Popular pets
52 Trumpet call
53 Tourist mecca
54 Roofing material
56 River: Sp.
58 Silent

ACROSS

1 English writer
5 Obnoxious guy
10 Coffee
14 Rangers' milieu
15 French income
16 Russian range
17 Italian saint
18 Triple-Crown horse
19 Year in reign of Claudius I
20 Sign on road under repair
22 Spiny anteater
24 Legal claim
25 Ostrichlike bird
26 Fenced in
29 Becoming abstruse
34 Hindu incarnation
36 Postponed
37 Taste
38 Zola
40 Cobh's land: Abbr.
41 Like some hangings
44 Sweater-knitter's problem
47 Emcees' specialties
49 Ancient
50 Contest
51 In the same place: Abbr.
53 Sailing vessel of India
56 Part of some splits
60 Above
61 Insult
63 Change
64 __ to terms
65 Plumed bird
66 Eastern country
67 College town
68 __ for (summons)
69 Festive time

DOWN

1 Italian river
2 Manner
3 Legal abbreviation
4 Place for fryers
5 Beldame
6 Go over one's darning
7 Spanish queen
8 Heavenly
9 Baker's treats
10 Man's name: Sp.
11 Like the Mojave
12 Futile
13 Inter __
21 Opera by Verdi
23 Mind
26 Spaghetti, for one
27 Birdlike
28 Slip
30 Omit
31 Word for some halls
32 Intrepidity
33 Inexperienced
35 Moves
39 Gasman's reading
42 Abrades
43 Cheese
45 Meat cut
46 Getting along
48 Erred
52 Holders for ship's cables
53 S.A. rodent
54 Source of power
55 Volume
57 Skin, in Paris
58 Hero
59 Pay through the __
62 Ode subject

ACROSS

1 Spume
5 Shrewd
9 __ of roses
14 Counteractive agents
16 Terra __
17 Old or New
18 "I wasn't there," e.g.
19 Plays the villain
20 Timetable abbr.
22 Gentle or Big
23 Harem rooms
24 Cloudless
27 Hound
28 "__ of bricks"
29 Imitations
32 Stake
36 "You're the __"
38 Strengthen defenses
39 Act in "East Lynne"
40 He's overboard
41 Nickname
42 Concerning
43 Texas college
44 The good guys
45 U.S. publishing family
47 Apple tosser
49 Golf accessory
50 Pluto
52 Beverages
56 Western Indian
57 Old __
58 Neighbor of Arizona
60 Sculpture piece
62 Specious
reasoning
65 __ space
66 Precedes
67 Last traces
68 Ointment
69 Fix over

DOWN

1 Nickname of sorts
2 Days __
3 Confused
4 Small sums
5 Space group
6 Western Indian
7 Five and __
8 To be: Sp.
9 In the distance
10 Sesame
11 Courts
12 Whale secretion
13 Kind of dance
15 Women's org.
21 Gov't agency
25 Streaks upward
26 Not identified
27 Heaven: Sp.
28 Ridge
30 Gets ready
31 Duck
32 Erode
33 "Yet Brutus says he
was __"
34 Pearl Buck topic
35 Musical study
37 Accustom: Var.
46 Greek letter
48 Came out
51 Highway to Alaska
52 Converts to Islam
53 Miss Lehmann
54 Mistook
55 Authority
56 Portico
57 Fate: Lat.
59 Shaped like: Suffix
61 Holy __
63 Collection
64 Not crooked: Abbr.

107

ACROSS

1 Mythical fluid
6 __ artium
9 Wild driver
13 Color
14 Tide movement
15 Harem rooms
16 Mountain crest
17 Vapor: Prefix
18 Wood tool
19 Certain Sundays
22 Social groups
26 All
27 Planned
32 Drinks
33 Golconda
36 River in Tell's land
37 Ex-gridman Walker
38 Wagnerian god
39 Fold
40 Architectural fillet
41 Check-payer
42 El __
43 See 45 Down
45 Pipe tool
47 Wild thyme
51 Famous narrator
55 Exchange rate
56 Rainbow
57 Dictation
62 Important age
63 Fish
64 Molding
65 Companion to now
66 Leaky noise
67 Handle

DOWN

1 "Is __ promise?"
2 Stanley, for one
3 Vietnamese port
4 Elect
5 Heavy jacket
6 Notwithstanding: Var.
7 Montague
8 Fencers, old style
9 Okie family name
10 Countess Ciano
11 Dim
12 Applications
14 Paris designer
20 Metric measure
21 U.S. pension org.
22 Fogbow
23 City in India
24 Filches
25 Tasket's cousin
28 Tree with banana-like fruit
29 Andean plateau
30 School item
31 Conduct oneself
33 Bucolic sound
34 "__ no use!"
35 King Cole
38 Light boats
44 Daisy Mae's son
45 With 43 Across, legal acts
46 Heretofore, in poems
48 Monsters
49 Entanglements
50 One to a shay
51 School subject
52 S-shaped molding
53 Row
54 Sharpen
58 Egg: Prefix
59 Kind of hold
60 Building part
61 Turf

108

ACROSS

1 European
5 Executes a sailing maneuver
10 Examine closely
14 Sandarac tree
15 Chou __
16 Thought: Prefix
17 Surrealist painter
18 Revoke a legacy
19 Flanders
20 Certain Iberian
23 Symbol of strength
24 Symbol of duplicity
25 Acts maliciously
28 French lawman
33 Seine sight
34 Old expletive
36 Eastern Indians
37 Port on Danube
38 Dried tubers
40 Showman Edwards
41 Sahara region
44 Filly's relative
45 Doublet's partner
46 Predetermines
48 Worships
50 Suds
51 Atlantic fish
52 Future salute for Charles
60 Awry, old style
61 Caravansary
62 Image
63 Harden
64 Allay, as thirst
65 Novel character
66 Place for a chapeau
67 Chemical compound
68 Traffic sign

DOWN

1 English writer
2 Song
3 Young salmon
4 Uprightness
5 Flowers
6 Go on __
7 Musical symbol
8 Scottish jackdaws
9 San __, Hearst showplace
10 Resembling
11 Matinee __
12 Hew
13 Enameled metalware
21 Poetic word
22 Look: Lat.
25 Team plus subs
26 Throb
27 Metrical feet
28 Parties
29 German river
30 Hardship
31 River of W.W. I note
32 Road hazards
35 Plucky
39 More wonderful, teen style
42 Bric-a-brac holder
43 Be unwilling, old style
45 Famous Johns
47 Tributary of the Oder
49 __ bill
51 Interest
52 Word for a Mohican
53 Type of arch
54 Undiluted
55 Bookbinding materials: Abbr.
56 Q.E.D. word
57 Adjective suffix
58 Definite refusal
59 Torment

ACROSS

1 Guitar device
5 Concoct
10 Auto tool
14 Dupe
15 Religious cape
16 Soviet range
17 Against
18 One bestowing a title
19 Immense
20 Certain allowance
22 Electrical unit
24 Unctuous
25 Bird sound
26 Part of Tanzania
29 Japanese reign
33 Steinbeck topic
34 Greek god
36 Among: Prefix
37 ___ Percé Indians
38 Place for a reader

40 Name in boxing
41 Wind: Prefix
43 Restrain
44 Farm feature
45 Began an inning
47 Atom part
49 Handle a bobsled
51 Face part
52 Worn
54 Orchard men
57 Eins, zwei, ___
58 Tile: Fr.
60 Lily plant
61 Record
62 Sheaf of a leafstalk
63 Satiate
64 Children
65 Toasted
66 Spanish pronoun

DOWN

1 Fellow
2 Superior
3 Condescended
4 Rust
5 Insect
6 Old Syria
7 Headwear
8 Evident
9 Recluse
10 Gear for a field event
11 Wing-shaped
12 Upper or lower
13 Soldier's equipment
21 Asian river
21 Asian river
23 Simple
25 Race horse
26 Of an area
27 One-seeded fruit

28 Rainbows
30 Building features
31 Greeting
32 Constellation
35 Zoo animal
38 High
39 Sandwich material
42 Decorations
44 Cargo placing
46 ___ clay
48 ___-Magnon
50 Develop
52 Cold, in Spain
53 Recline
54 Part song
55 Scoop up
56 Bristle
57 Insect spray
59 N.Y. subway line

ACROSS

1 Place for an oda
6 Kind of acid
11 Weather abbr.
14 City in Spain
15 Like a __ bricks
16 Adjective suffix
17 Gets down to business
19 Western state: Abbr.
20 Polishes up
21 Open gallery
23 French thoughts
25 Kind of turkey
26 Parking place of a sort
30 Commoner
32 On hand
33 Music group
35 Crow
39 Way
40 Rubber source
41 Apollo's mother
42 Thanksgiving concern
43 Russian city
44 Yielded
45 Maggiore
47 Leslie and others
48 Korean city
51 Claw
54 Upright
56 Certain certifiers
61 Conjunction
62 Seasonal event
64 Prefix for Gothic or classic
65 Wading birds
66 Hebrew teacher
67 Go wrong
68 Waves: Fr.
69 Make __ at

DOWN

1 Tricornes
2 Of grandparents
3 Peeve
4 Sommer
5 Kind of tape
6 In harmony
7 Dit-dah man
8 Printer's need
9 Holiday season
10 Days __
11 New York county
12 Former slugger
13 Fold
18 African people
22 Certain bird
24 Sales pitch
26 Title for old-time teacher
27 Lily
28 Horse
29 What to do on Thanksgiving
31 Delicatessen item
33 Fortune-telling pack
34 Map abbr.
36 Make over
37 Solar disk
38 Olympians
40 Record
44 Card game
46 South: Prefix
47 René of France
48 Scottish title
49 First-rate person
50 Witch of __
52 Joint
53 Soil deposit
55 Malaysian title
57 Musical selection: Abbr.
58 Hebrides island
59 Eternities
60 Depots: Abbr.
63 Free of

111

ACROSS

1 Al of comics
5 Land tax in Britain
9 Unrefined
14 Take a gander
15 Bowling alley
16 Make new charts
17 Matriculated again
19 Manifest
20 College, for one
22 Dilettante
23 Gifts for men
24 Letter
25 Energy
26 King of Israel
30 Concerning
33 Destination for Hansel
35 Chemical suffix
36 Redden
37 Une saison
38 Emulate thespians
40 French article
41 Large bird
43 Morals man
44 Vessel
46 Parts of the psyche
47 Time
48 News item
50 Lacking teeth
54 Courts
57 "Ici on __ français"
58 Certain college courses
59 French city
60 Exact
61 Street in Gopher Prairie
62 Certain fashion
   creations
63 Store divisions: Abbr.
64 Volcano

DOWN

1 French isle in Medit.
2 Author James et al.
3 Dress detail
4 Theban king
5 Openings
6 Town near Memphis
7 Cut, old style
8 Dull lecture, in a way
9 Hag
10 Emend
11 Final word
12 Puppeteer
13 Le Havre, for one:
   Abbr.
18 __ line
21 Icy crust
25 Yes and no
27 Anita
28 Voice
29 Dickens character
30 Up to
31 Took it on the lam
32 Yorkshire river
34 Most imminent
37 Measurement of a sort
39 Interval
42 U.S. journalist
45 Wave
47 Draws forth
49 Consecrate
50 Get rid of
51 Bay of Yugoslavia
52 An __ the hole
53 Polish town
54 Spy
55 Guthrie
56 Kind of drink
57 Hippie home

112

ACROSS

1 Fencer's cry
5 Hebrew measure
10 Paintings
14 Be next to
15 Arctic
16 A Louis
17 Greek promenade
18 Newspaper edition
19 Flirts
20 Baseball tactic
23 Ordinarily: Abbr.
24 Marie, for one: Abbr.
25 Laundry room item
29 Runt
31 Seized
33 Brace
34 Pallid
35 Agent
36 Namath was one
37 W.W. I outfit
39 One of the Taylors
40 Roderick __
42 Admit, with "up"
44 Winged
46 Anent
49 Oxford fellow
50 Descartes
51 Business expense
53 Goods sample
55 Money, in Lima
56 Treat for pigs
57 South Seas figure
61 Mod slogan
64 Shifts
65 Feminine name
67 Farm animals
68 Place again
69 Physicist's concern: Abbr.
70 Cowbarn
71 Kefauver
72 Practices

DOWN

1 Combo member
2 Bottomless pits
3 Pennsylvania river
4 Aleutian island
5 Worn out
6 Nobel or Pulitzer
7 Sharpen
8 Not care __
9 Printer's trashcan
10 Daisy
11 Eastern league
12 Name in U.N. lore
13 Family member
21 Compass reading
22 Synthetic resin
23 __ tree
26 Claim settlements
27 Signal
28 Weather word
30 Letter
31 Old-hat
32 Exude moisture
35 Scheme
38 Mockery
41 Chinese dynasty
42 G.I. wear
43 Astonished reaction
45 French port
47 Like Ferdinand
48 Antique
51 Perches
52 Slippery __
54 Steak
55 Rock debris
58 Big bills
59 Command, of yore
60 __ monde
61 Seaman
62 Chemical prefix
63 Language: Abbr.
66 __ Passos

113

ACROSS

1 Squabble
5 Vamoose
10 Bind with ropes
14 Indian weight
15 Tony of baseball
16 Shade of red
17 Like a bump on __
18 Prof's role
19 Rudiments
20 Jam makers
23 Action at Aqueduct
24 Is out of sorts
25 Kokomo product
27 With piety
30 Objection
33 City in Spain
34 Lugosi
35 Obi accessory
36 Trammel
37 Citizens of Canea

40 __ de vie
41 Leavings
43 Site of tree of life
44 NATO and SEATO
46 Man from Man
48 Tragedy by Tennyson
49 Slackening
50 Engine puff
51 Staff on a green
52 In a photo finish
58 Brainchild
60 Tiff
61 Czar's name
62 Cult
63 Beldam
64 Luxor's river
65 Invites
66 Jinxed
67 Actress Sommer

DOWN

1 Try: Colloq.
2 Game divided into
   chukkers
3 "Thanks __"
4 Sycophant
5 Grievously
6 Highland groups
7 Solemnity
8 With: Fr.
9 William Tell was one
10 "Conning Tower" man
11 Sightsee
12 Step up
13 Gnat or rat
21 Popular scent
22 Man's nickname
26 Silkworm
27 Asian capital
28 Skids past the base
29 Young quahog

30 Hinder
31 Joie de vivre
32 Awaken, country style
34 Eliot hero
38 Food fish
39 Disburse
42 Held court
45 "Strange Interlude"
   finale
47 Wimple wearer
48 Forbade
50 "Common Sense" man
51 Galileo's birthplace
53 Preserve
54 Fort __
55 Sinister
56 Tapered wedge
57 It's above the tibia
59 Siamese money

114

ACROSS

1 Bay
5 Gambling games
10 "__ a laugh!"
14 Drug-yielding plant
15 Turkish decree
16 "Othello" character
17 Special greeting
20 Blow __ cold
21 Beer
22 Grundy, for one
23 Attachments
25 "God bless our home,"
   e.g.
27 Girl of a song
31 More insignificant
34 Exclamation
35 Rouses
37 Moldings at base of
   a column
38 Kingfisher's home
40 __-la

41 Arm of Black Sea
42 __ dust
44 Creater of Gerald
   McBoing-Boing
47 Netherlands town
48 Toadies
50 Restrained
52 Plaza de __
54 Laugh, in Paris
55 Timetable abbr.
57 Peculiar: Prefix
59 Manias
63 Moneymaking film
66 Onion's cousin
67 Girl's name
68 Verne's captain
69 Companion of bitty
70 Laborers of old
   England
71 Destroyed

DOWN

1 Corned-beef dish
2 Medley
3 Habit
4 Envoy
5 Kind of regards
6 Energy unit
7 King Cole and others
8 Old Greek theater
9 Rarely
10 Head décor
11 Barbershop
   quartet man
12 Seaweed product
13 Turkeys
18 Monograms: Abbr.
19 Western park
24 Satisfies
26 Pacific bark cloth
27 Like some spinach
28 Reporter's query
29 Nice place to live

30 Wandered
32 Destroy slowly
33 Talked extravagantly
36 Braten or kraut
39 Wood of Japanese ash
43 Earnest: Prefix
45 __ a board
46 Fluid
49 Small lump
51 TV movies
53 Trig ratios
55 Legendary
   Scandinavian
56 Art of speech: Abbr.
58 Valhalla host
60 Island off Estonia
61 White frost
62 Tug's tow
64 Telescope's field
65 Bravo: Sp.

115

ACROSS

1 Lead-tin alloy
6 Stately
11 Show off
12 Gum resins
14 Cattleman
15 Mustard pod
17 __ table
18 Scottish name
19 Gem weights: Abbr.
20 "Faerie Queen" maiden
21 Yucatan Indian
23 Cuba __
25 Iotas
26 Erroneous
28 Actress Joanne
29 Port city of India
30 Faded: Fr.
32 Refrains from

34 Booms' opposites
36 Fawning people
38 Levantine vessel
41 Prefix for five
42 Prefix for parage or jointed
44 __ und Drang
45 Diving-bell inventor
46 Frost et al.
48 Comfort, in Paris
49 At all
50 Standard
51 Biblical well
53 Mongrel
54 Children's disease
56 In a dishonorable way
58 __ down (rejected)
59 Miss Gibson
60 Italian poet
61 Harrison's successor

DOWN

1 With 10 Down, lines by Ogden Nash
2 Curved line
3 Memorable Cowardly Lion
4 Perfectly suited
5 Sea nymph
6 Cleans again
7 Type size
8 Mucilages
9 French friend
10 See 1 Down
11 Kind of hat
13 Vacation goal for some
14 Plan anew
16 Bridge positions
22 Concurs
24 Golf club
25 Girl of song
27 Brownish shade

29 Covered walks
31 Poetic word
33 Thus: Lat.
35 Legendary goal of explorers
36 Fishgig
37 Kind of butter
39 Legendary British princess
40 Abrasive
43 Make a __ (try)
46 Stakes
47 Absurd
50 Lily of opera
52 One of the leagues: Abbr.
55 Time
57 Italian's who

116

ACROSS

1 Shooter fodder
4 Show place
9 Lacking interest
13 Harding and Sothern
15 Diadem
16 Slipper
17 Take issue with
19 Actor Walter
20 Saddle __
21 Discipline
23 Greek letters
26 Actress Terry
27 Like some wood
29 N.M. Indian
30 Resort
33 Broadway
35 Comm. system
36 Quick blows
37 Org. founded in 1890
38 Place for a stretch
39 Compass point
40 Good will
44 Indian cymbals
45 Indian money
46 Projecting pieces of wood
47 Vine
49 Unfledged bird
50 Passes over
53 Art figure
56 Pullets
57 Boone's forte
61 Stake
62 Doone
63 Roof part
64 Cartoonist
65 Door sign
66 Strong solution

DOWN

1 Moccasin
2 Seth's son
3 __ mundi
4 Stopping place: Abbr.
5 Help
6 Nonprofessional
7 Arrange music, in a way
8 Miss Wood
9 Tropical timber tree
10 Famous pianist
11 Martinique et al.
12 Printing direction
14 Gushes forth
18 Nerve networks
22 Small or grand
24 Blackbird
25 Columnist's ambition
27 African country
28 Certain sprays
31 Skins
32 Colleague
33 Waste allowance
34 Flight arm: Abbr.
38 Conclusion
40 "Too bad!"
41 Vestment
42 Tunisian ruler
43 Silly
48 Gore
50 Conjunction
51 Rockfish
52 __ of (rather)
54 Jargon: Abbr.
55 Covet
58 Direction: Abbr.
59 Spike
60 __ whiz

117

ACROSS

1 Pitching rubber
5 Porch
10 Long mantle
14 Moslem judge
15 Miss Hopper
16 Gamete
17 Wandering
19 Spice
20 Martinique volcano
21 Emulates an elusive quarterback
23 Varnish ingredients
25 French month
26 Shore, e.g.
32 Slalom gear
35 __-Neisse line
36 "__ trust a stranger"
38 Bronze coin
39 Clay boxes
41 Adjective suffix
42 Relative of bingo
44 Pen name
45 Charity
46 Choices
49 Balloon ingredient
50 Catch
54 Whirlpool
60 Wheat: Sp.
61 Mideast port
62 Spiral
64 Smart
65 Swelling disease
66 Division of Greece
67 Poet's command
68 Copal
69 Periods

DOWN

1 Scenic view
2 Name tag
3 Astaire
4 Galleys
5 Navigation abbr.
6 Asian holidays
7 Of Horace's works
8 Repute
9 Isthmus
10 Farm machine
11 Athletic field
12 Dark red
13 Uncles, in Scotland
18 Check
22 Gas pipes
24 Zeno's building
27 Lawn tool
28 French rule
29 Instruct
30 Kind of eye
31 Paper measure
32 Certain day: Abbr.
33 Maintain
34 Munich's river
37 Literary initials
39 Settees
40 Marathon
43 Dereliction
45 Bridging
47 Biblical wife
48 Internal: Prefix
51 Legislator's ploy
52 Lizard
53 Masts
54 Sound-speed word
55 Hurt
56 Greek goddess
57 Advise, formerly
58 Cheers
59 Chevalier song
63 Preserve

118

ACROSS

1 River of the Great Falls
8 Of a part of the mouth
15 Crimson Tide
16 Condensed account
17 Scene of first W.W. II Rhine crossing
18 Canary island
19 Bugle call
20 False gods
22 State: Abbr.
23 Native of: Suffix
24 Finishing material
26 Zoo denizen: Abbr.
27 Noted physicist
29 Relatives of aves.
30 Laurel's Hardy
32 Actor Davis
34 Is in store
35 Star-of-Bethlehem flowers
39 Musical compositions
40 __ the other
41 Spanish elevens
42 Site: Abbr.
43 Clergymen: Abbr.
47 Sun god
48 Member of a Biblical group
51 Of age: Abbr.
52 Indian titles
54 "__ song at twilight"
55 Love: Sp.
56 Wool grease
58 Place in a song
60 In the near future
61 Invalidated
62 Oppression
63 People seeking the light switch

DOWN

1 On the __ (in behalf)
2 Certain ester
3 Meddle, with "with"
4 Nigerian leaders
5 Periodical, for short
6 Shapeless thing
7 Area of Brooklyn
8 Skin: Lat.
9 Make __ at
10 Sass
11 P.I. natives
12 Fibbed
13 Mennonite
14 Watertight
21 Waiting places
24 Type of rayon
25 Querying words
28 Tout le __
31 Comedian Bert and family
33 Wall St. items: Abbr.
34 Scottish one
35 Small heraldic shape
36 Commencement degree
37 One who leans over
38 Fomenting
42 Like an easy chair
44 Mature germ cell
45 Pipe smoker's device
46 Violins, for short
49 Aladdin's servant: Var.
50 Lamp-lighter
53 East Indian shrub
55 Take __
57 Chaney
59 In the past

119

ACROSS

1 L.B.J. daughter
5 Culminating point
9 Girl's name
13 Clear
14 Corners
16 ___ facto
17 Resulting
19 British statesman
20 Teach
21 Poured
23 U.S. author
24 Fungi
25 Muse
28 Rascal, in Dublin
31 Beliefs
33 Is under the weather
34 Apart: Abbr.
36 Blackbirds
37 Company of lions
39 Latin warning, with
"canem"
40 Resembling: Abbr.
41 Ardor
42 Nomad
44 Clothing
47 Warning signal
48 Meat cuts
49 English gallery
51 Furnish
53 LSD of ancient times
57 Scarves
58 Sign-off words
60 Eng. title
61 Word in a Thomas
Wolfe title
62 British composer
63 Charity
64 Sticky one
65 Rules, for short

DOWN

1 Places
2 Immediately
3 Time periods: Abbr.
4 Puts in office
5 Ave ___ vale
6 Las ___
7 Get together
8 Poetic word
9 Greasy compound
10 Passwords
11 Common response
12 Auction word
15 Baby carriage
18 Rye fungus
22 Blanc and neighbors
24 Bit part on stage
25 Greek letters
26 Go back on a decision:
Var.
27 Orwell title
29 Name for a Western
horse
30 Emphatic denial
32 Magnificence
35 Saucy
38 Also-___ (losers)
39 Gregorian or Julian
41 Arabian prince
43 Relative of wheaten
45 Settles down
46 Cubic meters
50 Separate
51 Rhyme scheme
52 Colt
53 Glacial snow
54 Ran madly
55 Some juries
56 Summers, in Paris
59 Big shot

120

1	2	3	4	5	█	6	7	8	9	█	10	11	12	13
14					█	15				█	16			
17					█	18			19					
20				21				█	22					
█	█	█	█	23				█	24					
█	25	26	27				28				█	█	█	█
29					█	30				█	31	32	33	34
35				█	36			█	37					
38				39			█	40						
█	█	█	41			█	42							█
43	44	45	46			█	47				█	█	█	█
48					█	49				█	50	51	52	53
54				55			█	56						
57			█	58			█	█	59					
60			█	61			█	█	62					

ACROSS

1 David or scarum
6 Title
10 Rebuff
14 Kind of theater
15 Bath's river
16 Spanish nickname
17 At last: Fr.
18 Three-point landing places of a sort
20 Whitney's creation
22 Assign
23 Gratify
24 Guides
25 Hedda of drama
28 Turn right
29 Missile for Washington
30 Kind of angel
35 Philatelist's need
36 Forbid
37 Whim
38 Misunderstands
40 Defarge, for one
41 Tennis gear
42 Enough!
43 Foolishness
47 Tobermory's creator
48 __ Arden
49 Carriages
54 Magnet
56 Old Greek district
57 Beget
58 Prefix for gram or naut
59 Swarming, with "with"
60 Pegs
61 Barrymore forebear
62 More protected

DOWN

1 This one: Lat.
2 Florence's river
3 Deprived, poetically
4 Monad
5 Quixote
6 Macbeth's vision
7 Sidestep
8 Bewail
9 Photo-developer's word: Abbr.
10 Purloined
11 Thread
12 Man in a cast
13 Mails
19 V.I.P. on a low level
21 __-do-well
24 __ of Tranquillity
25 Musket ball, in India
26 Vestments
27 Blood: Ger.
28 Weapon
29 Weir
30 Phosgene
31 Pedestal part
32 Old Irish frock
33 Culmination
34 Humorist Bill
36 Stake
39 Clue
40 Pepe le __
42 Bigoted
43 Slightest
44 Release
45 __ Dame
46 Lands
47 Treasure
49 Silver: Abbr.
50 Montez
51 Star in Pegasus
52 Split
53 Early Irish tenant
55 Uncouth one

121

ACROSS

1 Space mission
7 Carousal
11 Presidential name
14 Contended
15 Type of falcon: Var.
17 Wild
18 Swiss Alpine region
19 "Bad __ to you!"
20 Spanish linen fabric
21 Brazilian macaws
22 Goddess of dawn
23 Jots
24 Moro chief in P.I.
25 Russian rocket ports
29 __ Downing St.
30 Gave the go-ahead
31 Humane group: Abbr.
33 Legendary Gaelic hero
34 Gum __

38 Can. province
40 Conversation: Sp.
41 Storage space
44 Rainy-day account
46 Nautical term
48 Faked blow
49 __ Alamos
50 What she wants, she gets
51 Cal Tec, for one: Abbr.
52 Low rating
54 Late risers
56 Kind of tiger
58 One way to dine
59 Offer for thoughts
60 Cambridge tutor
61 Hebrew lyre
62 Crack-troop headgear

DOWN

1 W.W. II fliers: Abbr.
2 Prepares fruit for shipment
3 Female blunderbores
4 San __ Obispo
5 Camera part
6 Pindar's forte
7 Portuguese city
8 Focuses a light anew
9 Makeup
10 Ending for law or saw
11 Noah's landfall
12 Double, as a leaf
13 __ a sour note
16 Flower, for short
20 Fuel-wood measure
22 Behold, in Italy
23 Earmarkers
26 Mother of Hermes

27 Exams
28 Scrawny animal
32 Young whale
35 French Channel port
36 Unaware of
37 New England food staples
39 Put __ (stop)
40 Power
41 Story-telling song
42 Port of Panay
43 "His wife could eat __"
45 Slangy word for face
47 W.W. II mil. woman
52 Pepper, in Rome
53 Unique guy
55 Bleat
56 Old Persian title
57 Belgian river

122

ACROSS

1 Convivial
7 Popular winter resort
14 Appearance
15 One with no future
16 Came home, at Shea
17 Repetition
18 Hirsute
19 N.L. player
20 "Kings __"
21 Unpropitiously
22 "For __ sake"
23 Dumb one
24 Acapulco wave
25 What the doctor did
26 "For I am poor and __"
27 Drink
28 Southern college
29 Bullfight-arena section
30 Parsimonious ones
35 Kennel sound

36 __ contendere
37 Dynamo data: Abbr.
39 Spikes, as a drink
42 Former V.P.
43 Slight difference: Abbr.
44 Homme d' __ (statesman)
45 Old Turkish coin
46 Bolivian river
47 Degree in religion
48 __ Bill
49 Fine vases
50 Coasts
52 Enthusiastic cry
53 Harmless
54 Of certain mountains
55 Most adroit
56 Informal word for a wife

DOWN

1 Vogue
2 Bake potatoes in sauce
3 Fruiterer's concern
4 Kind of cloth
5 __-deucy
6 Relative of inc.
7 Faced the pitcher
8 New World residents: Abbr.
9 V.I.P. of silents
10 Nabokov character
11 Smokeless-powder inventor
12 Harmony
13 High road
15 Grapevine's relative
19 Fabulist
22 Surgeon's problem

23 Take out
25 French muralist
26 Slangy negative
29 Hard: Prefix
31 Da's opposite
32 Roman date
33 Gets even
34 Spirit away
38 Folsom et al.
39 Admits
40 Greek goddess
41 Beach sight
42 Climb
45 Mosquito genus
46 Ties securely
48 Former Indian coin
49 Stage and screen name
51 Tipsy one
52 Rita of films

123

ACROSS

1 Runs for one's health
5 Receded
10 Olympian
14 Chkalov's river
15 Old Peruvian calculating device
16 Thruway sign
17 Family member
18 Pressed
19 Labyrinth
20 Be perfidious
22 Instances
23 Position
24 Exchange
26 Sandy's sound
29 Slighter
31 Get the better of
35 Thick soup
37 Publication
39 Popular signature
40 Speedy
41 Wading bird
42 Superposable
44 Moderate purple
45 Menu item
46 Cicero's knee
48 Certain voter: Abbr.
49 Dispossess
51 Bounce
53 Sprightly
56 Just
61 Retina features
62 Buddhist shrine
63 Aerobatic maneuver
64 Qualified
65 Think upon
66 Moab's neighbor
67 Lawn nuisance
68 Religious adherents of India
69 Size of paper

DOWN

1 Beginning advantage
2 In words
3 Vasco da __
4 Kills
5 Treat as comparable
6 Mock
7 V.I.P.'s
8 Fencing gear
9 Fiasco
10 The true bugs
11 Student's concern
12 Cold Alpine wind: Var.
13 French seasons
21 "__ and forget"
22 Not flabby
25 Opus
26 Expeditiously
27 Wax prolix
28 Face
30 Pleading
32 Impostor
33 Popular garnish
34 Plant tissue
36 Rapt
38 Took the necessary steps
40 Exam unit: Abbr.
43 Enlist again: G.I. slang
44 Sine qua non
47 Mayfly young
50 Numerical prefix
52 Harassed unnecessarily
53 Bird feature
54 Garment
55 At ease
57 Je ne sais __
58 Presage
59 Oar part
60 TV award
62 Mood in grammar: Abbr.

124

ACROSS

ACROSS

1 Perfume
6 Place for research
9 Joyce
14 No-good heel
15 Poetic output
16 Sound off
17 Cotton cloth
19 Unqualified
20 Place of refuge
21 Rocket projection
22 Cleric
23 Coarse herb of Europe
26 Youthful
28 Single
29 Athenians: Abbr.
32 Name in publishing
33 Dance
37 Nitrogen
39 Caldwell

40 Prepare ice in a way
41 What some people
   settle for
44 Kitchen feature
45 Wapiti
46 Female rabbit
47 Czech coins
49 Speak frankly
52 Hidden
55 Needle case
56 Enzyme ending
59 Performing
60 Shone unsteadily
62 Overact
63 Fish
64 Sheriff's décor
65 Man of Spain
66 Tiny
67 Bean or Welles

DOWN

1 Can. province
2 Duty period
3 Pompous person
4 Invite
5 Town officers
6 Doone
7 Revoke
8 Board's companion
9 Trips
10 Shaw
11 Other shoe
12 Paris seasons
13 Muralist
18 Marina visitor
22 Flat side
24 Remain stationary, as
   a ship
25 Meddles
26 Bored
27 European blackbird
29 Places to whistle past

30 Name for a dog
31 British guns
34 Turkestan native
35 Canapé item
36 Oar part
38 Imperil
42 Parcel out
43 Fringe of warp threads
48 Holding arms à la Puck
49 Musical direction
50 Giggle
51 Practical
52 Drinks
53 City in Georgia
54 Plant shoot
57 Lily of West
58 Former Downing St.
   name
60 Mend
61 Spike

125

ACROSS

1 Three-headed goddess
7 Fordhamite
10 Famous Roman
14 Christie
15 __ king
16 Garden occupant
17 Willa
18 Words for an egoist
19 Jade
20 Wood burr
21 Chinese dynasty
23 Boca __
24 White lie
26 Fishy group
28 Kind of potatoes
30 Christian hide-out
34 Counted noses
36 Vietnam holiday
37 Fete
38 Abbreviation on an envelope
39 China
42 Tar
43 Entre __
45 Medical org.
46 Kingly
48 Therapy
51 Crème de la crème
52 Sentinels
53 Brit. fliers
54 Started
57 Caesar's bane
59 Convenes
62 Lost
63 Indian of West
64 Wine grape
66 Coast Guard girl
67 Got the idea
68 She had a cow
69 Beginner
70 Letter
71 Revenue source

DOWN

1 Drudge
2 Actor Richard
3 Bier
4 Excited
5 Beverage, in Lyons
6 Rabbit __
7 Pour
8 Settled down
9 Month in printemps
10 Library user's aid
11 Passage
12 Root
13 Black cat, for one
22 Los Angeles campus
23 Elephant-eating bird
25 Ran, as dye
27 Horse opera
28 All in
29 Croatian peak
31 Bach opus
32 Swell
33 Fur
35 O'Neill work
40 Title for a retired person
41 Poetic word
44 Cactus
47 Tumblers
49 Cask
50 Lao-__
54 Egyptian goddess
55 Notice
56 Low or high
58 City-sky sight
60 Storied mansion
61 Charon's purlieu
63 Keats specialty
65 Gums

126

ACROSS

1 Misfortunes
5 Ocean-bottom covering
9 Bake in cream
14 Glean
15 Eye section
16 Italian city
17 Creating
19 Shoelace part
20 Sommelier
21 Stays on
23 Choler
24 Cassia shrub
25 Crept
28 Imperious
32 Capitol Hill group: Abbr.
33 Opening
34 Pornography
35 Away
36 Ancient Greeks
38 Self
39 Social groups
41 Dutch commune
42 Narrow valley
43 Dial
45 German state
46 Eskimo
47 Rover or Spot
48 Sustenance
51 Overland hauling
55 Earn
56 Giver of a certain party
58 Vacant
59 Bacchanalian cry
60 Miss Foch
61 Deep sounds
62 Headgear
63 Old area of Europe

DOWN

1 Flower
2 Spring period
3 Wash
4 Gushing out
5 Bizarre
6 Roman poet
7 Buddhist school
8 Two-under-par coups
9 Wrenches, in old Blighty
10 Wan
11 Groundless
12 Sorry person
13 Hairpieces
18 British stool pigeon
22 Modulate
24 Sagacious
25 Dred or Walter
26 Old French bagpipe
27 Up to
28 Deface
29 Gasses up
30 Impulses
31 Sierra ___
33 Old Hambletonian site
36 Exhausts
37 Summer drink
40 Radiant
42 Understanding
44 Beginning
45 Frau's consort
47 Leo and Paul
48 Among
49 Curtain material
50 Abadan's country
51 School dance
52 World area
53 Knee: Lat.
54 Of a time
57 Grape

127

ACROSS

1 Resort in West
6 Prince of Wales: Abbr.
10 Asian priest
14 Sun-dried brick
15 Assembly room
16 Building beam
17 Substantive in grammar
18 Share
20 Canadian football cup
21 Lightens
22 Chosen: Abbr.
23 Painted
24 French Guiana territory
26 Ground together
31 Excites
33 Like an egg yolk
34 Bearing
35 To __
36 Lack
40 Salt and cocktail
43 More untidy
44 Beach or bath
45 Mission
47 Relative, for short
50 Some tire workers
54 Sacrifice play
55 Aromatic herb
56 Completely
57 Manner
58 Chemical suffix
59 Extreme
60 Trapper's prize
61 Part of a parrot's bill
62 Nautical position

DOWN

1 Projecting strips
2 Worship
3 Simplicity
4 Mind
5 Poetic word
6 Lightweight fabric
7 Shout
8 Hay fever, e.g.
9 Serb or Croat
10 S.A. metropolis
11 Support
12 Hair
13 Buchwald and Carney
19 __ basin
21 Topnotch
23 Resident: Abbr.
25 Muses and others
27 Allay
28 Accommodation
29 Pitcher
30 Does a hair job
31 Caliph
32 Sneer at
37 More exact
38 Kind of arts
39 Learned
40 Catch unawares
41 Scuttles
42 Wonder
46 Spanish title
48 Prefix for mural
49 James Watt's medium
50 Hostess's letters
51 Fencing weapon
52 Linden
53 Carry on
54 Underground bud
56 Between sine and non

¹	²	³	⁴		⁵	⁶	⁷	⁸	⁹	¹⁰	¹¹	¹²

(crossword grid with numbered squares 1–62)

ACROSS

1 Ablution
5 O'Flaherty
9 Comply
13 Nymph
14 Book, in Spain
15 Neck area
16 Proofreading word
17 Mao or Gandhi
18 Gang
19 First of a trio from the Litany
21 Belmont features
23 Nautical word
24 Part of the earth's crust
25 Rickety planes
28 See 19 Across
32 Masks
33 Thin mortar
34 Asian gazelle
35 Eastern title
36 Town __
37 Certain party
38 Poker term
39 Lensmen: Abbr.
40 Setting
41 Sweetheart
43 Vice President under F.D.R.
44 Aida or Salome
45 English composer
46 Withdraw
49 See 19 Across
53 V.I.P.
54 __ show
56 Space org.
57 Delicate color
58 Series of woes
59 British P.M.
60 Lawyers: Abbr.
61 Dolt
62 "__ Mabel"

DOWN

1 Defeat
2 Hormone substance
3 Quaker word
4 Fix
5 Cotton thread
6 Researcher's abbr.
7 Macaw
8 Beaucaire, for one
9 Waiting by the phone
10 Hoarse cough
11 Foil
12 Evergreens
14 Deities
20 Arena sounds
22 Ohio name
24 Brake parts
25 Place for medals
26 Versifier: Var.
27 Parting word
28 Corny
29 Gnawed
30 Western movie
31 More titanic
33 Stand of trees
36 Splenetic
37 Examined
39 Walk heavily
40 Polish
42 Rears
43 Cupidity
45 In advance
46 Stiff hair
47 Word under a red light
48 Coin
49 Musical work
50 __ mecum
51 Czech river
52 Byway
55 "__ is forgiven"

129

ACROSS

1 Corn leaving
4 Attention-getting
  sounds
8 Door part
12 People
14 Marianne or Grace
15 Port of Honshu
16 Benes, for one
19 Bohemian spa
20 Blasting material
21 Scottish uncle
22 Dropsy
24 Bar
28 Obeisance
32 Odd: Scot.
33 Congolese river
36 Beatle name
37 __ mater
38 Home of the Braves

40 Bigwig
41 Anesthetic
43 __ avail
44 Line of soldiers
45 Buddhist's duty
47 Kind of head
49 Famous poem, with
   "The"
52 "__ was saying"
53 Latin light
56 Give power to the
   people
61 Former Czech leader
63 Large number
64 Class
65 Hook together
66 Name in Yugoslavia
67 Terminuses
68 Ref. book initials

DOWN

1 __ of the walk
2 Spanish weight
3 Brew
4 Flower
5 Unravel
6 Site of the Iliad
7 City noted for its
  porcelain
8 Initials on a sheet
9 Relative of soir
10 Medit. port
11 Penchant
13 Eyeball covering
14 Vacate
17 __ sapiens
18 Forerunner of the Inca
23 Eastern name
24 Drank
25 School subj.
26 Capital for 61 Across
27 Liquefy
29 Middle-ear bone

30 Deft
31 Brooded
34 Pathet __
35 Austrian river
38 Fleet
39 Facing
42 Be wrong
44 Pass, as a butterfly
46 Vindicate
48 He sold his birthright
50 Port in Hanover
51 Very many
53 Essayist
54 Suffix for sec or pop
55 Alien: Prefix
57 Shank
58 Holy image
59 Former infielder
   Bonura
60 Pieced out
62 Famous papers

130

ACROSS

1 Roll of stamps
5 Jug handles
9 Jostle
14 City on the Jumna
15 Garment
16 Opera-box sight
17 American
20 Mr. in Belém
21 Uncorrupted
22 His: Fr.
23 Word with mat or mate
24 Retardations
25 After avril
27 Classify
29 Something secondary
31 Subventions
33 Lbs. and ozs.
34 Fund-raising medium
38 Thinks
40 Coarse tobacco
41 Wound
42 Vehicle
43 Dry: Prefix
44 Wreath in Waipahu
45 Fervor
47 Lamb, old style
48 Pole, in Pamplona
51 Sparse
53 German physicist
55 Maryland proving ground
57 __ time
60 American of note
62 Of musical keys
63 __ now
64 Portend
65 Citizen of Tabriz
66 Grecian Jupiter
67 Scientist-author

DOWN

1 Hansoms
2 Blunderbore
3 Old __
4 Shaping machine
5 Pitcher
6 Timetable entry
7 Certain Hindus
8 Mutation, in biology
9 Greek letters
10 Spoiler of Biblical vines
11 Brazilian state
12 Zoo favorite
13 Draws to a close
18 The shay's motive power
19 Nebraska river
23 Carney and Linkletter
25 Armor
26 Adjutant
28 Nineteenth cent. U.S. utopianists
30 Pacific island
32 Bluejacket
35 Member of a world-wide order
36 Zhivago's love
37 N.C. college
39 Drive a nail obliquely
40 French port
42 Shade of red
46 Bodily vigor
48 Operatic great
49 Loathe
50 Woman's name
52 Region containing Mecca
54 Rue and thyme
56 Spanish surrealist
57 Switch positions
58 Fuss
59 Once more
61 Foolish: Fr.

131

ACROSS

1 Ducks
6 Peer
10 Ingenuity
14 Pilasters
15 Elm or oak
16 Rat-__
17 Toasting need
18 Poise
19 "Woe __"
20 Made an analysis
22 Photo
23 Prove false
25 Fix up, as a play
27 Pallid
28 Most recent
29 Primp
30 "It tolls for thee" poet
31 Sally Rand's prop
34 Grampuses
35 Common Latin abbr.

36 Golfer's word
37 Oriental holiday
38 On a __
40 Miss Eggerth
41 Bred
43 Projecting window
44 Holdup-man's need
45 Soprano Emma
46 Word book: Abbr.
47 Cornet valves
50 Pioneer movie director
51 Turkish weight
52 Red dye
56 Headliner
57 Grape juice
58 Indian coin
59 __ de combat
60 Anglo-Saxon slave
61 Sudden movement

DOWN

1 Child's game
2 Photo lab abbr.
3 __ standstill
4 Defunct relatives of
   Cadillacs
5 Meeting
6 Miss Kett of comics
7 __ of sunshine
8 Backward movement
9 Disappoint
10 Blouses
11 "__ to Say," Mathis
   song
12 Daughter of David
13 Progression
21 Stitch
23 Guitar-player's term
24 Anti-air pollution
   proposal
26 Letter

27 Name for a dog
28 Observed
30 Skid-row people
32 TV comic Johnson and
   others
33 Approach
36 Sends work to another
   shop
38 Calendar abbr.
39 Plan
40 Complaining people
42 Organic compounds
43 __ volente
44 Pony
46 Kind of cloth
48 Give a wide berth to
49 Insipid
53 Bath, for one
54 Comparative suffix
55 Trapeze insurance

132

ACROSS

1 Falling-out
5 Coronet
10 Author's output: Abbr.
13 Military cap
14 Lands
15 P.I. people
16 Land on Caspian Sea
17 Castle areas
18 Niche
19 Late G.O.P. figure
21 Parsonage
23 Pipe joints
24 Keeper of rabbits
25 Earth pigment
27 Military area
28 Departs
29 Immobile
33 Dish for Kamehameha
34 Loud and clear
35 Maiden-name word
36 Slinky motion
38 Solar disk
39 Glossy fabric
40 Seed coverings
41 Suitors
44 __ a coin
45 Long S.A. river
46 Quiver
49 Phone
50 Wolves
52 Autocrat
53 Spreads to dry
54 Equivalent of a miss
55 "__ boy!"
56 Classifieds
57 Baltic seaport
58 Kind of food

DOWN

1 Winter driving danger
2 Persian sprite
3 Controversial topic in Pretoria
4 Fools around with a job
5 Brings under control
6 Image
7 Brazilian macaw
8 Eating of one's words
9 Declaration
10 Water or musk
11 Outlet
12 Sylvan deity
15 Nautical position
20 Observe
22 Sing like Bing
24 Becomes fatigued
25 Former Soviet police initials
26 Fur animal, for short
27 Ship accommodations
29 Firebrick ingredient
30 Italian tidbits
31 Lively dance
32 Intense desires
34 Light cigar
37 Belongings, in the vernacular
38 Grain bristles
40 __ to the good
41 Artery
42 Partner of cut
43 Intellects
44 Melted together
46 Silents' Negri
47 Genus of armadillo
48 Of a time period
51 Went for the hook

133

ACROSS

1 Cut of veal
5 Drawing room
10 Electric catfish
14 Wife of Zeus
15 Barton
16 __' acte
17 Moslem priest
18 Carouse, in olden days
19 Willow genus
20 Focus
22 One of a scheduled nine
24 River to North Sea
25 Course
26 Capital of Croatia
29 Placed in a certain way
33 Building wing
34 "Hellzapoppin" name
36 Important French river
37 Gil __
39 Sea duck
41 American Beauty
42 Fortification
44 Stair part
46 Male sheep
47 Windflowers
49 Talks back
51 Ship part
52 Where Zeno taught
53 Tree similar to the apple
56 Renegade
60 Plan of lily family
61 Use the mutuels
63 Major or Minor
64 Fashion name
65 Adjust
66 Inlets
67 Projections
68 Prior times: Abbr.
69 __ a one (none)

DOWN

1 Candy piece
2 Prefix for sphere
3 African port
4 Coddle
5 Scrawl
6 Singly
7 Milk: Fr.
8 Correlatives
9 Part of a D.W. Griffith title
10 Seasonal steed
11 Opposed
12 Solar ring
13 Kind of race
21 Spread
23 Baseball team
25 Bring up-to-date
26 Veld sight
27 Leader of Green Mountain Boys
28 Forest opening
29 Surrenders
30 Disturbances
31 Follow
32 Oceans, poetically
35 Muscle
38 Needlework items
40 Brings back
43 Actress Bayes
45 Asian land
48 Peer Gynt's home
50 Space vehicle
52 All in
53 Fashioned
54 Pen name
55 Dutch or front
56 Spartan king
57 Concert passage
58 Nicholas, for one
59 Simple
62 Bar order

134

ACROSS

1 Provençal love songs
6 Feigns
10 Bulldog
14 Gaiety
15 Arab sailing vessel
16 Asian range
17 Watered silk
18 Region
19 Byway
20 Actress Dickinson
21 Seasonal chandelier décor
23 Beset
25 Light upon
26 School subject
28 Blind part
29 Animal identification
33 Autumn pear
35 Hard wood
36 Asian capital
37 Building pier
38 " __ on earth . . ."
41 S.A. wildcat
42 Meager
44 Roman god
45 European river basin
46 Large numbers
48 One waiting in ambush
50 French marshal
51 Jabber
52 Oppressive things
54 Holiday fireplace décor
58 French parent
61 Yakutsk's river
62 Eye makeup used in East
63 City near Florence
64 "Unto us __ is given"
65 Within: Prefix
66 Capital of Nord
67 Skirt feature
68 Biblical verb
69 Display frame

DOWN

1 Abbess
2 Symbol of Britain
3 Guide for the Wise Men
4 Roman halls
5 Swerves
6 Water
7 Festive seasonal sight
8 On one's __
9 Envelop
10 Evergreens
11 Smell __
12 Woolen: It.
13 Robt. __
22 English limestone
24 Syrian city, to Frenchmen
26 Disconcert
27 Atlantic croaker
30 Items in Santa's bag
31 Emanations
32 Dazzling
34 Sweetshop holiday novelty
39 Part of a vending machine
40 Kind of power: Abbr.
43 Ship wood
47 Like some fences
49 Become mussed
53 Princewood
54 Lava
55 People of Uganda
56 __ about
57 Emphatic negative
59 Tamarisk
60 December song

135

ACROSS

1 Offspring: Abbr.
5 Short ride
9 Scarlett's milieu
13 Pale color
14 Bustle
15 Customers
17 Dentist's gear
18 Prolific writer
19 Legbone
20 Transmit
22 __-Magnon
24 Postal initials
25 Bit
26 Iroquoian
28 Scrap
29 Ocean routes
30 Gets on
31 Sack
32 Green light
33 Gather
34 Yak away
37 Crowlike
38 Seafood
39 Most brief
41 Biblical underdog
42 City on the Yser
43 Predicaments
44 __ mode
45 Incorrect
46 One of the Andrews
   sisters
47 Hairy
49 Munich's river
51 Adduce
53 La Scala unit
54 Bookbinding material
55 Choir member
56 Asian sea
57 Give ear
58 "How have you __?"

DOWN

1 Smidgen
2 Outfit
3 Conjectures
4 Décor features
5 Hard look
6 Seine feature
7 Altar words
8 Cool
9 Coaching
10 "__ was saying"
11 Check
12 Springs
16 Unvarying
21 Topnotcher
23 Join
26 Casals, for one
27 With 28 Down, street
   sign
28 See 27 Down
29 Tarpon
31 __ call
33 Army man
34 Youngster
35 Liqueur
36 Bankroll
37 Neck: Fr.
38 Part of the street scene
39 Quartz ingredient
40 Faith __
41 Richard of silents
42 Snoozes
43 Got on
46 Confusing place
48 Odds and ends
50 German pronoun
52 Ages and ages

136

ACROSS

1 Cat, in Spain
5 Subway grip
10 Dernier __
13 Scent
14 Second-rate stuff
15 Greek letters
16 Abominable snowman
17 House area
19 Residue
21 Torme
22 Ejects
23 Geometric shape
25 Consumes
26 Of a pouch, in anatomy
28 Somewhat: Suffix
29 Salutation
30 "Once __, twice shy"
34 She loved Narcissus
38 Tide
40 Zodiac sign
41 Fashion name
42 Noble
43 Cast a pall
45 Chick
46 Madison Ave. output
48 Traffic circle
50 Pretty
52 Sound from a tree
55 "Green Hat" author
56 Fleming
57 Shelve
60 Funny Girl
63 Kind of case
64 Literary collections
65 Flower part
66 Lab equipment
67 Enclosure, in Scotland
68 Paradises
69 Printing direction

DOWN

1 Spanish painter
2 Drinks
3 "Step __"
4 Windows
5 Ship: Abbr.
6 Bridge term
7 Icy deposits
8 Kind of sauce
9 Little: Fr.
10 Made a selection
11 Haymarket and others
12 Doctrines
15 Put down
18 Old French coins
20 Pitcher's plate
24 Epic narratives
26 Something destructive
27 Part of the eye
28 Add to the interior
31 Refrain syllable
32 Shooting match: Fr.
33 Cry by woman on chair
35 Ashtray item
36 Frost
37 Paris airport
39 Typewriter parts
44 Norse giantess
47 Gainsay
49 Fluffs the hair
50 Stretch one's neck
51 Arm bones
52 Spent
53 Chief Justice, 1874-88
54 S.A. Indian
55 From a distance
58 Seven of eleven on offense
59 Coup d' __
61 Athlete's degree
62 Certain trains

137

ACROSS

1 See-through item
5 Navy specialist
10 Asian prefix
14 Early explorer
15 Take out
16 Service clubs
17 Tortilla
18 Demanding
20 English novelist
22 Dispatch
23 Youth org.
24 Food for bees
26 Sports initials
28 __ standstill
31 Aviation initials
32 Method
35 Hoist
37 Sale words
39 "... in corpore __"
40 Piled up
42 Relies
44 Role
45 European capital
47 Tête-__
48 Diva's exercises
50 Noun suffix
52 Mayday's relative
53 Letter
54 Sidereal
56 "__ were you"
58 Small whales
60 Asian donkey
64 Private
67 Western alliance
68 Siege
69 Gaggle components
70 Sudden noise
71 Predicament
72 Heroic tales
73 French pronoun

DOWN

1 Leases
2 Part of Q.E.D.
3 Finicky
4 Contumely
5 Desert
6 Gershwin
7 Flunkies of yore
8 Chemical compound
9 Restraint
10 __ generis
11 Fuel gases
12 Entre __
13 Thessaly sight
19 Memorable date
21 Cozy places
25 Amphibians
27 Something of value
28 Conform
29 Daughter of David
30 Covetous
32 Direction: Abbr.
33 Put an __ it
34 Lawgiver
36 Agave fiber
38 Wedding surprise words
41 Greek goddess
43 Song of praise
46 Roped
49 __ majesty
51 Indian monetary units
54 Lent a hand
55 Fer-de-__
56 Missile
57 Cold sheet of sorts
59 Plain or deckle
61 Effrontery
62 Latin abbr.
63 Line
65 Relatives of aves.
66 Female bear: Sp.

138

ACROSS

1 Cutter
5 Besides
9 Cheese
13 100 centavos
14 Crowbar user
15 Partner of yep
16 Sloth
17 Rod of tennis fame
18 Trick
19 Household item
21 Clad
22 Scientists' places
23 "__ things!"
25 __-Powell, Scouts' founder
28 Flowed in a noisy way
30 Orally
31 Sun-dried brick
32 "What's up, __?"
34 __-garou

35 Young fowl
36 Traveled
37 Coming-out girl
38 Fry lightly
39 Dud
40 Elapses
42 That is: Lat.
43 Surpass
44 Of an Asian nation
46 Terra __
48 Take second helpings
53 Grandparental
54 Defunct car
55 Family business abbr.
56 Erase
57 French river
58 Unaspirated
59 Blackens
60 Printing error
61 Pitcher

DOWN

1 Potato
2 Cotton fabric
3 Son of Isaac
4 Share quarters
5 Sheiks and others
6 Vivid
7 React, as to twins
8 Hockey star
9 Enlist
10 Highbrow
11 Church part
12 Reward, old style
14 Academy freshman
20 Set down
21 Anger
24 Fuse by heat
25 Undisguised
26 Bitter __
27 Mumbo jumbo

28 Swollen
29 Extinct birds
31 Baseball name
33 Coin
35 Bullfighter's maneuver
36 Bridge call
38 Animal org.
39 Typesetter, for short
41 Tropical fibers: Var.
44 Shorthand gal
45 Inactive
46 Moslem judge
47 Kiln
49 Wet
50 Beer
51 Ranger or wolf
52 River to North Sea
54 Superlative suffix

139

ACROSS

1 __ the morning
6 Trade
10 Type of coal
14 Kind of acid
15 Gully
16 Canadian Indian
17 Picnic treat
19 Pro __
20 __ artium
21 Rumor
22 Humperdinck girl
24 Spin a floating log
25 Gushed
26 Port near Naples
29 Light-colored
30 Tooth problem
31 They keep falling on heads
35 Guinness
36 Human __

37 Oil country
38 W.W. II general
40 Egg-shaped
41 Express sorrow
42 Euclid or Madison
43 Tooth décor for the young
45 __ Rabbit
46 Add, as syrup
47 Black: Fr.
48 Former columnist
51 Large lump
52 Kissing
55 Lily
56 Connery
57 Covered the floor
58 Camp item
59 Organism
60 Hostile one

DOWN

1 New Zealand tree
2 Bradley
3 Grain exchanges
4 __-horse town
5 Strengthen
6 Puff up
7 __ the plank
8 Bustle
9 Indoor game
10 Drink or tool
11 Make a speech
12 Celebrated
13 Greenish blue
18 Husband, in Lyon
23 Tear
24 Concomitant of scarcity
25 Move furtively
26 Bede
27 Indian festival

28 Maple genus
29 Child, in Glasgow
31 Brings up
32 Algerian port
33 Maori weapon
34 Snick-or __
36 Prude
39 Chanel of fashion
40 Failed as a dieter
42 Seed covering
43 Casino game
44 Keep going
45 "I'm Alabamy __"
46 Type that's easily set
47 College sports org.
48 Single or double
49 "Trees," for one
50 Griffith
53 Time div.
54 Type of can

140

ACROSS

1 Lessen
5 Seed vessels
10 Diner drink
14 Swiss river
15 Base for glue
16 Baker's need
17 Story unsuitable for a bald man
20 Juice
21 Serais
22 Reference book
23 French silk
24 Biblical weed
26 Find
29 Easter
32 Particle
33 Flowing hairdos
34 Recent: Prefix
36 Local action groups
40 Shoe size
41 Annoys
42 Greek letter
43 Did a hostler's job
45 Singer Geraldine
47 Scottish negatives
48 St. __, French port
49 Unadorned
52 Glut
53 Blackjack player's word
56 Opposite of summer in the country
60 Forbidden
61 Top-notch
62 State
63 Signs of success
64 Gloomy Gus
65 Greek community

DOWN

1 Cries of disdain
2 Good report card
3 Some users' aim
4 Relative of eterne
5 Cap
6 Think
7 Football setback
8 First-century date
9 Opposite of ant.
10 Wrote
11 Written pledge in law
12 Soft palates
13 French donkeys
18 Public disorder
19 Showy
23 Author Baker
24 Stage awards
25 Fish sauce
26 Trimming
27 Indians
28 Celestial body
29 Had strong feelings
30 Goose genus
31 Girl's name
33 Priscilla's proxy suitor
35 Sandy ridge
37 Suave
38 Shade of green
39 River to the Mediterranean
44 Hostility
45 Family member
46 Opposite of aweather
48 Having a dull surface
49 Attention getters
50 Ananias
51 Early pulpit
52 Small amount
53 Home for a queen
54 News release
55 Ancient city
57 In __
58 Workers' group: Abbr.
59 Bounder

141

ACROSS

1 Place for a nest
5 Wicker: Var.
10 Moslem priest
14 Eastern name
15 School, in Nice
16 "Then there were __"
17 Auto-racing city, with "Le"
18 Compacts
20 Karamazovs, e.g.
22 Spreads rumors
23 Early astronaut
24 Wood support
25 Lorn
27 Adam's possession, in a way
31 Woman with __
32 Son of Noah
33 Finished
34 Taste
35 Petty tyrants
38 Famous fifty: Abbr.
39 Educ. place
41 Onion's relative
42 Beer
44 Hardened
46 Adorns, old style
47 Brought up
48 Vessel
49 "My Sister __"
52 Moon area
55 Building foundation
57 Entrance
58 Headquarters
59 Eastern queens
60 McCarthy, to friends
61 Gardner
62 Viewpoint
63 Raw materials

DOWN

1 Farm animal
2 Structural unit
3 Certain treatises
4 Moves with energy
5 Not long since
6 Kind of squash
7 Weights
8 Liquor ingredient: Abbr.
9 Illumination unit
10 Put in writing
11 Struthious birds
12 Prefix for bellum
13 Dinner of a kind
19 Surf sound
21 Lifts
24 __ one's piece
25 Singer
26 Memorable works
27 Fragment
28 Cavalryman with T.R.
29 Garment addition
30 Pooh's cousins
32 Arab
36 Transferrers of property
37 Move furtively
40 One of a French trio
43 Long in the past
45 Word with port or lance
46 Most serious
48 High-school subject
49 Actual being
50 Relative of via
51 Faithful, in Scotland
52 Famous editor
53 Eat
54 Seasons in Nice
56 Remainder: Abbr.

142

ACROSS

ACROSS

1 Bumpkins
6 Hardened
11 Composer of 55 mazurkas
12 Holmes
14 Defunct N.Y. paper
15 Origins
17 Harness parts
18 Farm animal
20 Charity effort
21 Birds in general
22 Positive photo
24 Corner
25 Part of W.W.
26 Pious
28 Blunder
29 Gregarious bird
31 Clinic workers
33 ___ jury
34 Arrived
35 Prance
38 Klondike resident
42 Winglike part
43 Intersecting lines
45 Roman 502
46 Phony coin
48 Blows one's top
49 For fear that
50 Lodge doorkeeper
52 North or Ross
53 Prominent clergyman
54 Starts
56 Insulting person
58 Wooden bench
59 Salvation and others
60 Considers
61 Scrutinizes

DOWN

1 Wild fancy
2 Rounded parts
3 Work of 11 Across
4 Clamor
5 Scornful
6 To the point
7 Bar order
8 Category
9 Turn inside out
10 Yens
11 Apparel item
13 Busy man on April 18, 1775
14 Relents
16 Prophets
19 Plane part
22 Mountain lion
23 Apartment dwellers
26 Slanders
27 D'Artagnan's creator
30 Greek letter
32 Morning-after eyes
34 Choral works
35 Theater program listings
36 Associates
37 Like many cathedrals
38 Chastise in a way
39 Forms an opinion
40 Church sections
41 Gunpowder ingredient
44 Brahman, Sudra, etc.
47 Exploit
49 Famous Russian
51 Set system
53 Cougar
55 City on the Danube
57 Spark stream

143

ACROSS

1 Gush forth
5 Creole potpourri
14 Italian Paul
15 Color named for Goya
16 "__ is Born"
17 Baking dish
18 Source of soup stock
20 Drainage, for short
21 Gov't agency
22 Greek god
24 Six, in Italy
25 Fool
27 Fiber knots
29 Yonder
31 Table center-piece
33 Mud
35 Cooking utensil
36 Loving
40 Lichen
41 Explosive force
42 Italian poet
45 Space initials
46 Flightless bird
47 Pub order
48 Fury
51 Ace
53 Bordeaux miss: Abbr.
55 Brawl
59 Certain highways
61 Conclusion
62 Dialers' concerns
63 Part of a gem
64 Breakfast item
65 Prune, in Scotland

DOWN

1 Dress feature
2 French chef's specialty
3 Feelings of zest
4 Marginal economic group
5 Witty, in Scotland
6 Mexican cabs
7 Greedy one
8 French ski resort
9 Donkey: Fr.
10 Alphabet units: Abbr.
11 Waken
12 One who shouts
13 Penguin
14 __ de deux
19 Mangos of P.I.
23 Certain kinds of beef orders
25 Faroe winds
26 Military address: Abbr.
28 Antes
30 Greek goddess
32 Car mechanics' concerns: Abbr.
33 Relative
34 __ March
37 Repetition
38 __ de plume
39 African antelope
42 Hindu gong
43 Then: It.
44 Vendor
45 Required
49 "__ and his money. . ."
50 Step: Sp.
52 Of a geologic period
54 Ancient kingdom
56 First word of N.C. motto
57 Prevaricated
58 Landing craft: Abbr.
60 Parent org. of N.B.C.

144

ACROSS

1 Belmont winner, 1955, or city in N.H.
7 Derby winner, 1958
13 Predetermine
14 Without weapons
16 Vends again
17 Vestment band
18 Harem room
19 Disappoint
21 New Guinea port
22 Swing around
24 "Who's ___?"
25 Curve
26 Alabama city
28 French conjunctions
29 Count of jazz
30 Spend the summer
32 Classified
33 Marine worm
35 Roman orator
38 Derby winner, 1887
42 George Eliot's real name
43 Tire mount
44 ___ Anita
45 Hold on
46 Art style
48 Region: Abbr.
49 Explosive
50 Measles
52 Wire measure
53 "___ tell you I do"
55 Period of decline
57 Busy official in whodunits
58 Conclusions
59 Ancient ascetic
60 Follows

DOWN

1 Derby winner, 1956, or thread holders
2 Triple Crown winner, 1946
3 Sault ___ Marie
4 ___ Gail, Derby winner, 1952
5 Vacant
6 Art lover
7 Swellings
8 ___ of (impressed)
9 Horace or Thomas
10 Three: Prefix
11 Most sufficient
12 Girl in "Gone With the Wind"
13 Tiller rope: Fr.
15 Transferred legally
20 Derby winner, 1954, or decide
23 Famous
25 Farm pest
27 Asserts strongly
29 Marina sights
31 I love: Lat.
32 Japanese coin
34 Preakness winner, 1965
35 Boston player
36 Scott hero
37 Namesakes of Pollux's twin
39 Eight furlongs
40 Walks in a way
41 U.S. inventor and others
43 Drill again
46 ___ abend (good evening)
47 Conceal, in law: Var.
50 Coty of France
51 Barley beards
54 Opposite of neg.
56 Greek letter

145

ACROSS

1 Caesar, for one
6 Hunk
10 Humorous poet
14 Rub out
15 Southern favorite
16 Preposition
17 Ocean vessel
18 Bit
19 Insect
20 Bazaar's relative
22 Breed's or Bunker
23 Currier's partner
24 "What have you done for me __?"
26 Dance step
30 Details
32 Balcony
33 Gallic name
35 Musketeer
39 Mushroom
41 Win
43 Risk
44 Tool
46 Men
47 Fragrant
49 Los Angeles five
51 Small cap
54 Cease
56 Spin like __
57 Fragrant shrub
63 Cocktail variety
64 Angry
65 Michigan town
66 __ many words
67 Adduce
68 Picks out
69 Appear
70 Origin
71 Mini or maxi

DOWN

1 Word with him or her
2 Seed coat
3 Alley
4 Cruising
5 Skin layer
6 Steeple
7 Emulates Peeping Tom
8 Stake
9 Ringo, for one
10 Billy
11 Ado or Orphant
12 Booth
13 With passion
21 Prevent
25 Oriental nurse
26 Burst of thunder
27 Certain plate
28 Lab medium
29 School dance
31 Shipbuilding wood
34 Work for
36 Now's partner
37 Done
38 Does needlework
40 Latin pronoun
42 Instrument
45 Letter winner
48 Moral system
50 Athenians
51 Grounds
52 Agreed
53 Waken
55 Gave a hand
58 Cleveland's waterfront
59 Defeat
60 However
61 Capsule
62 Relax

146

ACROSS

1 Four-bagger
6 Handy Latin abbr.
10 First name of Mrs. F.D.R.
14 Maine town
15 S.A. bird
16 Biblical kingdom
17 Biblical victim of hanging
18 Headland
19 Covet
20 Unusual fellow
21 Legacies, in old days
23 Fictional captain
25 Gardner
26 Loop travelers
27 Matched group
29 French dugout
31 Nautical direction
33 Reeds
35 Tourist stop in India
37 Antarctic sea
41 Elusive quest of explorers
44 Part of Saturn's rings
45 Kind of joint
46 Port of ancient Rome
47 Part of a Scottish name
49 ___ miss
51 Conrail takeover: Abbr.
52 Fast plane: Abbr.
55 Underpinnings
57 People of old Gaul
59 Detailed report
62 Soil: Prefix
65 "Othello" role
66 Former ruler
67 Horatio
68 Old-World duck
69 Roof finials
70 Blabbermouth
71 Hindu weights
72 English sand hill
73 Lands

DOWN

1 Santa sounds
2 Algerian port
3 Kind of occasion
4 Lake in Finland
5 Swoboda
6 Sea eagle
7 Words for Franco's regime
8 Odin and followers
9 Subject of Holmes poem
10 Sobeit
11 Present occasion
12 Variety of orange
13 Chasm
21 What trouble-makers raise
22 Roman bronze
24 Spar
27 Living-room piece
28 Black
30 Shore bird
32 Greek god
34 Hindu grant
36 Cable
38 South Sea island boat
39 Agitate
40 Wild sheep of India
42 Generally recognized
43 Olden days
48 Beverage
50 Timetable abbr.
52 Type of cheese
53 Disgrace
54 ". . .___ burning bright"
56 Quebec area
58 Of apples
60 Pulls
61 Gaelic
63 Dream, in Paris
64 Wolframite et al.
67 "Not ___ Stranger"

ACROSS

1 Subdivision of the Constitution
8 City on S.F. Bay
15 Item for a cap
16 Not exaggerated
17 Vacationing, military style
18 Mother of Arthur
19 Coagulate
20 Trait of verbose writers
22 Bronze, for one
23 Do fancywork
24 Kind of corporal
27 Builder of London churches
29 Passing fancies
33 Embellishes
35 Over an earthquake's center
37 Dugout canoe
39 Violently angry
40 Dovish
42 Steadying device
43 Capital of old Elam
44 "__ Here to Eternity"
46 Cuts of meat
47 Mail car: Abbr.
49 African people
51 Relating to a police officer's duties
55 Bond
58 Halos around the sun
59 Chiller
61 Sums
62 Arms storehouse
63 Young women
64 Birds, generally

DOWN

1 In __ (bewildered)
2 Chateaubriand title
3 Lofty
4 Inhabitant: Suffix
5 Throw down the gauntlet
6 Horizontal
7 Heretofore
8 Came to rest
9 Franklin's aid
10 Roman halls
11 "I was __"
12 One of "H.O.M.E.S."
13 During: Fr.
14 Pub drinks
21 Vortex
22 Bearing fruit at the end of the stem
24 Northern Scandinavians
25 Farewell
26 Mrs. Charles and others
28 Prefix with gram or sode
30 Mites
31 Philistine deity
32 Snow vehicles
34 Stifle
36 Free from defect
38 Continent: Abbr.
41 Timber wolf
45 Robin Hood's Maid __
48 Coin of Finland
50 Mother-of-pearl
51 Adjective suffix
52 Honshu town
53 Sings of a hit
54 Mrs. Dick Tracy
55 Melody
56 Letter-shaped beam
57 Slippery ones
60 This, in Rouen

148

ACROSS

1 Mast support
5 Salad gelatin
10 Big-Ben sound
14 Mine, in France
15 Flat surfaces of the skull
16 Cuchulainn's wife
17 Autoists' reading matter
19 Sonoran Indian
20 Swiss Alpine group
21 Period of trial
23 Work on shoes
25 Australian native
26 Elusive thing
33 Grant
36 Italian finger game
37 Ethiopian lake
38 Philippine tree
39 Joint units
41 Scottish violinist
42 Neighbor of Sverige
44 __ part
45 Pillow material
46 "For I'm to be __"
49 Siouan
50 Zoroastrian writings
54 Some travelers
60 Round-Table knight: Var.
61 "Not __ to stand on"
62 Investigate
64 Immense
65 Used up
66 Department in France
67 N.M. art colony
68 Wading bird
69 "Ancient of __"

DOWN

1 Little elephant of juveniles
2 Chemical compound
3 Large pill
4 Surging
5 Service-mail initials
6 Kind of dash or happy
7 Young salmon
8 __-European
9 "Come with me to the __"
10 Confers on
11 Chinese peak
12 Emperor
13 Pleased look
18 Island east of Java
22 Encourages
24 Sailors' saint
27 Former Yankee pitcher
28 Garden plant
29 French pastry
30 Shakespearean villain
31 Sled's milieu
32 Put in hock
33 After quatre
34 __ ben Adhem
35 Infrequent
39 Hundred: Prefix
40 Town in central Iowa
43 Bizet
45 Lumber yielding color bases
47 Scads
48 State
51 Mountain people of India
52 Like a flimsy metal
53 Llamas' home
54 Thai money
55 Hawaiian food fish
56 Western lily
57 Of the dawn
58 Roast: Fr.
59 Farm basket
63 Suffix in chemistry

149

ACROSS

1 Caprice
5 Pitch's tag-along
9 Evening, in Berlin
14 Yorkshire river
15 Stratagem
16 Mischievous
17 Orating
20 Old coin of Italy
21 Has a bite
22 Meadowland
23 Men
24 Possessive
25 Botch
26 Leaf nuisance
29 Catlike
31 Unsuccessful
32 Make one
33 Milky Way, for one
37 Resident of: Suffix
38 Gab at length

39 Distrustful
40 Helms's outfit
41 Move swiftly
43 Hollywood area
44 Roil
45 Matured
47 Settled
48 Complacent
51 Family member
52 German article
53 Sesame
54 Family member
55 African river
59 Ad-libbing
62 Thick soup
63 Undressed
64 __ Bator
65 Boxes
66 Egyptian deity
67 Allocate

DOWN

1 Funny people
2 Charter
3 Where Basra is
4 Famed violinist
5 A.L. team
6 Painting
7 Floundered
8 Follow-up
9 Honeybee genus
10 Show __
11 Banish
12 5 Down et al.
13 French impressionist
18 Faded out
19 Honest
25 Cooperstown name
26 Birds' class
27 Bygone
28 Yesterday: Fr.
29 Not numerous
30 Vote against
32 Rouses

34 Recorded proceedings
35 Chapter heading
36 Play area
38 Preserve container
39 Douceur
42 Menu item
43 Five-year period
44 Sheet of rock
46 City on the Mississippi
47 Immunological items
48 Units of progress
49 Confusion
50 Way-out
52 Retail unit
54 City north of
   Des Moines
56 El Bahr
57 Fall guy
58 Nine: Prefix
60 Noun ending
61 Ceremonial words

150

ACROSS

1 Come into view
5 Swamp
10 Foot soldier, in India
14 Monster
15 Type size
16 Choir voice
17 Make out
18 Strong man
19 Picnic spoiler
20 Personal sacrifice
22 Trial data
24 Step lightly
26 School in England
27 Cage bird
31 Certify
35 Sends forth
36 Social division
38 Sailor
39 Carry on
40 __ blanche
41 Overfill
42 Native of: Suffix
43 Narrow boat
44 Brown pigment
45 Sidewalk nuisance
47 Urban dwelling
49 Ex-Card Slaughter
51 Persian fairy
52 Splash
56 Lease-signer
60 Fly the __
61 Decree
63 Double-reed
64 Besides
65 Brazilian port
66 __ majesty
67 Symbol of redness
68 Growing out
69 First home

DOWN

1 Nobleman
2 Molding
3 Algerian port
4 Reflect
5 Ear of corn, in Africa
6 Height: Abbr.
7 Vex
8 Part of a poem
9 Waver
10 Top company in a group
11 Enthusiasm
12 Of the ear
13 "__ but the brave . . ."
21 Scows
23 Lavish fondness on
25 Praline ingredient
27 Risk
28 Violin maker
29 Metal bolt
30 Mystic card
32 Warehouse
33 Smooth
34 Something pleasant
37 Soak
40 Vitamin A source
41 Florida Indian
43 Coin
44 Arid
46 Certain container
48 Prickly plant
50 Type of auto
52 Strikebreaker
53 Propel a punt
54 Be on the short end
55 Rio __
57 Retired
58 Meddle
59 Number ending
62 Library list: Abbr.

151

ACROSS

1 Humorous fellows
6 Soft or no
10 Agreement
14 Concerning
15 Spaniard's hello
16 Capri
17 Subject of a tongue-twister
19 Converse
20 Diminutive suffixes
21 Hearing aids
22 Keepsakes
24 Celebration
25 Helper
26 Inhabitant of Mideast
29 Give in
33 Then, in Paris
34 "__ of my dreams"
35 Winglike
36 Grimace
37 __ Hawkins Day
38 Cordage fiber
39 Art medium
40 Zounds!
41 Piano part
42 Death __ (certainties)
44 Le Mans entries
45 Takes steps
46 Gloom
47 Lettering on a cheerleader's sweater
50 Spanish painter
51 Range of sight
54 Biblical trio
55 Like some tails
58 Corn-oil product
59 Places
60 Migratory birds
61 Campbell or Cove
62 Israeli leader
63 Cut off

DOWN

1 May or Ann
2 Give aid to
3 Goes bad
4 Owing
5 Easy and one-way
6 Dorset, for one
7 Word before sorry
8 Beverage
9 Small bit of matter
10 What 17 Across did
11 Tennis player
12 Family group
13 Asian holidays
18 Spread
23 Poetic form
24 Garage for red vehicles
25 Sharp
26 South Pacific islands
27 Remove oneself: Var.
28 Form, in England
29 Operatic heroine and namesakes
30 Pass over
31 Early Asian
32 Tests
34 Green plums
37 Double triple
41 Cut-off apple skins
43 Top pilot
44 Hold sway
46 Naval historian
47 City problem
48 Word for some stories
49 Awry
50 Ten: Prefix
51 City on the Dnieper
52 "Do it or __"
53 Poetic word
56 Steal from
57 Observe

152

ACROSS

1 Haggard heroine
4 Mythical source of gold
9 Dress-shirt feature
13 Careless
14 Chemical compound
16 Prefix for drome or dynamics
17 Mohammedan name
18 British botanist
19 Gloomy Dean
20 Old prcs
22 Wild spree
24 Crew
25 Salt grass
27 Filaments
31 Paint like Seurat
35 Learned
36 Oriental nursemaid
38 "Ah, me!"
39 Central American Indian
40 Anoint
41 Bronzes
42 Sports area
43 Rafter
44 Actor Vincent
45 Metal workers
47 Salty springs
49 Insects
51 Varnish base
52 Participated in
55 Drips
60 Man from Lodz
61 Lily Maid
63 Poem
64 Put up
65 Punch-card device
66 Hockey team
67 Kind of light
68 Useless growths
69 Pen

DOWN

1 Serb or Croat
2 In the pink
3 Door sign
4 Get the wrong impression
5 Coney or Midway
6 Scottish river
7 Collect
8 Capitol man: Abbr.
9 Big name in Tara
10 Incline
11 Exhort
12 Man of action
15 Shower again
21 Pre-spring color
23 Silkworm
26 David's specialties
27 Cast
28 Hoist
29 Of a branch
30 Most reasonable
32 "For 2¢ __"
33 Spear
34 Letters
37 __ culpa
40 Grates
44 Gold-bearing deposits
46 Compass point
48 Straightened
50 Gaze
52 Pair
53 Sharpen
54 Vocal range
56 Customary practice
57 Defeat
58 Do city-room work
59 Spicy
62 Moo

153

ACROSS

1 Tilting
6 Paid in a way
11 Statue support: Abbr.
14 __ voce
15 Lady of song
16 Word in a Salinger title
17 Finn
19 Mouths
20 African country: Abbr.
21 Very, in Rouen
22 Man or bird
24 __ majesty
25 Poplar
27 Compelling effect
30 Abridge
33 Highest points
34 "__ Bulba"
35 Freuchen subject
36 Classmen: Abbr.
37 Off-base dress
38 Spill the beans
39 Summer clock reading
40 Judith Anderson role
41 Dull finish
42 Twisters
44 Hungarian
45 Capp creation
46 English gallery
47 Seaport of Chile
49 Chaplin spouse
50 Angle
53 Plant science: Abbr.
54 One kind of story
58 Old card game
59 Ghastly
60 Be indebted
61 Valid: Abbr.
62 Indians
63 Hoosier poet

DOWN

1 Court champ
2 Bumpkin
3 Desire
4 Wall St. purchase: Abbr.
5 Nahuatlans
6 U.S. playwright
7 Scottish negatives
8 Asian goat
9 Stray
10 Living-room pieces
11 Leaning
12 Jane of fiction
13 Kind of reckoning
18 Formerly, of old
23 __ de France
24 Swedish districts
25 Artery
26 __ Brith
27 Part of a map
28 World, in Italy
29 Part of a Joyce title
30 Eating places
31 Actress Berger
32 Avid
34 Royal house
37 Early Asian
38 U.S. desert sight
40 Restraint
41 Man with a cape
43 Initials on a TV screen
44 Buddenbrooks' creator
46 Insect eaters
47 Competent
48 Word in a Williams title
49 Migrant worker
50 Fight
51 Der __ (old one)
52 Maneuver
55 "__ Town"
56 Dernier __
57 Caribbean islands: Abbr.

154

ACROSS

1 __ Volta
6 Composition
10 Worker
14 __ better (outdo)
15 Completed
16 Song
17 Salvation Army item
19 __-do-well
20 Purchase of 1853
21 Fresh-water fish
22 Doggie-bag contents
25 Formulated
27 Prissy
28 Road curve
31 Part of a movie dog's name
32 Track event
33 Settle
35 Caught __-handed
38 Dispatch boat
40 Timetable abbr.
41 Jostle
43 Two handfuls
44 Young cods
47 Europe's neighbor
48 __ loss
49 Manicure the lawn
50 Window part
51 Soft-colored sketches
55 Bear witness
57 Creep
58 Flippered sea creature
61 Ibsen heroine
62 Generous
66 Anthony __
67 Duck!
68 French lifeline
69 Legal document
70 Cleaving tool
71 Clean a blackboard

DOWN

1 Word of disgust
2 Kentucky bluegrass
3 "__ my word"
4 Final stages in chess play
5 Update an atlas
6 Probabilities
7 Russian weight
8 Single
9 Mack of the silents
10 Have a __ (participate)
11 Fields of study
12 Relative
13 Challenged
18 Auto that was
22 Certain choosy eater
23 Have a yen for
24 Castor-oil plant poison
26 Contends
29 Tower
30 Rude word of dismissal
34 Constellation
35 Miss O'Grady
36 Satan's specialties
37 Delivered
39 Bone: Prefix
42 One in a hurry
45 Get rid of deviously
46 Reaper's wake
48 Ready to use
51 Languished
52 Electrode
53 Rocky debris
54 Taste quality
56 Back-comb hair
59 Detective-fiction name
60 Freshly
63 Circle's width: Abbr.
64 Letters
65 Metal loop

155

ACROSS

1 Cicatrix
5 Tennis stroke
10 Beseech
14 Player on dealer's right
15 Garment
16 Let up
17 Ending
18 Greta Garbo word
19 Nothing, in Paris
20 Moon, for one
22 Reference book
23 Shows emotion
24 Silk maker
25 U.S. agency: Abbr.
28 Craft
29 Bee, for one
33 Fitzgerald
35 E.S.P.
37 Drink: Fr.
39 Vehicle
40 Growing out
41 Gets under the skin
44 Migration
45 __ Assembly
46 Legal man: Abbr.
48 Old draft agency: Abbr.
49 Anne, for one
50 Smudge
52 Half a fifth
55 E.S.P.
59 Double curve
60 Rhino's relative
61 Bakery items
62 One beyond belief
63 Shallow
64 Concerning
65 Vipers
66 Gave the eye to
67 Ruminant

DOWN

1 Hot and Warm Springs
2 Part of a comet's head
3 Dill herb
4 Resume
5 Alpinists
6 Oval
7 Digs
8 Wind indicator
9 Make out
10 Apt
11 Fence part
12 Befuddled
13 Hankerings
21 Meadow
22 Become active
24 Biblical verb ending
25 Package again
26 Funeral oration
27 Adjust
29 Teardrop contour
30 Growls
31 __ Park, Colo.
32 Gives off
34 Lightning guards
36 Totem pole
38 Mother or Good
42 __ victus (woe to the conquered)
43 Used a tiller
47 Kind of dance
50 Flower part
51 Quick
52 Weight of India
53 Sponsorship
54 Tide
55 Strong flavor
56 Antler point
57 Roll-call response
58 River in Belgium
60 Spanish relative

156

ACROSS

1 Organic compound
5 Béchamel, for one
10 Sod
14 Art movement
15 Test
16 Type of eye
17 Worldwide
19 French name
20 N.Y.-Wash. liner
21 Open space for walking
23 Guarantee
25 Gabor
26 Itinerant
32 Marbles
35 Growl
36 Fortification
38 Nabokov book
39 Fig-bearing plants of India
41 Position
42 Volcano of Martinique
44 Verve
45 Mailed
46 Word for Big Brother
49 Double helix
50 Most positive
54 Defame
60 City in Bengal
61 Norwegian king
62 See 46 Across
64 Gull
65 Return
66 Charity
67 Cheers
68 Venner or Dinsmore
69 __ majesty

DOWN

1 Swelling
2 Church parts
3 U.S. dramatist
4 Thrashes
5 Adage
6 Tennis star
7 Takes advantage of
8 Nag
9 Small hole
10 Threefold
11 Eye part
12 Cheese covering
13 Escape
18 Bygone times
22 States
24 Therefore
27 Among: Prefix
28 Speak: Fr.
29 Spaces
30 Useless
31 Biblical brother
32 Vanishing gas-station gift
33 Conception prefix
34 Ointment
37 Snare
39 Human
40 Chemical suffixes
43 Greens
45 Layered
47 Matched set of jewels
48 Bare: Prefix
51 Lycée's relative
52 Drosses
53 Armor plate
54 Old fogy
55 Jewish month
56 Neck part
57 Actor Walter
58 Twitchings
59 Same: Prefix
63 English river

157

ACROSS

1 Inaccurate plus
9 Singing star
15 Senior citizens' insurance
16 Babe Ruth, once
17 __ head
18 "South Pacific" role
19 Where to find dumbbells
20 Emulate a girl-watcher
21 Savile Row man
22 Certain doctors
23 Way to go: Abbr.
25 Old draft agency
26 Road men of a sort
29 Exact satisfaction for
32 Make __
33 Kind of bill
37 Not certain
40 Wed
41 Bouncy
43 Certain soldiers
44 Coats with metal
45 Suit
46 Novel title
49 Men of letters, for short
50 "Home of the bean and the __"
51 From first __
54 Poetic contraction
56 Concealed danger
59 Old love token
60 Paul Revere's signals
62 Capital of Saskatchewan
63 First name in stage lore
64 Goodies
65 Put up with

DOWN

1 Atmospheric hybrid
2 Tax
3 Footnote word
4 Moslem saint
5 Kitchen utensils
6 Displays, in a way
7 City 200 miles south of Moscow
8 Be worthy of
9 Argues
10 Coded region
11 Flowery girl's name
12 Sprawls
13 Inter __
14 Intuitive ones
22 Words of encouragement
24 Beliefs
26 Rapunzel's pride
27 Without: Ger.
28 Figures of a kind
29 Be present at
30 Political initials
31 Escaped, in a way
34 Head into the wind
35 Spore sacs, in botany
36 Halting place
38 Diminutive suffix
39 Caps
42 Cuddles close
45 See 50 Across
46 Get off
47 Grand slam, at times
48 Praise: Fr.
50 Capital of Crete
52 Tenor's specialty
53 Caused to go
55 Disney
56 Campus V.I.P.
57 Oriental case
58 Ruler
61 Word with play or run

158

ACROSS

ACROSS

1 Prefix for aircraft and trust
5 Excuse
10 Entreaty
14 Prisoner's concern
15 Club sandwich ingredient
16 Biblical symbol of power
17 Stumble
18 Show off
19 Mine access
20 Reluctant
22 Quality of some penmanship
24 Proclaim loudly
26 Command to Pussy
27 Greek letters
29 Shock
33 Like some treaties
37 "As good __"
38 Native of Yemen
39 Egyptologist's quest
41 Bog
42 Seethes
44 Laid waste
46 Of certain mountains
48 Small branch
49 Printing word
51 Pacific island group
55 Harassed
59 Of the nostrils
60 Voice
61 Undermine
63 Peculiar: Prefix
64 Deceitful one
65 Tiny land area
66 Old Greek contest
67 "Contrary" mistress
68 Vales
69 Telescope part

DOWN

1 Essential oil
2 Strength
3 Attempts
4 Errant husband's forte
5 One intentionally not present
6 Part of a race
7 Religious object
8 Uses an auger
9 Not broken
10 Like some dreams
11 Comstock, for one
12 Tosser of a mythical apple
13 Aardvark diet
21 Tallow
23 Home of Irish kings
25 Ventured
28 Base of some taxes
30 Specific quantity
31 Bare
32 Overcame in a way
33 Rum cake
34 Mashie or wedge
35 Put down
36 Speech troubles
40 Tiaras
43 Glut
45 Actress Lee
47 Sea nymph
50 Brief
52 Gnat
53 Gibson ingredient
54 Certain signs
55 Part of the hand
56 Pen name
57 Arcturus
58 Plaything
62 State: Abbr.

159

ACROSS

1 Operatic ruler
6 Be effusive
10 Jug
14 Precise
15 Grayish mineral
16 Inter __
17 Current playwright
18 Modern form of hauling
20 Josh
21 Medium's messages
23 Puts a certain ball in play
24 Thicket, in Britain
26 Asian
27 Racetrack character
28 Bar tidbits
32 Wallop
34 Howe
35 River island
36 Indian nurse
37 Fair-haired boy
38 Indian tourist mecca
39 Via
40 Thoroughly
41 Distance runner
42 Storms
44 Bus rider
45 __ of laughter
46 Disheartens
49 Accent
52 Escape slowly
53 Aloha concomitant
54 Transplant for Richard I
56 Wild-apple tree
58 Toward the mouth
59 Season
60 Kind of eagle or owl
61 Old Greek platform
62 Pieces out
63 Ford

DOWN

1 Chicago team
2 Hybrid primrose
3 TV adjunct
4 Diamonds: Slang
5 Breast bone
6 Aquarium favorite
7 Author of "Armageddon"
8 __ Harbor, N.Y.
9 Large cask
10 City of Iran
11 Norwegian saint
12 Hue of blue or green
13 Guffaws
19 Irish poet
22 Of age: Abbr.
25 Danny Kaye role
26 Threefold
28 Conspires
29 Farm cultivators
30 Money in Salerno
31 Headliner
32 Spanish cloak
33 Cereal grasses
34 The Four Hundred
37 Marksman's goal
38 Yorkshire river
40 Annul
41 Lese __
43 Program
44 Headgear
46 Goes gaga over
47 Lead and tin alloy
48 Prophetess
49 Clumsy fellow
50 Exhaust
51 Gad
52 Voided escutcheon
55 Sea diver
57 No gentleman

160

ACROSS

1 Successful shows
5 Aleksei Peshkov
10 H.H. Munro
14 Neglect
15 Violently
16 Football infraction
17 Information
18 Shops
19 Charged atoms
20 Jean Baptiste Poquelin
22 Ohio port
24 Knows, old style
25 Spin a floating log
26 Old-hat
28 François Marie Arouet
32 __ Haute
33 Brooks
34 Nest: Fr.
35 Item on a handbag: Abbr.
36 Commends
37 Pledge
38 Soft food
39 Least particles
40 Vladimir Ulyanov
41 Marie Henri Beyle
43 Tunneled
44 Violinist Bull and others
45 Common contraction
46 Chatters
49 Eric Weiss
52 Hideout
53 Type abbreviation
55 Italian resort
57 Eye
58 Rodents
59 Hebrew month
60 Hardy heroine
61 Lyric poem
62 Ship

DOWN

1 Bricklayer's need
2 Mosque priest
3 Josip Broz
4 Valiant
5 Mature germ cell
6 Sharif and Khayyam
7 Underdone
8 Small fiddle
9 Imparts gradually
10 Liliaceous plant
11 Century plant
12 Type
13 __ facto
21 Captive of Hercules
23 Scraps
25 Tree trunks
26 French political body
27 Rubbish
28 Essential
29 Empty
30 Exacting
31 "East of __"
32 Handy hints
33 Hayworth and Tushingham
36 Bringing together
37 Christians
39 Not in use
40 Swedish soprano
42 Ours: Fr.
43 Dessert
45 Distributed
46 Scheme
47 Vogue
48 Troubles
49 Headgear for some
50 Shade of green or blue
51 Wife of Norse myth
54 Tip's partner
56 Word with maid or master

161

ACROSS

1 Repudiations
11 Become crusty
15 P.T. Barnum, for one
16 Sashes
17 Hundred-yard dash, e.g.
18 Grooves
19 Water, in France
20 Hideout
21 "__ Terrible"
23 Shaving hazard
25 Metric measure
26 Cultivated
27 Western Indian
29 Brought up
33 Quantities: Abbr.
34 Broadcasts
36 Coeur d'__
37 Eur. country: Abbr.
38 Features of German vowels
40 Undermine
41 Virgil hero: Var.
43 Suffix with trick or prank
44 Vapor: Prefix
45 Come forward
47 Hue's companion
48 Kind of school
49 Scorch
51 Egyptian abode of dead: Var.
52 Base runner, at times
55 Muhammad
58 Indisposed
59 Fatigue
60 Its capital is Nouakchott
63 Regarding
64 Enclosure with stakes
65 Army officer: Abbr.
66 "And __ in a pear . . ."

DOWN

1 Detaches
2 Deterioration
3 Evergreen
4 Uris hero
5 Peddle
6 Bone: Prefix
7 Caution
8 Parseghian
9 Lawful
10 In any degree
11 Of an eye part
12 Border on
13 Kin's partner
14 Actual being
22 Vicinities
24 Elec. units
25 Start from __
27 Famous Uncle
28 Troubles
30 Curbed
31 Doing fingernails
32 Force migration from an area
35 Litigant
38 Commonplace
39 Test
42 Garb
44 Brazilian tree
46 Bonuses
50 Swimmer's hazard
52 Greedy gulp
53 Filament: Suffix
54 Make a living
55 Sandarac tree
56 Tune
57 Latin journey
61 __ tree
62 Friend: Fr.

162

ACROSS

1 "Deer Park" author
7 These, in Paris
10 Scotsman's to
13 Use a match
14 Algerian port
16 Bird
17 George's wife's grapes, so to speak
20 River area, in France
21 Parisian co.
22 Furnishings of a kind
23 Old terms of address
26 Fatty
27 Malayan sir
28 Antelope
29 Indian flour
30 Discharge
31 Come to the __
33 Kind of plane: Abbr.
34 Neglected in a way
37 Baseball statistic: Abbr.
40 Ericson, for one
41 Relative of alas
44 Weapon in Rouen
46 __ low
47 Bore out
48 Lawn layer
50 Physiognomies
53 Expression of relief
54 John, in Scotland
55 Alfonso's queen
56 Certain dressings
60 Gas: Prefix
61 Asian ox
62 French relatives
63 Three, in Turin
64 Culinary meas.
65 Dater's word

DOWN

1 Puccini heroine and others
2 Variety of talc
3 __ natura
4 Illuminated
5 African country: Abbr.
6 Get there
7 Place for a marina
8 Silk worm
9 Cape Cod sight
10 Places for brewing
11 Checks
12 One on the aisle
15 Italian saint
18 Family member
19 Palm-leaf mat
24 Racetrack position
25 Dvorak
26 Old womanish
28 Furze
31 Jeopardy
32 Peter and Alexander
35 Flying
36 Stadium
37 Knocking sound
38 Person asked to spare a dime
39 Supplicate
42 Purple color
43 Edited
45 Genesis name
49 Mountain of Thessaly
50 Liberian native
51 Horns and oboes: Abbr.
52 Fresh
54 Castor's killer
57 __ Hill
58 Map abbr.
59 French donkey

163

ACROSS

1 Small handful
5 Blas and others
9 Ad men's concerns
14 __ Domini
15 Black
16 Rectify
17 Commandos' job
18 Snow field
19 French reading matter
20 Within: Prefix
21 Flock of larks
23 "__ yourself"
25 Utter heedlessly
26 Angler's casting hazard
28 Summary
33 Banish
36 Prefix for dynamics or gram
38 Malaysian canoe
39 Procrastinator
41 Page sizes for books
43 Organic compound
44 Verne character
46 Related through one's mother
47 Happy
49 City in need of a bell
51 Six tricks, in bridge
53 More easily cut
57 Honey factory
62 Solemn declaration
63 "You're __"
64 Spanish direction
65 Certain negative
66 Bread necessity
67 Jewish month
68 Cheese
69 Seasons
70 Jack of old Westerns
71 French resort

DOWN

1 Merchandise
2 Fatuous
3 Subtly catty
4 Group of aquatic mammals
5 Classes
6 Wild goat
7 Sweet and attractive
8 Fishhook holder
9 Ester of acid in apples
10 Utter
11 Consort of Siva
12 Japanese case
13 Arabian port
22 Old card game
24 Barely
27 Steak order
29 Pair of draft animals
30 Crab-eating mongoose
31 Debatable
32 Mitigate
33 Earl of Avon
34 Strange: Prefix
35 Cabal
37 Crucifix
40 __ the road (terminus)
42 __ 'clock scholar
45 Barely gets along
48 Stops, as a missile flight
50 Maintain
52 Fetish
54 Late, in Rome
55 African antelope
56 Poet's concern
57 Former film czar
58 Suggestion
59 Butcher-shop item
60 Down __
61 And others: Abbr.

ACROSS

1 Irreligious one
8 Two of a kind
13 Cattle owner, in Southwest
14 Romantic hero of old
16 Fleeing
17 Exact satisfaction
18 Harmonize
19 Spring up and down
21 Racetrack item
22 Rank, as contestants
23 Intolerant one
24 Lollobrigida
25 Italian numeral
26 Upbraided
27 Vegetable cutter
28 Marquette
29 Hollywood hopeful
31 Large snail
33 Play direction
34 "_ and Fall . . ."
36 Son of Adam
37 Answer to a stimulus
38 River to the Rhone
40 Ninny
43 Prefix with date or cede
44 In a sufficient way
45 French relative
46 Moisture
47 Pillar of stone
48 Port of Iraq
49 Gives the slip to
51 Indian, for one
53 Contraption
54 Visual recollection
55 Vaquero's rope
56 Hunting dogs

DOWN

1 Clothes-closet item
2 Access
3 Was sore
4 Quaker pronoun
5 Possessive
6 Up on book learning
7 Period of youth
8 Modified leaf
9 Divagate
10 Brew
11 Hymn
12 Contrive
13 Menu item
15 Deviate
20 Shows boredom
23 Speaks explosively
24 Dimensions
26 Started up a dead fire
27 "Inferno" man
28 Nez __
30 Relative of itty-bitty
31 No matter the time
32 Summer occurrence
34 Sent to another club
35 Girl's name
36 Sun parlors
39 Sang-froid
40 Stanza
41 Attires splendidly
42 U.S. portrait painter
44 In a tizzy
45 Clergyman's house
47 Cut: Suffix
48 Resting places
50 Prefix for gram or meter
52 Officeholders

165

ACROSS

1 An old saw, with 31, 40, 46, 51, 57, 66 and 67 Across
5 Respecting
10 Did a farm chore
14 Site of Taj Mahal
15 Page number
16 __ now
17 Pour
18 Expels
19 Grape refuse
20 Home of the Muses
22 Stars: Fr.
24 ". . . __ nisi bonum"
25 Got: Abbr.
26 Heaven
31 See 1 Across
35 French frend
36 Certain schools: Abbr.
38 Solos
39 Soldiers
40 See 1 Across
42 Rank below maj.
43 "__ of robins in her hair"
45 Sea bird
46 See 1 Across
47 Teaparty greeting for Alice
49 Babies
51 See 1 Across
53 West
54 Mayor: Sp.
57 See 1 Across
61 Othello
62 "Let __ where it is"
64 Arabian gulf
65 Skinner
66 See 1 Across
67 See 1 Across
68 Prefix for gram or meter
69 Jinxer
70 Hangs down

DOWN

1 Fashion name
2 Pointed arch
3 Russian city
4 Layers
5 "Ask __ question . . ."
6 Certain word
7 City trains
8 Saltpeter
9 Try __ the tide
10 Container for smokes
11 Gem
12 French verb
13 Blanchard and Severinsen
21 Spanish hero
23 Indian, for one
26 Heathen
27 Kind of acid
28 Stair part
29 Usher's quest
30 Irish patriot
32 Recess
33 Prank
34 Western park
37 Withered
40 Kind of pigeon
41 39.37 inches
44 "__ good"
46 Pull __ over . . .
48 Fashionable
50 Do handwork
52 River of Hades
54 In a frenzied manner
55 French novelist
56 Wind
57 Silent actor
58 "__ angel"
59 David, for one
60 Chemical endings
63 Band instrument

166

ACROSS

1 Attire
5 Logan or elder
10 Mussorgsky's mountain
14 Love in Toledo
15 In turmoil
16 "Un Bel Di" for example
17 Instrument
18 N.Y.C. events of 1863
19 Ohio team
20 Irreverent rhymes
22 Junk
23 __ ex machina
24 Greek goddess
26 Rill
29 Poisonous plant
33 Gave audience to
34 Popular kind of fur
36 Hog feed
37 __ one's word
38 Classroom needs
41 Freshwater fish
42 Outward bound

44 B.P.O.E.
45 Give the slip to
47 Type of government
49 Civil War photographer and family
50 Russian body
51 Good flying conditions: Abbr.
52 Ormandy's aid
55 Role of son of James II
60 Corrida plaudits
61 "A __ the Races"
62 "Oz" dog
63 Money-changing fee
64 Faced the dawn
65 This: Sp.
66 "And all I ask is a __ ship"
67 Aquatic mammal
68 Describing Latin or Sanskrit

DOWN

1 British prison
2 Both: Prefix
3 Leeway
4 Poultry man
5 Metallic element
6 The Red and others
7 Chess piece
8 Reptiles
9 Time periods: Abbr.
10 Wastelands
11 Environs
12 Jar parts
13 100-yard item
21 British novelist
22 Boxing term
25 Bakery aid
26 Batch of papers
27 Tantalize
28 Chided

30 Long account
31 Hot beverage
32 Fencer's tools
34 Collapse
35 Call for
39 Scan
40 "They also __ ..."
43 Modern kind of can
46 Boasted
48 Operated
49 Cake base
51 Break off
52 Dinghy
53 Seaweed
54 Linden
56 Indian peasant
57 Portion
58 Girl's name
59 Way
61 P.I. tree

167

ACROSS

1 Tackle
6 Numbers man
9 Nothing: Sp.
13 Ukase's relative
14 Midwest state: Abbr.
15 Servant of a sort
16 Actor Alan
17 Soviet chessmaster
18 Stage offering
19 Literal enclosures
22 Verb ending
23 Reckless ones
24 Difficulty
26 Doctors' org.
27 Social occasion
30 Sea of __
33 Historic Bible
36 Particles
37 Mine output
38 __ France
39 Aware
41 Green spots
42 One of the Carsons
43 Plus
44 Letterhead abbr.
45 The U.K.
48 Parrot
51 19 Across, in England
55 "... if __ cares for me"
56 Estuary
57 Deserves
59 Eminent
60 Hebrew letter
61 Locations
62 Keep __ cool
63 Girl of song
64 Brakes

DOWN

1 Drop bait lightly
2 Mideasterner
3 Panama lake
4 Picture writings
5 Aerie
6 __ del Vaticano
7 Tartan
8 Distributes
9 Palms
10 Insist
11 Dagger
12 "Oh, my!"
15 Pal
20 Diplomatic V.I.P.
21 Dub
25 Without blemish
27 Stockton's river
28 Earth: Ger.
29 Ripens
30 Car-trunk item
31 Thine: Fr.
32 Bridge: Fr.
33 On __ with (amicable)
34 Neighbor of Arg.
35 Extort
40 Monogram: Abbr.
44 Wife of Athamas
45 Czech hero
46 Farewell
47 What "veni" means
49 Give __ (listen)
50 As good __
51 __ time (instantly)
52 Time of day
53 Do a civic chore
54 Jumble
58 Draft org.

168

ACROSS

1 False god
5 Fuel
9 Caught up in
13 Very, in music
15 "__ fellow well met"
16 Dies __
17 British crown jewel
20 Yorkshire river
21 Man: Lat.
22 Stationed
23 Enzyme ending
24 Compass direction
26 Cathedral city on the Ouse
27 What one should call
33 Devise
34 Haw's partner
35 Old oath
39 Flightless bird of N.Z.
40 Unpolished
42 Hindu melody
43 Blyth and Sothern
44 Stood for election
45 Detroit player
46 Intimate
50 Resort
53 Overwhelm
54 Swiss river
55 City on the Nile
57 Greek letter
58 Southern state: Abbr.
61 Society dating to 1860's
66 Kind of watch
67 Wheel holder
68 Nuance
69 Bad actors
70 Mail
71 Fire escape, e.g.

DOWN

1 Caspian city
2 Hebrew zither
3 Tennis star
4 Chou En-__
5 Nervous disorder
6 Scull
7 Make fun of
8 Biblical priest
9 Long aperture
10 Words from Gertrude Stein
11 Jury
12 Kind of bear
14 Intrude upon
18 Seine tributary
19 Retired
24 Violated a traffic law
25 Alike
27 "__ silly question"
28 Part of the leg
29 Hock
30 Imitative
31 Electrical by-pass
32 Weird
36 Foolish
37 Dyeing apparatus
38 Pub weapon
40 Crop
41 Distinctive
45 Violent pangs
47 Merit
48 Arrow's destination
49 Hickam Field's island
50 Sloppy stuff
51 __ Arenas
52 Self-evident truth
56 Surprised sound
58 Linen fiber
59 Roman public games
60 "Not on __!"
62 __ of luxury
63 Outside: Prefix
64 Jolson and others
65 Fidel's late cohort

169

ACROSS

ACROSS

1 Manuscript leaf
6 Prince
10 Spurious
14 Maurice of stage note
15 City in Russia
16 Western bulrush
17 Common contraction
18 Soup vegetable: Var.
19 Wide-mouthed jar
20 Lenten time
23 Actual
24 Weather word
25 Places of worship
28 O'Neill subject
32 Arranges
33 Light wood
34 Star of India, e.g.
35 Peau de __
36 Real estate sign
37 Egyptian goddess
38 Literary scraps
39 Flying gear of a sort
40 One at the polls
41 "I'll see you in __"
43 Socially-shunned persons
44 Overhang
45 Golf pro Dave
46 Bunny's calling date
50 French town
51 Utters sharply, with "out"
52 Spirits: Lat.
55 Kind of pupil or gazer
56 Partner of snick
57 Scenite or Arab
58 Took off
59 German river to Elbe
60 Alexis and others

DOWN

1 Infrequent
2 Egg cells
3 Scourge
4 Show the way
5 Stablemen: Var.
6 Like some soil
7 Roguish
8 Historic city
9 Chicken Little, for one
10 Prosaic
11 Dance
12 Confederate
13 __ culpa
21 Time periods: Abbr.
22 Marsh bird
25 State of India
26 Daft
27 Musical chord
28 Aureoles
29 Playing marble
30 Fisherman of Galilee
31 Arab princes
33 Australian club
36 Extend over
37 Opera notables
39 Mix rapidly
40 Inexperienced
42 Vacation spot
43 Wool: Prefix
45 One who ponders
46 Suffix with usher or kitchen
47 Ladd or King
48 Graf __
49 Persian demigod
50 Compass point
53 Deface
54 Ego sources

170

ACROSS

1 Local movie,
   Variety style
5 Determined
8 Japanese coin
11 Spoken
12 Surfacing
13 City of Bolivia
16 River known
   for water gap
18 Vixen: Sp.
20 Meat curer
21 Awned
23 Manor
25 Down
26 Courage
29 Home of Hoover
   Dam
31 Sign
32 Ignores
34 Flaccid
38 Year in Nero's
   reign
39 Zodiac animal

40 Musical direction:
   Abbr.
42 Cutting device
43 River to North
   Sea
45 New York college
47 Football player
48 Precisely
50 Habit
52 Weapon
55 First-born
57 Supersede
59 Accentuate
63 Tilted
64 Czars' protectors
66 Growl
67 Spanish relative
68 Math branch:
   Abbr.
69 Alkaline solution
70 Cunning
71 Quest

DOWN

1 Signals in a way
2 Tract
3 Social event
4 Snapping beetle
5 Show surprise
6 Attention
7 Picked up the tab
8 Clusters on
   ferns
9 Removed
10 Matrimonial
14 Course
15 Bone: Prefix
17 Certain wind
19 Gas: Prefix
22 Changed
   direction
24 Vivacious
26 Handle
27 Begrudge

28 Compatible
30 __ Minor
33 Cinders
35 "The very __!"
36 Chinese dynasty
37 Suffix for centi
41 Industrial giants
44 Kind of triangle
46 Picks out
49 Planetarium
51 River valley
52 After fa
53 Birds in general
54 Vegetable
56 Theme
58 Waste time
60 Pale color
61 Rind
62 Army rating: Abbr.
65 Pomade

171

ACROSS

1 Legend
6 Relative of 1 Across
10 Stars and __
14 Utopian
15 Comprehending words
16 U.S. author
17 Like soil
18 Approach
19 Fad
20 John Jacob's wife
22 Coquettish
24 Comparative suffix
25 Thrashes
29 Error
33 Sea god who rode a dolphin
34 Divest of weapons
35 Seed spreader
36 Famous West Point dropout
37 French town
38 Window parts
39 Naldi of silents
40 Tosspot
41 Buenos __
42 "Stop __" (traffic sign)
43 Target of the Seven against Thebes
45 Runs over a page margin
46 Broadway producer's goal
47 Shout
48 Celtic sea god
49 Hireling
54 Nobel physicist
57 Actor Novello
59 Irish goblin
60 Egyptian deity
61 Early Japanese
62 Dark
63 Sharp sound
64 Negatives
65 Gorges

DOWN

1 Shutterbug's need
2 Biblical name
3 Lillie and namesakes
4 Tibetan monk
5 Perfect abode
6 Secondary
7 French river
8 Social affair
9 Strong man
10 "__ not, on the lone . . ."
11 Constellation
12 Equipment
13 Compass point
21 Golfing area
23 Famous Persian
25 Parts of ratchet wheels
26 Word for N.Y. State
27 Plundered
28 Sam and J.C.
29 Freshwater clam
30 Entirely
31 "Bambi" author
32 __-Magnon
33 Natives of Cracow
35 Temptress
38 Geological era
39 Direction
41 "God's Little __"
42 Grecian gods' abode
44 Eyeing amorously
45 "__ it's cold"
47 Persian king
49 Condition: Suffix
50 Hebrides island
51 Dunce
52 Steinbeck figure
53 Turner and King Cole
54 Don't care a __
55 French friend
56 __ ton
58 Routing word

172

ACROSS

1 Alms box
5 Familiar palindrome
10 Fiddler
14 Stringed instrument
15 Fragrance
16 System of exercises
17 Corrupt
18 Painter famed for pastels
19 Friars, for one
20 Home of the anoa
22 "Prometheus Unbound" author
24 Guildhall sight
25 Wheys
26 Jan. 1 mecca
31 Artful Dickens character
35 Mulberry
36 Stains
38 Suiting
39 Disease: Suffix
41 Ibsen output
43 Marsh bird
44 African waterbuck
46 Sends forth
48 Finished, in verse
49 Nothing to __ at
51 Range of Africa
53 Kind of door
55 Metric measure
56 Art form
59 Smothered laugh
63 Cruising
64 Moroccan port
66 Edible root
67 Marshall __
68 Fragrant resin
69 Stew
70 Water lily's milieu
71 Oozes
72 Feature of N.E. Australia

DOWN

1 With: Fr.
2 Split
3 Twist
4 Maintain
5 Succeeded
6 Greek god
7 Follow closely
8 Pile up
9 Certain potatoes
10 Aegean islands
11 Parker House, for one
12 Sassafras tree
13 Coddle
21 Curtsies
23 Cupid
26 Stock-list group
27 Made of a grain
28 Cut
29 Telegram
30 S.A. ruminant
32 Curry
33 Plume
34 Rises up
37 Enamored, old style
40 Pony or wool
42 Mythical island
45 Pound
47 Hindu garment
50 Tidal floods
52 Military area
54 Norman Vincent __
56 Famed cartoonist
57 Northern capital
58 Tilt
59 Porridge
60 Cabbage
61 Canal
62 Kind of garden
65 Drone

173

ACROSS

1 V.I.P.
8 Volcanic depression
15 Word for a Manx cat
16 Invaded
17 Italian Mrs.
18 Self-flagellation
19 Smart __
20 Q E2, for one
22 Bearing
23 Croesus's empire
25 Impertinent
27 Time zone
28 __ rose
30 Nut tree
32 Kind of burglar
35 Poet Edgar
37 Vampire
41 Shaded walk
43 Island republic
45 Child
46 Summarize
48 Expand needlessly
49 Edmund Hillary gear
51 Kind of blanket
53 C.P.A.: Abbr.
56 __ as a fiddle
58 Ladies of Berlin
62 Roman 554
64 Fords a stream
66 Prefix with phile or stat
67 Fine cigars
69 Olivine
71 Spice
72 Counterfeit
73 Dupe
74 Pestered

DOWN

1 Kind of metabolism
2 Frigidly
3 Pledged, old style
4 Papal delegate
5 Stir
6 Earthy deposit
7 Goddess of oil
8 Fine and dandy: Var.
9 Opposed
10 Writer Deighton
11 Small amount
12 Ford
13 Sped
14 Concerning
21 Arrests
24 Medit. republic
26 Named, in olden days
29 Failure
31 Linden of TV
32 Machine part
33 __ Baba
34 Thrash
36 Non-purse material
38 Cartographer's concern
39 __ hurry
40 Subjoin
42 Swab
44 Cry of a bird
47 Wife of Geraint
50 Southern African
52 Where Gaugin painted
53 Kind of committee
54 Barton
55 Catlike animal
57 Warm
59 Decoration
60 Affect feeling
61 Renowned
63 Hobos, for short
65 Dotted, in heraldry
68 Downy coat
70 Miss., for one

174

ACROSS

1 Guy
5 Subway for René
10 Spat
14 Part of ship or nut
15 Not this
16 Sea east of Caspian
17 Spanish bit of land
18 Soviet mountains
19 Minor taboo
20 Underhand doings
22 V.P. under Nixon
23 Museum offering
24 Battle site in France
26 Indian chief
30 "The __ Roman . . ."
34 Dies __
35 Charged particle
37 "From __ dewy eve"
38 Boy's name, for short
39 Ill-starred
41 Having had it, with "up"
42 Verbal noun
44 Kicker
45 Star in Cetus
46 Willowy
48 Despotism
50 More recent
52 Posed
53 In a while
56 Pranks
61 Cupid
62 Asian city
63 Alone
64 U.S. weapons system
65 German city
66 Yul Brynner's kingdom
67 Sneaky name
68 One of the five W's
69 Sea bird

DOWN

1 Smart
2 Kind of puppies
3 "Monarch of __ survey"
4 Appease
5 Corn squeezin's
6 Common French verb
7 "__ gold in them . . ."
8 Trust
9 Conjunctions
10 Hybrid fruit
11 Press
12 Temple, old style
13 Course
21 Onassis
22 Perth __
25 Prank
26 Little noises
27 Projecting window
28 Mother-of-pearl
29 Bird-wearing officer: Abbr.
31 At last: Fr.
32 Austere
33 Yesterday tomorrow
36 Bolt's complement
39 Place to get out from
40 Trigonometry abbr.
43 Flabbergast
45 Post-impressionist
47 Go over again
49 Indian sovereignty
51 End of washing
53 Gooseneck, e.g.
54 Gallic friend
55 Civil wrong
57 Word with party or theater
58 Rouge et __
59 Part of K.K.K.
60 Part of
62 Chop

175

ACROSS

1 Went bathing
5 Egyptian queen
9 Companion to tush
13 Vegetable
14 Catch-all place
15 Two-toed sloth
16 Major or Minor
17 Ruth's mother-in-law
18 Cake ingredients
19 Formerly
21 Tolerate
22 Ivan
23 German: Prefix
25 Entrance
27 Canadian area
30 Maxim
31 Talkative
32 Spanish relative
33 Chill
34 Yacht-club sights

35 Disagreeable one
36 Civil War man
37 Trinity Church feature
38 Ruminant
39 Versatile
41 Spent
42 Merits
43 Old __
45 Little, in Tours
47 Allowed period
52 W.W. II group
53 Hourglass, e.g.
54 Belmont entry
55 Instance
56 Miss Post
57 Spirit
58 Chemical suffixes
59 Baltic native
60 Firm-name ending

DOWN

1 Large sea bird
2 Kind of hog
3 As well
4 "__ back at the ranch"
5 Riser and tread
6 Jot
7 Traveler's aid
8 Here, in Brest
9 Door, in San Juan
10 When appropriate
11 Starch palm
12 Corn feature
14 Theater group
20 Italian family
21 "__ me not on . . ."
24 Recedes
25 Theatrical figure
26 180 steps a minute
27 Scottish proprietor

28 Fixed a squeaky door
29 Drum sound
30 Irish lake
31 Gets an advantage
34 Made thread
35 Shuffleboard, canasta, etc.
37 Kind
38 Gather
40 Poker moves
43 Food fish
44 Nest
45 __-cake
46 Red-letter word
48 Not genuine: Abbr.
49 Saint-__, Channel port
50 Asian land
51 Numbers
53 Far: Prefix

176

ACROSS

1 Melchior and companions
5 U.S. painter
10 Primers
14 Image
15 Backward: Sp.
16 Fuel source
17 Certain uninvited guest
19 ___ as a rock
20 Native of an African area
21 Acrobats' garb
23 Doorway: Abbr.
24 Sterile
25 Movie, in Madrid
27 Flees from the cops
28 Former tennis star
32 Vestment
33 Woof's companion
34 Change dies
35 Dressing-down
37 Knee part
38 Trip asea
39 Ready
40 Insecticide
41 Follow
42 Command, in days past
43 Harem rooms
44 Injury
46 Uris hero
47 Transfer liability
50 Greek letters
53 African plant
54 Near-nemesis of 007
56 Kind of store
57 Kind of ink
58 Fluid: Prefix
59 Some are split
60 Ruhr city
61 Greek god

DOWN

1 Russian fighters
2 Hear: Prefix
3 Holden and Luther Adler roles
4 Hydrocarbon
5 Precipice, in Hawaii
6 W.W. II area
7 Certain light
8 L.A. five
9 Flight, in France
10 Dark rock
11 Honey hunter
12 Prizefight program
13 Norms: Abbr.
18 Bankbook abbr.
22 Cylindrical
24 Starr of football
25 Do intaglio work
26 Village on the Mohawk
27 Fabric
29 Channing played one
30 Meir
31 Louvers
33 Bets
34 Engrossed
36 Strained condition
37 City known for biased view
39 Merges again
42 Midwest Indians
43 Province of Spain
45 Saul Bellow's ___ March
46 "What a good boy ___"
47 Plane staircase
48 Robt. ___
49 New Rochelle college
50 "... wings ___ angel"
51 Flight: Prefix
52 Sellouts: Abbr.
55 Cutting device

177

ACROSS

1 Warplanes
5 Competently
9 Chemical compound
14 Guinness
15 Girl's name
16 Reduce
17 Become understandable
19 Did lawn work
20 Harmonious
21 Makes accessible
22 Fur-bearing animal
23 Oranges
26 Show-offs
29 Part of a courtroom
32 Recognize: Abbr.
35 Links
36 Eye part
37 Coiffure
39 Coins
41 Modern Christiania
42 Dress
44 Caviar
45 Cheer
46 Inclement
47 Agatha Christie character
49 Rich cake
54 Neighbor of Quemoy
56 Excess amounts of type
59 __ Jack
60 Specify
61 Entire range
62 Certain serves
63 Occasion
64 Printing marks
65 Police rounds
66 Greek letters

DOWN

1 Mr. of cartoon
2 "__ My Heart in San Francisco"
3 Reach
4 Leafless stalk
5 Israeli port
6 Coalition
7 Suffer defeat
8 __ man
9 Succoth fruit: Var.
10 Developed favorably
11 Assumes control
12 Tied
13 Buttons et al.
18 Entertainment
24 Minted money
25 Classify
27 Perturbed
28 Very small amount
30 Mackerel-like fish
31 Cheese: Ger.
32 Sea call
33 Ablative, for one
34 Keeps busy
38 Gets the barrel ready
40 Fictional Place
43 Patio
48 Relatives
50 Roundish
51 Pay up
52 Tropical shrub
53 Letters
54 Tobies
55 Med. study
57 City in Sweden
58 Fit together easily
60 Seize

178

ACROSS

1 French cake
5 Headwear
8 Jewelry unit
12 Sullies
13 Big bird
14 Brother of Moses
16 Pentateuch
17 Relative of Mayday
18 Metric volume
19 Fish sauce
20 Ann Corio specialty
22 Rubber rings
24 French city
25 Poem
26 Greek letters
27 Knot lace
30 Naturally spoken
33 Jack of TV
34 Good guy
35 Words on an old burlesque marquee
38 Composer Charles
39 Indigo
40 Pet peeves
41 Author Rand
42 Large deer
43 Chap
44 Figure-skating move
45 Slight
49 Some comics
53 Frivolous
54 Serve
55 Where Salome dances
56 Bulb
57 Poet Stephen or William
58 Mother of Julie
59 Proofs of payment: Abbr.
60 Cape
61 Pen
62 Crumbs

DOWN

1 College-song word
2 Buenos __
3 Some skits
4 Residue
5 Lab jobs
6 Love god
7 Theater
8 Stitches
9 Eroded
10 Space
11 Beetles
12 Kind of party
15 Born: Fr.
20 Holy woman: Abbr.
21 Couples
23 Spinning air
26 Old-World capital
27 Subject
28 Commedia del' __
29 Trifles
30 Eastern area
31 Impost
32 Bovines
33 Spots that flatter
34 Star
36 Greek physician
37 Rug type
42 Ennobles
43 French article
44 "__ Irish Rose"
45 Smart
46 Command
47 Lumps
48 Some bills
49 Bar I.O.U.
50 Hot place
51 Flat side
52 Great, to the younger set
56 Gold: Sp.

179

ACROSS

1 Kindly
7 Flabbergasted
13 Pooh's creator
14 Noble's headpiece
16 Second word of "Jabberwocky"
17 Adriatic port
18 Pony up
19 American and Western
21 Depression initials
22 Op. __
23 Shams, in Scotland
24 Farm sounds
25 Rummage-sale purchase
27 Few and far between
29 Old absolutions
30 U.S. dramatist
31 Snacked

32 Life substance
33 Greek length
36 Nonconforming
40 People with deeds
42 Onetime tenth month
43 Radiate
44 Sly __
46 Baboon
47 Village in Sweden
48 Garden implement
49 From Dixie: Abbr.
50 Fatty
52 Put into symbols
54 Greeted via the back
55 Insect-eating plants
56 Ancient ascetic
57 Chemical compounds

DOWN

1 Food enhancer
2 Signal sender
3 Khartoum's river
4 Out of sorts
5 Liqueur
6 Envoys
7 Take steps
8 Quagmire
9 Uris hero et al.
10 Writer Akins
11 Catch
12 Belittle
13 Eastern computer
15 Tantalizes
20 Family member
23 Word with weight or shop
24 Cause of poor archery score
26 Royal headpiece
28 Like a camera lens

32 Proper
33 Remnants: Sp.
34 Dum or dee
35 Liar
36 Linebacker's forte
37 Hit __ (pitch too close)
38 Relatives
39 Poll findings
41 Druid stone of England
42 Newscaster Rather
45 Leather
48 "Essay on Man" author
49 Marquis de __
51 Letter adjunct
53 Explosive

ACROSS

1 Slip up
5 Umpire's call
9 Out of range
13 Prefix for bus or potent
14 Cat, in old Rome
15 Ridged area in Balkans
16 Stare in a way
17 Roman roads
18 Spanish ladies: Abbr.
19 House warmer
21 Verse
22 Toward shelter
23 Pinnacle
25 Arabic demon: Var.
27 Human dynamo
30 Marsh feature
31 Loses color
32 __ Juana
33 Compacts, e.g.
34 Chemical suffixes
35 Follow orders
36 Paris pal
37 God's Little and others
38 Transport for Cleo
39 Autumn sights
41 Sixth __
42 Entire range
43 Harmonized
44 Golf-club parts
46 In quick succession
51 Arabian noble
52 Drawing room
53 Favorite
54 Hindu queen
55 Separated
56 Buttons and others
57 Word with hand or boot
58 Old domestic slave
59 Common Latin verb

DOWN

1 Drivers' game
2 Sacred Buddhist mountain
3 Unique person
4 Pistols, etc.
5 Bristles
6 Guinness
7 Homes
8 Curve
9 Take in
10 Certain circus performers
11 "__, poor Yorick"
12 Incarnadine
14 __ mignon
20 Ballet bend
21 Simple Simon's quest
24 V.I.P.
25 Poplar
26 Target area
27 Churches, in poetry
28 Feudal figure
29 Burden
30 Tomboy's knee décor
31 Certain buildings
34 Light color
35 Pend
37 Directs
38 River feature
40 Spenser's Queene
41 Lo or Louis
43 Germ cell
44 Helot
45 Khayyam
47 Ladd
48 __ of March
49 Reels' companions
50 Other
52 So, old style

181

ACROSS

1 Piscatorial pursuit
8 __ as a ghost
14 Provokes
15 Greek pastoral region
16 Lover's opening line
17 Corroborate
18 Move suddenly
19 Fogs
20 Upstate N.Y. resort
22 Attention-getting sound
25 Pouch
28 Head: Fr.
29 Frame of mind
31 Rockne
33 Wine vessels
35 River to the Moselle
36 City in India
37 Eat away
38 Brood of pheasants
39 Port Authority income source
40 Millstone support
41 Units of force
42 Fails to be alert
44 Hip bones
46 Italian three
47 Army acronym
48 Spoors
50 Ballads
52 Palms
55 More ostentatious
58 Pianist Oscar and others
60 Sharpened again
61 Built
62 Parts of double boilers
63 Postulates

DOWN

1 Mast support
2 Chemical endings
3 "Go away!"
4 King of Tyre
5 Repeat
6 Snuggle up to
7 Basic time initials
8 Son of Zeus
9 Criticize severely
10 Trait of Scrooge
11 Fuss
12 Eastern campus
13 "__, drink . . ."
15 Stage husband
19 Memory study
21 Eared seal
23 Short race
24 Harbor craft
25 Widows in a card game
26 Luanda's land
27 Shore bird
29 Half a fly
30 Peewee
32 Tearful earful
34 Befuddle
37 Hesitating sounds
41 Grammar cases
43 Lament
45 Soccer positions
48 Chalcedony
49 Set apart
51 Dregs
53 Sinus: Prefix
54 Proofreading word
55 Hindu title
56 Kind of party
57 Exclamations
58 Meadow
59 Noises: Abbr.

ACROSS

1 Magna __
6 Something extra
10 P.M.'s
14 City in New York
15 Disclaim noisily
16 Beseech
17 Some of the media
20 Rorschach material
21 W.W. II agency
22 French pronoun
23 Airline listings: Abbr.
25 Pens
26 Tanner
29 Greenback
32 Remote
33 Italian love
35 Poetic word
36 Section
37 Nicholas and others
38 Word for Cassius
39 Neighbor of U.S.
40 Pallid
41 Representation: Prefix
42 Heraldic star
44 Red-necked chicken
46 Organic compounds
47 Gaelic
48 Early mind-reader
49 Vestment
50 __ Jima
53 What a TV fan does
57 Celestial handle
58 Traveled
59 Clouded
60 Former French President
61 Burl
62 Mary or Vincent

DOWN

1 North Atlantic fish
2 Jai __
3 Guide
4 Run on and on
5 Some
6 Annie Oakleys
7 Rules
8 Us, in Bonn
9 Vatican neighbor
10 Washington product
11 First Amendment guarantee
12 Defiles
13 Method: Abbr.
18 Standard
19 Adjust
24 Brit. fliers
25 Raconteur
26 Fare for the gander
27 Forearm bones
28 Have __ in (be bored)
30 Harangue
31 Part of dovetail joint
34 Picture border
37 __ and handsome
38 How to tell it
40 Devout
41 Duos: Abbr.
43 Kind of street or ticket
45 To the city: Lat.
48 Driest Spanish sherry
49 "Then __ dash of . . ."
51 Bridge seat
52 Preposition
53 Time off: Abbr.
54 Negative prefix
55 Scotsman's tiny
56 Mideast land: Abbr.

183

ACROSS

1 N.L. team
5 Reverie
10 Writer Munro
14 Biblical ruler
15 Rope
16 Group of three: Abbr.
17 Legal hold
18 Seasonal saps
20 Arabian guides
22 Downright
23 Area of Africa
24 Foil
25 Patterns: Fr.
27 Checked
31 Tapestry
32 Food fish
33 Chinese weight
34 Light
35 Hone
36 His and __
37 Motel of yore
38 Personnel man
39 Rembrandt __
40 Forms deltas
42 Feats
43 Beatle's cry
44 Musical group
45 Hazardous skating surface
48 Part of a day
51 Mischievous ones
53 Amino __
54 Large rooms
55 Smell __
56 Biblical weed
57 One of the senses
58 Coeds
59 Dash

DOWN

1 Penicillin source
2 Arabian prince
3 Holding dear
4 Unusual
5 TV offerings
6 Become ready
7 Merit
8 N.Z. tribe
9 Famous Mrs.
10 Mall units
11 Venezuelan town
12 Oast
13 Part of M.I.T.: Abbr.
19 Ungirdled
21 Tributes to skylarks, et al.
24 Baseball statistic
25 Underworld group
26 Ape
27 Estate
28 Flamboyant
29 Former Governor of Penna.
30 Medicates
32 __ throat
35 Edges
36 Waver
38 German biologist
39 Laborer
41 Of the nose
42 TV wraiths
44 Lobster roe
45 Audit men: Abbr.
46 Calla lily
47 Account
48 Tiber tributary
49 Star in Cetus
50 First home
52 Child's game

184

ACROSS

1 __ cry
5 Witticism
9 Remove
13 Minnow's role
14 Repeated
16 Invention
17 Name in law
19 Lemon part
20 Noted Victorian
21 Augurs
23 Ad topic
25 Edsels' relatives
26 Worshipers of Allah
29 Mean
33 First, second, etc.
34 Obscure
36 Eur. country
37 Old oath
38 Jutland people

39 __ boy!
40 Young
41 Eurasian vine
42 Propeller
43 Places
45 Cougar
47 Merit
49 Italian coin
50 Faint
54 Contemporary
58 Parted
59 Special vehicle
61 Bit
62 Take off
63 Girls' nicknames
64 Ruler
65 Glacial ridges
66 Holds a session

DOWN

1 Medieval poem
2 Parking garage sign
3 Ali Baba, for one
4 Like an alcove
5 Elbow
6 Amphibian
7 Defeat
8 Stamp
9 Most dreadful
10 Norse god
11 Protect
12 In-things
15 Poseidon's attendants
18 Early Slav rulers
22 Broadway award
24 Bovary and Goldman
26 Black __
27 Kind of orange
28 Time of day
30 __ nous
31 One who observes

32 Chess-game ending
33 Supplicates
35 __ en pis (from bad to worse): Fr.
38 Prepare to bathe
39 Greeks
41 Jungfrau or Everest
42 Thurmond
44 Fruit juice
46 Fabulous water monster
48 Void, in Italy
50 Eur. country
51 Durocher and others
52 Stage group
53 Art colony center
55 True, in Rouen
56 "__ we got fun?"
57 Miss
60 Calculator: Abbr.

185

ACROSS

1 Musical refrain
5 British servicewomen
10 Dunderhead
14 Oriental name
15 Roman halls
16 Cuchulainn's wife
17 Famed Alp
19 Less, in music
20 Outmoded
22 Civil War initials
24 Sea goddess
25 Make effervescent
26 Subtle stimulus
28 Crackers
31 Stock units: Abbr.
32 Hat features
34 Israeli port
36 Fielding Yost or Don Shula
41 Mideasterner
42 Brawls
44 Gazelle of Asia
47 Confused
50 Conclusions
51 Cinnamon bark
53 Pronoun
55 Letter
56 Friend of Disraeli
60 Wavy, in heraldry
61 Lacking in taste
64 Live __
65 Acknowledge
66 French composer
67 Recipe abbrs.
68 Palms
69 Unimproved

DOWN

1 On the __ (fleeing)
2 Rhyme scheme
3 Philanderer
4 Parking problem
5 Well-known concerto
6 Phidias statue
7 S.A. copper center
8 Granular snow
9 Resin-yielding tree
10 Object
11 Last items
12 Dimension
13 City south of Paris
18 Misdo
21 Get the __ (defeat)
22 Truck feature
23 Beach feature
27 Mine: Fr.
29 Mendelssohn
30 Architect's concern
33 Musical passage
35 Run swiftly
37 Resident of an upstate N.Y. city
38 Miscellany
39 Choral compositions
40 London park
43 Wind direction
44 Exculpate
45 Frequents
46 Spent
48 Yugoslav peninsula
49 Shallow African lakes
52 Oozes
54 Silkworm
57 Blue: Prefix
58 Rough it
59 __ de Pinos
62 River of Asia
63 Lettuce

186

ACROSS

1 Chair back
6 Fleece
10 Netherlands town
14 Restraint
15 Wings
16 Tuscany river
17 Ready
19 Firearms
20 Third of a crowd
21 __ breve
22 Archery gear
24 Penzance people
26 Dry periods
27 Pipe joint
28 Gumbo ingredient
29 Light color
32 Animal trail
35 Kind of peach
37 Betel leaf: Var.
38 Sub-chaser's device

39 Writer Murdoch
40 Consider
42 Small fish
43 Freudian topic
44 Smorgasbord items
45 Insect
46 Clotho and friends
48 Small round molding
52 More downcast
54 Hindu caste
55 Born: Fr.
56 Old oath
57 Orchid-like plant
60 Classify
61 Asian desert
62 Records
63 MacMurray
64 Gaelic
65 Bizarre

DOWN

1 Sailing vessel
2 Finnish coin
3 Subsequently
4 Shade tree
5 Scene of action
6 Prison features
7 Olive shrub
8 Put one's __ in
9 Sign printer
10 Tidal flood
11 Shopping-mall unit
12 Stratford name
13 Greatest
18 Mariner's term
23 Macaws
25 In harmony
26 Old Irish dagger
28 Avifauna
30 Dye plant
31 Aerie
32 Graf __
33 Sharp feeling

34 Passe
35 Young horses
36 Officiated at a track event
38 Immigrants' quarters
41 Network
42 Learn the real nature of
45 Greek letter
47 Annexed
48 Fiber shrub
49 Awkward
50 "__ a dull moment"
51 Brants
52 Slave
53 Seaweed product
54 Fighter's maneuvers
58 June bug
59 Relative: Abbr.

187

188

ACROSS

1 "Pretty maids all in __"
5 Bear-like animal
10 Cudgel
14 Branches
15 Affirms
16 Like a June day
17 Roof ornaments
18 Populace
19 __ est percipi
20 Precipitately
23 Guitar part
24 Starchy
25 Harmony
28 Begin
32 Members of the jet set
33 Rendered
34 Cleaving tool
35 Paul Newman movie
36 Extreme in opinion
37 Grain appendage
38 Speed horse
40 Picture
41 Understand?
43 Exotic dancer
45 Coercion
46 Asian tree genus
47 French father
48 Dab
55 Indian dance drama
56 Girl's name
57 Novice: Var.
58 At variance with
59 Equip anew
60 Potpourri
61 Trade center
62 River of the Left Bank
63 Stupid mistake

DOWN

1 Vicinity
2 Absorbed
3 Fail to mention
4 Yearn
5 Cushioned
6 Prevent
7 "__ me impune lacessit"
8 Paid an informal visit
9 Miscellaneous
10 "I __ Jeannie"
11 Venturous
12 Constellation
13 Borscht ingredient
21 Deviates from aim
22 Smyrna product
25 Turkish titles
26 Kind of plaster
27 Tree
28 Theatrical family
29 Provoked
30 First words of a typing exercise
31 Men, for short
33 "Only God can __"
36 Maturing agents
39 Movie maid or butler
41 Maharishi
42 Builder
44 Greek letter
45 Contention
47 Silk fabric
48 Sixty grains
49 Eastern prince
50 Gravelly ridges
51 Family-room unit
52 European measure
53 Greenland colonizer
54 Appropriated

189

ACROSS

1 Plods heavily
6 Name for a meatman's boy
11 Gushing out
13 Patronizing
15 "More __" (gumshoe's observation)
17 Give it the gun
18 Evades
19 Hockey players: Abbr.
20 Period before a Jewish holiday
22 Seniors in a group
23 Burns, for one
24 Creepy
26 Sea distances: Abbr.
27 Macedonian mountain
28 Complicate
30 Hasten
31 Stupid
32 Infielder Tony
33 Sultan of Turkey
34 Thug
36 Quit a habit, with "off"
37 Luau dish
38 Tilts
40 Dutch painter
41 Turkish province
43 Modern insecticide
44 Hawaiian bonito
45 __ in mind of (recalls)
47 Christian, for one
48 Story going around
51 Musicians' delights
52 Cold cuts
53 Chases away
54 __ up (prearranged)

DOWN

1 Fields of activity
2 Desert
3 Possess
4 Hobbling walk
5 Golfing great
6 Morsels
7 Expressions of disgust
8 Article
9 Gumshoe's task
10 Labor leader and I.W.W. founder
11 Scatter
12 African antelope
13 Confucian cardinal virtues
14 Students' concerns
16 Hike
21 Certain bulls
23 Hardened
25 Beauty-parlor gear
27 Spring month
29 Math abbreviation
30 Indian weight
32 Arsenic and strychnine
33 Stirs
34 Furze
35 Human automaton
36 __ up (develop)
37 Golf strokes
39 Castor and Pollux
41 Public vehicles
42 Wall piers
45 Pueblo Indian
46 Writer Gardner
49 __ Canals
50 Detroit-based org.

ACROSS

1 Teacake
6 Direction: Abbr.
9 Egyptian king
13 Showy flower
14 Israeli port
15 "This one's __"
16 Inn
17 Entree
19 Goal
20 Smelt
22 French co.
23 Go!
25 Bargain
26 Blacksmith
28 Author of "The Golden Bowl"
31 Caen's river
32 Cherub
33 Extinct
35 Kerchief
37 Billiard shot

38 Fanfare
40 Money in Modena
41 As well
42 Close
47 Ne plus __
49 List
50 Algerian port
51 Pagoda
52 Lulus
55 Broke bread
56 Stray
58 "__ man . . ."
60 Channels
61 Well disciplined
62 Elliott
63 Rail complex: Abbr.
64 Tree
65 Washes down

DOWN

1 Display
2 Select
3 Hemingway character
4 Beverage
5 Supervisor, for short
6 Outcry
7 Sang
8 Prefix for sphere
9 Instead of
10 Creatures of myth
11 Milieu
12 Utahan
14 Loom up
18 Naval off.
21 Postpone
24 Farm machine
27 __-house salesman

29 Youth org.
30 Advanced class
34 Variety of brown date
35 Decline
36 Trices
38 Blackfish
39 Insulation
40 Fresh gossip
43 Play __
44 Asp
45 Bovines
46 Makes dough
48 U.S. dept.
53 Der __
54 Sound of longing
57 Founded: Abbr.
59 Barnyard sound

191

ACROSS

1 Kind of party
7 Poker Flat figure
14 Deceive
15 Region of Ghana
16 Covered, as a seed
17 Native of Erivan
18 __ me tangere
19 Offense
21 Anoint the roast
22 Nitwit
26 Disney animal
29 Stretches out
33 Strange
34 Scout's good thing
35 Gardner
36 Put on airs
38 Birds __
41 Compass point
42 Helper: Abbr.
46 Appliances
47 Profane
50 Junior bingo
51 Was hip
53 Rule
56 So-so grade
57 Demolish
61 Useful picnic beast
64 For adults only
66 Most bleak
67 Product of applause
68 Builder's afterthoughts
69 C or K item

DOWN

1 Marshall, for example
2 Lofty prefix
3 Prison
4 Extemporized
5 One of the Three Stooges
6 __ it goes
7 Put one's __ in
8 Service branch: Abbr.
9 "It's in __"
10 Northern neighbor
11 Black cuckoos
12 Law: Abbr.
13 Prong
17 Part of the leg
20 On the rocks
23 Date or party
24 Before down
25 Inner: Prefix
26 Bundled
27 One way to walk
28 Bogs down
30 Mystic card
31 Happening
32 Final word
37 Feathered missile
39 Latin threads
40 Stretch out
43 Jig or buzz
44 Lollipop part
45 Mal de __
48 Seasonal color
49 Like some lenses
52 Spell caster
53 Indian music
54 Deserve
55 Country on the Caspian
58 Thine: Fr.
59 Cold forecast
60 Snake's home
62 Chemical suffix
63 Privileges: Abbr.
65 Biochemical initials

ACROSS

1 Salad
5 Take the sun
9 Chicken, for one
14 "Zhivago" girl
15 __ the minute
16 Chou __
17 Revolutionary figure
18 Get a result
19 Then: Fr.
20 Elba to St. Helena
23 Moon goddess
24 Oast
25 Date in the Forum
28 More embarrassed
32 Prefix in chemistry
36 "__, you're dead!"
38 Location
39 Crapshooter's cry
42 Stravinsky
43 __ about
44 Lariat
45 Size AAAA
47 Pop
49 Feminine suffixes
51 At a bargain, maybe
56 Sensation
60 Part of Africa
61 Last of the banquet
62 Author Paton
63 Party food
64 Kind of blue
65 Talks
66 Proboscis
67 Pitches in
68 Itemize

DOWN

1 One-armed bandits
2 Turner
3 Tricksy spirit
4 ". . . a merry old soul __"
5 Got mad
6 Did the same
7 Be the best
8 Red cent
9 Ceremonial macebearer
10 Caspian, for example
11 Maneuver
12 Front-page boxes
13 Prefix for play or band
21 Part of U.S.S.R.
22 Requiem
26 Black
27 Greek island
29 Military units: Abbr.
30 Seasons on the Seine
31 City for 1 Down
32 It's __ to tell a lie
33 Prefix with phone or cycle
34 Novello
35 Knightly courage
37 Mr. Wolfe
40 Overawed
41 Grassy plain
46 Baseball situation
48 Hunts water
50 __ Fe
52 Tangle
53 Stevenson
54 "My heart __ up . . ."
55 Director Lubitsch
56 Between A.M. and P.M.
57 __ hurry
58 Russian spaceman
59 Bosom bauble
60 DiMaggio and Mantle: Abbr.

193

ACROSS

1 Seafood
6 Rabbit's tail
10 Tree stem
14 Goddesses of the seasons
15 Draw near
16 Overthrow
17 Posture in yoga
18 Like many suburbs
20 Looks after
21 Heckle
22 Noted British family
23 Actress Ruth
25 Picks out
26 Green rust on old bronze
29 Puff up
31 Kind of agreement
32 Fauna and flora
34 Lou Costello's partner
37 Roman 1971
39 Ecologists' concern
41 Suffix with journal or Canton
42 Copy from an original
44 London park
45 Humble
46 Playful monkey
48 Jaunty cap
50 Bret Harte man
52 Like gold
53 Crooked
54 Rain clouds
58 Parade unit
60 White of egg
61 "Is there anyone ___?"
62 State
63 Top class
64 Nautical chains
65 Make over
66 Strikes out

DOWN

1 Small talk
2 Squander
3 Galway Bay isles
4 Blue-faced baboon
5 Ripen
6 Certain diver
7 Bridal adornment
8 Break of a bivalve shell
9 Light snack
10 Jockey's control
11 European thrush
12 Debtor's headaches
13 Make ___ meet
19 Gender
24 Certain pet
25 Runs rapidly
26 Fleshy fruit
27 Lights for stars
28 Unexciting
30 Put up with, if you don't like it
33 Holms
34 Tempting bargains
35 Pakistani tongue
36 Mascaras
38 Three-masted Medit. vessels
40 Fabric for bedspreads
43 Longed for
45 Comes up
47 Pivoted on
48 Strapping
49 Remove
51 Spa, in Britain
52 Second in evildoing
53 Silent salute
55 Classed matter
56 Angler's delight
57 Angers
59 Drinking place

194

ACROSS

1 Cantina fare
5 Fokker's foe
9 Diving duck
14 Not care __
15 Now's companion
16 Medieval guild
17 Reveal
18 Copies slavishly
19 Chairman's call
20 Pend in a big way
23 Saps
24 Deteriorates
25 Fracas, informally
27 Unfrequented
31 Declines
32 City official
33 Forefront
34 Arden
35 Creator
36 Adjective ending
37 River of England
38 Like some windows
39 Ex __
41 Costume jewelry
43 Bill
44 __ about
45 Regional animal and plant life
46 Precarious spot
50 Bouquet
51 Town of Vietnam
52 Literary work
54 Man of Athens
55 Nine: Prefix
56 Pianist Peter
57 Orgs.
58 Pipes up
59 Soft drinks

DOWN

1 Dinner check
2 Irish exclamation
3 Cavalry soldier
4 Scarce kind of store on Sunday
5 Seedy
6 Famed diarist
7 Region
8 Ruined
9 More pithy
10 Fond touch
11 Time __ half
12 Accustomed
13 Wall St. word
21 Pantheon
22 Recognition
25 European
26 __ heart
27 Finger __
28 Had something in common
29 Devilfish
30 Record
32 Swamp trees
35 __ the hour
38 Pyramidal trees
39 Meager
40 City of Pennsylvania
42 Surveyor's aides
43 Cups, saucers, etc.
45 Famed comedian
46 Misdoes
47 Votes against
48 15th-century caravel
49 Seine tributary
50 Eastern V.I.P.
53 Help!

195

ACROSS

1 Variety of pear
5 U.S. geologist
9 Water carriers
14 Cotton fabric
15 Trade discount
16 On reserve
17 Sufficient, to poets
18 Bligh or Ahab
20 U.S. statesman
22 Lupin and others
23 Muscle
26 P.I. fruit tree
27 Bankhead of theater
29 Anti-infection drugs
33 Island in Taiwan Strait
34 Horse, at times
36 Musical direction: Abbr.
37 Marble
38 Usher's concern
40 'arry's place
41 French article
42 German industrialist
43 Genu
44 Long-suffering one
46 Albany or Buffalo native
49 High note
50 Shorten
51 Making a living
55 Direction markers
58 Creeping plant
61 Dies __
62 Book for an eleve
63 Crystal-gazer's first words
64 Behold, to Caesar
65 French thoughts
66 Vital-statistic word
67 Visit a mall

DOWN

1 Air bubble
2 Wine prefix
3 Winter road machine
4 Marsh marigold
5 Pendant
6 Iron or teen
7 Estuary
8 Cape of Portugal
9 German royal house
10 Bony
11 Shensi city
12 Miss Adams
13 D.C. men
19 Up
21 Old French coin
24 Pacific island group
25 Track-meet event
27 U.S. jazz pianist
28 Iowa religious sect
30 House part
31 Gallic name
32 Guide
35 Browning girl
38 Urban vistas
39 Trip of a sort
43 N.Z. timber trees
45 Term in office
47 Cape of Jutland
48 Thrice: Prefix
51 He: It.
52 Dull
53 Gad
54 Talkative
56 Texas city
57 Small spring
59 Atomic prefix
60 Biblical name

196

ACROSS

1 Night spot
5 Sheiks, e.g.
10 Ancient Asian
14 Word for Wellington
15 French soldier
16 Jazzman Hines
17 Like green apples
18 One kind of legislation
20 Gift for May
22 Gin drinks
23 Male and female
24 Claim on property
25 Members of an Eastern sect
27 Signified
31 __ Unis
32 Kind of blow
33 Chemical suffix
34 Grapevine: Sp.
35 Resources
36 Keats work
37 One of a Latin trio
38 Approaches
39 Went for
41 One hemisphere
43 Indian lutes
44 Certain news item
45 Star in Cygnus
46 Dog-faced ape
49 Resort to in excess
52 Fatuous one
55 In __
56 Liberal
57 Prefix for graduate or handed
58 English actor
59 Stitched
60 Take out
61 Diner sign

DOWN

1 Quote
2 Biblical land
3 Presage
4 Solicit
5 Bobbing necessities
6 Crosses
7 Area of pollution
8 Inky: Abbr.
9 Makes do
10 Hardy breed of sheep
11 Merit
12 Residue
13 Cloth measures
19 Hebrew letter
21 W.W. II powers
24 Inclines
25 Late British Socialist
26 One at __
27 Boy Scout founder
28 Australian kingfisher
29 One of the Plinys
30 Requisites
32 Did a card chore
35 Pie adornment
38 Jockey-board listing
39 Ancestry
40 Repeat
42 Of a certain cloth
43 Unornamented
45 Medication amounts
46 Degree for diplomats
47 Yorkshire river
48 Took it on the lam
50 Filler for bird feeder
51 Vacation times in Paris
53 Wash. agency
54 Harem room

197

ACROSS

1 In a frenzied way
5 One kind of keeper
8 Later cost
14 Benzell
15 Grain
16 Earth pigment
17 First residence
18 Certain kind of shoe or brace
20 Hum
21 Joint
22 Lyric form
23 Ginza drink
25 __ facto
27 Arctic sight
30 Americans, to Mexicans
34 Aloof
35 "__ of some people!"
36 Galway Bay islands
37 Subject of many sculptures
39 Fly
40 Wets
42 Truman
44 Grasping claws
45 Wearing a certain garment
46 Business letter abbr.
47 Shot and shell
48 Having a 5 o'clock snack
51 Word on a French valentine
53 Greatest
57 City legislator
59 Division word
60 Small amounts
61 Skill
62 Memento of a scrape
63 Straightforward
64 Graduate degrees
65 Scary

DOWN

1 Ben William's middle name
2 Skirt length
3 Sign
4 Responsibility of Britain's Lord Chancellor
5 Word with three double letters
6 Breadwinner
7 Feminine suffix
8 Service org.
9 Brings water from a main
10 Show responsibility
11 Inner: Prefix
12 Geraint's love
13 Tempo
19 Elevation
24 Small island
26 Tiresome sermons
27 Family member, familiarly
28 Poet Jones
29 Forcefully
31 Dutch name
32 Egg-shaped
33 Became withered
35 Thy, in Rouen
38 Put in office: Var.
41 Bridge holdings
43 Goal
45 Elm-tree fruit
48 Arthritis aid
49 Arena figure
50 Master, in Malaysia
52 Moslem leader
54 "__ upon a time"
55 Canopus, e.g.
56 Uncle of fiction
58 Doer: Suffix

198

ACROSS

1 Handle rudely
4 Misses
9 Grand Canyon geological group
14 Cuckoo
15 Transfer point
17 Free
18 England, 1660-1688
19 Brain channel
21 Old card game
22 Sing monotonously
23 Crusader foe
25 Early laborer
26 English letter
27 Office hookup
31 Volcano that erupted in 1902
34 Inner, in anatomy
35 Shade
36 Le Gallienne and others
37 Scuffle
38 Hog food
39 __ gestae
40 Bathroom worker
41 Menu
42 Place between
44 Demure
45 Praise
46 Hiked
50 Nymphs
53 Grasp
54 Kind of review
55 Uniform item of W.W. I
58 Glib
59 Scatter
60 Summer cooler
61 Headliners
62 Moslem noble
63 Pulpit talk: Abb.

DOWN

1 Son of Priam
2 Santa __
3 More vast
4 Douglas, for one
5 Anointed
6 "__ the house"
7 Mother of Apollo
8 Theater sign
9 TV number
10 Mad party figure
11 Genus of mussels
12 Greek contest
13 French name
16 Ridges, in anatomy
20 Does a bulldozing job
24 Letter
25 Go onstage
27 Cove
28 Overdo the steaks
29 Throw out
30 Dole
31 Persian sprite
32 Balanced
33 Certain straw
34 Fished
37 Takes unfair advantage of
38 City Hall tenant
40 Wall St. men
41 Murmur
43 Beetle
44 Wrinkle
46 Land, in France
47 Hemingway et al.
48 Dodge
49 Hinder
50 Eyes: Suffix
51 Small animal
52 Girl's name
53 Originate, with "from"
56 Health center
57 Through

199

ACROSS

1 Movie-ad word
5 Ensign
9 Ledger entry
14 Drink mix
15 City near Lake Tahoe
16 Aquarium fish
17 Critical juncture
20 Capp character
21 City problem
22 Assemble
23 N.Y. summer hours
25 Snoop
26 Gorge
28 Piccadilly, for one
31 Kindled
32 Samovar
33 Ibsen girl
37 Part of a Darwin title

41 Boil down
42 Dawn goddess
43 French month
44 Moore specialty
46 Topic of discourse
48 Family member
51 Denial
52 Pair
53 Neat as __
55 Store specialist
59 Item in a certain book
62 Wicker basket
63 Want __ of
64 Island of exile
65 Bold
66 Pitcher
67 Take it easy

DOWN

1 Intuition, for short
2 Word of disdain
3 Having a distinct style
4 Riviera town
5 Top off a cake
6 Kind of wing
7 Mongkut's tutor
8 Peanut
9 Had brunch
10 Collections
11 Baffle
12 Diamond slip
13 Flavorsome
18 Swarm
19 Certain carriers
24 Air
26 Boor
27 Charter
28 __-Magnon
29 Conclude
30 Thus: Lat.
32 Brainwash
34 Reference work of a sort

35 Twenty quires
36 Land mass
38 Party initials
39 Byzantine art work
40 Sauce
45 Family in O'Neill drama
46 Ballet skirt
47 Sewing-machine attachment
48 Contest
49 Lyric drama
50 Track-team member
52 Quick-lunch stop
54 Require
56 Sufficient, to Omar
57 Alaskan Indian
58 Tips
60 Work at
61 Rodent

200

ACROSS

1 Secret store
6 Wallflower's kinsman
10 Bovine's booth
14 In a tangle
15 Assam silkworm
16 Charter
17 Ballcarriers of earlier era
20 Aching
21 It hath 30 days: Abbr.
22 Aerie
23 Monsarrat's cruel domain
24 Marx
25 Gender: Abbr.
26 Rumanian coin
27 Fully paid
29 Popular tune
32 ". . . secure in __ persons . . ."
35 Water or gas carrier
36 Herb of West
37 Hearty roar
40 Sight from Finsteraarhorn
41 Moon site
42 Some dispositions
43 Oath-taker's words
44 Vehicle for Amos of radio
45 Machine cylinder
46 Knight's companion
48 Pre-med subject
50 See 13 Down
53 "It's __!"
55 Nautical speed
56 N.H. river
57 Components of a word game
60 Half: Prefix
61 Waste allowance
62 "A votre __"
63 R.N. to M.D.
64 Barrelhead commodity
65 Feminine suffix

DOWN

1 __ belli
2 Glowing
3 Lesson from Madame La Zonga
4 Enormous
5 Hardly 'eaven
6 I.L.G.W.U. member
7 Pacts of 1668 and 1795
8 Familiar solecism
9 Villain's muffler
10 Disorder
11 Bounces off
12 Galls
13 Witness of a sort, with 50 Across
18 Biblical twin
19 Chaff of grain
24 Deborah or Walter
25 Gourmand's reading
26 Taradiddler's tales
28 Chemist's vessel
30 "__ a kick out of you"
31 Royalist of '76
32 Native of Bangkok
33 Freighter area
34 Market places
35 Roman 1109
36 Bogus
38 Date-producing country: Var.
39 Punky or midge
44 Sepulchral sound
45 Anti-Carthage Roman
47 Path of Pluto
49 Mariner's guide, with 56 Down
50 Quebec's neighbor
51 Madison Ave. clients: Abbr.
52 Countable items
53 Po tributary
54 Functions
55 Russian river
56 See 49 Down
58 Appendant abbreviation
59 Newsworthy jet

201

ACROSS

1 "Male and Female" author
5 Loops
9 Hag
14 As well
15 Catch
16 Wealthy ones
17 Signature
19 Like some gases
20 Alert
21 Persian water wheel
22 French historian
23 Spiritually cherish
26 Old clerical cap
29 Commotion
32 __ Mahal
35 Existing: Lat.
36 Utah town
37 Reconnoitered
39 Roll
41 Chemical prefix
42 Writer Norman
44 Violation
45 Silk: Sp.
46 U.S. painter
47 __ spheroid (football, to sports writers)
49 Russian peaks
54 Singing sounds
56 Dressed fit to kill
59 Prepared bread
60 Strike a response
61 Sharp ridge
62 Diminutive suffix
63 Fitzgerald
64 Do lawn repairs
65 __ stat (Irish for free state)
66 At long __

DOWN

1 Greater
2 Do the Gretna Green bit
3 Gray
4 Actress Reed
5 People in general
6 First-class
7 Places for fringe
8 Out of a clear __
9 Tough cotton cloth
10 Left
11 Persons of power
12 Italian saint
13 This, in Spain
18 Weed with purplish flowers
24 Cuddle
25 Cordwood measures
27 Lack of vigor
28 Insect
30 Food store, for short
31 Portent
32 Cookbook abbreviations
33 Yearn
34 Man in the street
38 Lacking power
40 Martyred saint
43 Unpublished literature
48 Put aboard
50 Mutineer
51 Miss St. Johns
52 Soothes
53 Chair-back piece
54 Ski lift
55 Thin
57 Aware of
58 Teutonic language group: Abbr.
60 Matter, in law

202

ACROSS

1 Repeat
8 Vinegars
13 "Do not fold, spindle or __"
15 Radio converting device
16 Stormy
18 "__ at Oxford"
19 Netherlands town
20 Tobacco juice
22 Sesame
23 Play part
24 Swindler
25 __ majesty
26 Scotsman's to
27 Organism requiring no air
29 Beings: Fr.
31 Andean herb
33 Bridge positions
35 Certain bridge card
37 Certain marble
41 Old Turkish coin
43 Roundabout
45 One, in Paris
46 Small city
49 "O! what __ and peasant slave am I"
50 Pourboire
51 Unclose, to poets
52 Get the beer keg ready early
53 Argentine tune
54 Cather
56 Table treats, of old
58 Shoreline feature
59 Feedback of speaker's words
60 Witnessing clause
61 Declares

DOWN

1 Copy
2 Layered
3 Odds and ends
4 Brook
5 Pub drink
6 Plug for a wound
7 Everlasting
8 Arabian garments
9 Islet
10 Inspire
11 North African port
12 Tarsus
14 Glossy paint
17 Opera-box wear
21 Horsy sound
24 Add knitting stitches
25 "__ be gay"
28 Rebuke
30 Pail, in England
32 Surgeon, at times
34 Weather radar system
36 Contrite
38 Wearied
39 Cherubs
40 Finery
42 Stays quiet
44 Figures on Valentines
46 Namely
47 Express an idea
48 Author of "Invisible Man"
52 Meat spread
53 Stadium receipts
55 Tennis term
57 These: Fr.

ANSWERS

1

```
SCUPS TIAS CONS
HORAE ORLE IMAM
IMAGE PROD RATE
MOLOKAI EATCROW
   DOLCE TAU
BEDAUB SPELLING
LAR TUTTI CANOE
UTAH MERES REVE
NEMOS SEDER RES
TRAVIATA NESTLE
   EFT TASSE
WHARTON RETRACE
HONE LEER IVIED
OVER LAVA VERDE
MEWS STAY ESSEN
```

2

```
EQUABLE BOASTER
GUNROOM UPBORNE
RACKSUP STUDIES
ESO SPECIES BMI
SHUN ERRED RUIN
SETUP OER PANES
SHARERS DUDES
NILS HARI
COCOA TAXICAB
SAVER BAN MADAM
IRES LARGO LARA
MAR MISSIVE MBS
IMAGINE NELLIES
LEGUMES GRISTLE
ELEMENT STATELY
```

3

```
WASP PALOS IRAN
ECHO AGORA MICA
EROS DOUBLEPLAY
PEWTER SOVIETS
WAVERS NEO
AGILE EAR RUSTS
BUN NAPLES STOW
AID TRELLIS AWE
SLOB CLIENT GEE
HEWER SEN ALERT
TIM STATIC
OBLIGED SETOFF
DRAMATURGY MAIL
DIME ANNIE UCLA
SEES LEAST SHAG
```

4

```
CAW CORES MILO
BARI OPERA INIT
AVES NAVAL DEVI
NICHES UTILIZES
CLAYPIGEONS
WISE ETHANE
RHFACTORS SATON
EELS SLUMS NORD
AMAHS SEALSKINS
PONYUP CITY
BLACKPEPPER
FIRESALE SPARTA
AMID SLUSH NUNS
TIME MATEO KNAP
STAN AYARD YES
```

5

```
LIONS ITSA HAHA
ONTOP SAIL OXEN
FROTH OKLAHOMAN
TEE ISLET URARE
ONETO BRAND
MCMLXX NEEDY
OOID KAREL FED
ONCEINALIFETIME
DYE MALLS ALME
MAGIC BURSAR
SLOGS OLENT
STORE UMIAK DIA
CROSSOVER ISING
OISE HERA NORGE
TAEL MASS DIKES
```

6

```
NASA SNAFU ABCS
OWNS TALON GOOP
REAL OTTER ASTA
ASPIRATE ESTHER
KATY TAPE
PREENS DESISTED
LOPAT PITON ELI
APOS QUEEN SPUR
TEC BURTS CHIDE
ASHTREES GOODER
EASE BLOC
EXTANT SWANKIER
PROP IOWAN ECRU
IAGO OLAND ROIL
CYST NEMAS SNEE
```

7

```
SARAH TEENER
ALAMO WANDERED
SHIVER ABNEGATE
LABE SULLA ASIF
ARAL ENTE STUNT
TABS SIE SPIRAL
ENA DEAR LIVELY
CANT MICE
MOTORS GAPE DEM
EVINCE RIP PINA
NETTY DAZE AVIS
ARAR BODED TOSS
CANALIZE OVERLY
ELICITED FENCE
LATTER FETED
```

8

```
SQUID CHIMERA
TUNDRA AERONAUT
RATION BRINGSTO
AIROUT BONA POT
FLUTTERING DUCT
EYESHADES LITRE
TVS CAVIAR
AMPERES FOMENTS
TERROR POX
ANENT TRACKSTAR
LESE PROMONTORY
OLS LAIT MORBID
SAUTERNE BLAISE
SURNAMES SLIDER
SETFAST STENS
```

9

```
HORSE SWEDE ODA
AROOM PALED NAN
SCUBADIVING ENG
PAT NOTE IMAGE
LANE PAEAN
RELATE GEMSTONE
IRATE BESET TOP
VASE SENOR OHNO
EST ELLIS FREED
REIGNITE HEARSE
NEEDS POLL
BELEM POLO PFC
ARI INFLUENTIAL
LIN EELER RETIA
LEE SOYAS YEARN
```

10

```
ANC TAMPA HEP
LEAS URALS SAVE
SOPPINGWET EVEN
ONTARIO BEARERS
INKS ERIE
BOIS INSOMNIA
PLUS PRO ISDONE
GOSH REBID IDES
ABLATE LDS POLE
SYRETTES LIME
METE PATE
SALADIN COCOTTE
PROD ENCLOSURES
ANNA SISAL SILT
DOE TSADE CEE
```

11

```
LUNA  HAS  NUBIAN
APOTHEGM  ATAXIA
MOVEABLE  BORING
ANA TREES  PEATS
   WHET  TAIL
NARROW  MALAYANS
OSIER  DIVAN  GOP
LIMN  VOTER  COMA
ADE  SEMES  CARAT
NERVEGAS  PARADE
   ALAI  SARD
SNARK  NAIVE  BEA
CANDIA  CREEPERS
ASTORS  MERRIMAC
THANKS  ESS  GASH
```

12

```
MASTS  SWAT  RECD
ALOHA  TOBY  OVER
RODIN  ERIC  BADE
GUARDS  LEONIDAS
   SLOYD  BONERS
PISTOLES  BUS
ARI  TOMES  NOBEL
GOLF  SERAC  NOSE
ENOLS  NIORD  LAS
   AHA  ENORMOUS
POTTER  SEPIA
SCUBARIG  SENORS
ARRU  AGAR  STRAW
LENS  NOME  ULTRA
MASH  TRET  PEHAN
```

13

```
META  AGATE  CAPA
ABET  CUMIN  OVAL
CONFECTION  NELL
ENTIRE  SOLACES
   RADII  BEN
REASSESS  LATEST
OMIT  LOVES  NCO
SIS  REALIST  LOW
ELL  IRMAS  PAWN
SEEING  TOPSOILS
   AGO  ERUPT
PROMOTE  RAIDER
AHAB  IRIDESCENT
PERU  ZANDE  HATE
SASS  ETTES  EROS
```

14

```
EGEST  MTNS  AQUA
LEFTA  OHIO  SUNG
SAFETYBELT  PATA
RUN  OME  LICIT
BLOCKANDTACKLE
BOG  RENDERS
OXEYE  OVA  USDC
CENTEROFINERTIA
ESTS  ORT  ROOST
   SWAHILI  NCO
HARDLINEBACKER
ALARY  LAN  ACE
SOJA  SHINGUARDS
TEAK  AONE  ABOIL
ASHE  OYEZ  RAPTO
```

15

```
LEIS  PACE  CARIA
AXLE  ERRS  OBOLS
GILA  REASONABLE
STERLING  RITES
   COLA  CAFE
AMAHS  CATERING
BALES  GONER  DIN
ENDS  BREED  SETA
ANE  PRODS  START
MARPLOTS  ORLES
   RAKE  STOA
PEACE  CHANNELS
MISTERCHAN  GRIT
INNER  HARK  ESSE
DEEDS  ATES  REAR
```

16

```
SCRIMP  SUNSET
FOREVER  TRAPPER
EMULATE  IGRAINE
RES  NESTLED  TAP
ROAM  RIOTS  BOCA
ENDOW  DAS  TAMES
TEETERED  LATEST
   HIED  TAMA
ASSERT  SHRIVELS
THIRD  HUE  LIMIT
MOBS  SIEPI  AINE
OWE  BANDIED  NEA
SERVANT  PROTEAM
TRIESTE  ENRINGS
YANKED  REMOTE
```

17

```
CLAP  STIRS  JENA
HOHO  KORAN  AVER
AWORMINAFURCOAT
PST  ARAN  BAKERY
   PILL  ABIE
SKILLS  SWELTER
ANNAS  BOARS  NAP
ROSY  BEAKS  MDIII
AWE  DRAKE  HOUSE
STARERS  GAPPED
   BOAS  LANE
UNMASK  EERO  ICC
SCISSORSGRINDER
IONE  FUSEE  OLLA
ASKS  FEAST  GELT
```

18

```
DOMAIN  ATROPA
EVILLY  PROPOSE
STERILE  POLENTA
AARON  CALENDAR
LIS  ATALL  HERL
ALEP  BALL  MARTY
DEERPARK  BAN
DRIEST  RAIDER
NEH  MALDEMER
CROCK  SINK  DIVE
HARE  HANKY  NEP
AVAILING  STEAL
SINGING  WOMANLY
ENGORGE  ATONCE
EERIER  RAGGED
```

19

```
CAM  MOTELS  PSIS
UDI  IMARET  RULE
POLYDIPSIA  OPEN
RIANT  AGR
PATRI  SOURCREAM
ORING  PANORAMAS
LEASH  ATRO  MERS
   TORMENT
ANTA  IRES  ALOFT
SCAPEGOAT  NACRE
SOUPBOWLS  TREAT
   REB  PAGAN
EMIT  CORPULENCE
RANI  ORMOLU  IES
DIET  TRAILS  ASP
```

20

```
SALP  RAP  PICK
ADAR  ERAS  ADANA
GIVESBACK  RODIN
BAYOU  KEG  LIFT
EXTEMPORIZE
FOLD  TAE  PAZ
IRE  DARNS  JERK
BEDROLL  QUASHES
GAEA  YOUTH  UNA
ALI  LII  ASTO
BULLFIDDLER
LOKI  ETH  IRENE
AMAZE  TANZANIAN
IBSEN  ONCE  ORSO
SESS  DOS  TATS
```

21

```
JANE  MASON  DADS
IRON  OSTEO  ABIE
LORD  ICOSI  TORT
TOMORROW  SLEUTH
   ROAN  BIER
GRASPS  PRESSING
RANEE  CRASS  LON
ABED  SHUNT  SIVA
IBA  SPANS  UPPER
LIRIPIPE  TRIALS
   GALE  CHAT
UNFURL  GAROTTES
NORA  ANODE  IOTA
DION  GOUGE  NUNS
OLGA  ESTES  GRAS
```

22

```
POMP  DIPS  SEWED
ALEE  IDEA  TREVI
READ  NELL  UNTIE
COLDCOMFORT  BLT
   LOS  PETAL
SIDEWALK  DETAIL
ARR  SUERS  RINSE
BEYS  ROOTS  SKEW
INGER  SNAKE  ERE
NEUTER  AGITATES
   LADED  LID
CIC  WARMBLOODED
ACHOO  EIRE  POGO
SEENO  SLOT  TRAM
ADDED  SOWS  SALE
```

23

```
BALTI JAY  ACTS
AGAIN OURS CLAP
RELET INSINCERE
REORIENT AERATE
   SMUT ALTERED
SIR ARSONISTS
CREATE CID ITAL
AMILE BTS MOOLA
RANT DEE CONRAD
 SERRATION YES
PATROON TRAM
ELANDS ACADEMIE
NOTASSUCH IDIOT
CHET YARE SIENA
EASE WED MANAS
```

24

```
FARGO UTAH  REST
OPINE RELY  ESPY
BIFURCATES CAIN
SSE SALE TRIUNE
   STRS BEEP
PATES AUROREAN
CASED LILI ONNO
RUHR SAMBA CATO
ALEE TIES PATEN
MINOTAUR CITES
   GILS DOTE
FURROW OILS ARE
AREA ASBESTOSIS
LISP RIOT ORION
ACTH TRES PEASE
```

25

```
TESLA SHAH EKED
ODEUM REDO XERO
GARLICSALT HAIL
AMBUSH PITTANCE
   SOW BEAU
TUSK IRA ABSORB
ANTE CASK ATSEA
XRAYTECHNICIANS
IRISH KEEN OGEE
SARTRE SAD NEWS
   OONA DIZ
GARNERED GESTIC
OBOE OREGONPINE
BLUR LIEU DATED
SEES LEMS AROSE
```

26

```
CAR LTCOL LEAD
LIEU AROMA ETTE
EDEN VIRES TUNA
FALSEIMPRESSION
   USETO ROC
RAMIT ORA SALEM
EMOTES ALL LEDA
CIGARETTEFILTER
ANUB ARE STIGMA
POLLS IFI STOAT
   ETD INDIA
JAPANESESANDMAN
ALEC COLUM AERO
DUET ADDLE YAMS
EMPS LASTS LYE
```

27

```
FAST ADOPT TANK
OMAR SULLA ALAI
GILA ABEAR NEIN
GRANT LONDONFOG
   SAKI SYNE
CALAMINE CRAWL
OTIC LESLIE VIA
DONT TRAIN SONS
ENE ASSUME EWES
SENSE SARGASSO
   ARAS BTUS
TOKYOROSE TODAY
ISEE GLEAN NONE
ASER OVINE ETNA
SANS TENSE DEAR
```

28

```
ECCE MOTA HARSH
CHAT AMOR ORATE
LAMELLATE LAMIA
AFIRE RENAL IRR
TENNER MADAM
  OATER ONEWAY
CARLSTADT DRAMA
OLE SPEWS SIR
LEAST TAILGATED
TELLER NIOBE
  YAHOO TREPAN
OFF COPRA ELATE
SILVA EDGARAPOE
SNEAK REED REND
ADDLE ARES DREY
```

29

```
SRI TEAKS OMNIS
HEM HOSEA REEFS
APPLESEED ALFIE
KLIEG ANDANTE
OYSTER SERG RMS
  TOOK NEE TOE
CHERRIES OFHIDE
MYLEG GAR RATED
DOESIT CHEERILY
RIV ART OWED
SDA PIES ESTHER
 THEMATA TOILE
ITISA PINEAPPLE
STOIC OPART PES
MYNAH TEPEE ONE
```

30

```
JONAH DET SPEAK
ELOGE ILO PODGE
EDSEL NIE ASIAN
PEENING RANTERS
 RETARD RUDE
  SAO SARONG
GREAT NOCTUIDAE
ROMP GRR OEIL
IMMODESTY CRASS
SEALER BAA
  OVID ALPACA
IMAGINE BLATANT
NOVIA ANI BRINE
CREST LEE LARID
HASTE SOS ESNES
```

31

```
AMPS UPAS ADAMS
LOOP NAMA MEDAL
MLLE ASIF AFORE
SELLOUT ADHERED
 ULE OGRE NESS
ENTER RAISES
LAIR BAL THEISM
AZO COLLARS NEO
MINION ERY SFAX
 NONCOM CALLA
SLOT EONS ALA
POVERTY REBATED
IMAGE ORAL BINE
RATES TICS LODE
EXERT EPEE ENOS
```

32

```
SPOUT SALE BAGS
CURSE OBAD AURA
ARDEN RING TROW
REND HANDY MOTS
ELA COSTA FAROE
FINGAL RUMINANT
UNCASE ASIA
LEERED ANNALS
 OUSE SCORIA
ONCEUPON MEDIAL
ROAMS CURIE EKE
ANTE DORIC OTOS
TENN OTIC DATUM
EGAD ERNE OHARA
SOPS SAGS SUSAN
```

33

```
AMBLE LAHR IMPS
SILAS ISEE NOLO
HEADSTREAM HIER
ENC AHEAD CARAT
 KAYE WALLETS
OAHU AHEADOF
SPENT ERIES HER
LOATH ANT ELEMI
ODD EDDIE TEAMS
 HOOTERS ADAK
INFERNO EARP
RELAY FOURS IDE
EGAD HORSESHEAD
NEMO AONE TACNA
EVEN STES STEAM
```

34

```
ACCT VOLGA ULAN
SHOEMAKING LOBO
TENNESSEAN YORE
ACCENT DRAMATIS
 KIITS ROSTEN
PRES LOW ERODES
EER MEANS EVENT
RIG ODD ODS SCI
SNELL SPLIT POE
ESSENE RON DEUS
 SALMON CORN
NEWSROOM SENATE
ISEE PROMENADER
SNAP ESTIMATORS
HERS REESE ESSE
```

35

```
BLOC LAPPS SCOT
LAVA EERIE TRUE
OVER TROPE RAGS
TENON OVERSIGHT
   MIDGES HASTY
EBB PARR ART
VOID TAB DEICES
INTERIM REDOUBT
LESSON GEM NERO
   TAG EVAN SOW
USERS CHISEL
THROTTLES WALKS
TONY IONIA SANE
ERIE PUNTS EMIT
REED STASH RATS
```

36

```
AGAS BOMB BASAL
LABOROVER BRINE
ELABORATE LATIN
SEC BOLERO BOLD
  SKEINS ALINES
IBSEN KOREA
SUER SIDER SHE
BRAYLIKEADONKEY
AGT ONERS OESE
  ANDES ALLIS
FARMER FILLET
ATEE ASTART TAP
CORES PICKABONE
ENURE UTTERANCE
SENSE ROOD YSER
```

37

```
CALL SANTAS EAT
ABEE AROUSE ROE
BLOWININTHEWIND
SES MEDE ERASE
    EAR ASST
SLANG SAP ERNS
PORTERAGES ROOT
AREA ALOMA FAMA
ANTI SUGARDADDY
KEEL TON ELSES
    INRE PAL
CANOE SEAR MBA
SINGININTHERAIN
INN SAMETO INTO
TEA ELUDES PEEN
```

38

```
WACO NBS DEW
AVILA FOIE MIRA
GENERALIZATIONS
ESQ ILEX OLDEN
  POLA DARKEST
ARIES CRONES
BANJO IOWA HELP
ENTO BRUNT AQUA
DIOR ACTS SKULL
  ADJUST WEILL
WHITEAS ACES
IONIC SIRE BIS
PRIVATEPROPERTY
EDGE OURS STAIN
DEO PRY ESSE
```

39

```
IAL VAST SITE
ANTE ONEIF URAL
ADOT LITTLEROCK
LULU ALEX NOS
ELPASOTEXAS
  NAH MALES
MARYLAND STOVE
SARI TRIED ALIT
PROVE EXTERNAL
ATWAR ANO
  LIBERTYBELL
AMI EIDE DIET
PITTSBURGH ISMS
AREA SCAPE CLUE
TOMB ENOS TER
```

40

```
HELP BLAH CIRCA
OVAL RORY AREAL
MESA EARMARKING
ENTICEMENTS TOE
  NOD ASE BEER
ASP TIER SAAR
LOAF NOSE ISAAC
ARRAIGN SCRATCH
SATIN SCAR LETO
  ILKS HUES SEW
SACS ASA AID
PLU INTROSPECTS
ILLUSTRATE ALEE
LEADA ODOR RUSE
ERROR PENS SETS
```

41

```
AWNS TIGHT SWAB
SHUT ARNEE LIME
SOMERSAULT ENID
TABLET PENATES
  LAYON SIZE
OFFAL NET GYROS
ALAR BEWITH TAW
TAL BABYSIT IKE
ERL ICIEST AMIA
RESAT TAU SNEER
  AHEM REMIT
EXPOSES ANIMAE
ARAR SPRINGBACK
CARS SCONE ERLE
HYTE YAWNS SEED
```

42

```
MAST PSHAW ERAS
IGOR AMORE TELA
MICA LETTERHEAD
INKWELL HANKIE
  ILLAT TONI
HOTELS CRUTCHES
ENTRE SOURS EAT
RIO SAVES AGE
DOM TYRES LADRA
SNEERSAT CALLED
  PATH SOUCI
ARIOSO CADENCE
PUNCHLINES SEAR
ITCH ICENT TRIS
AHAS CEDES ESNE
```

43

```
XRAY SPIRO BOWS
EIRE AESOP AGIO
BAIT SPINESCENT
ETE BIOS NIKES
CASEINS TINS
  INS SONGLESS
ADAGE VENGEANCE
LASH BETAS PTAS
EDITORIAL APERS
PONYRIDE IRE
  PLOT ONEROUS
DUROC ARLO STY
XENOPHOBIA ETTE
ENDO ELBOW LIEN
REEF SEANS FARE
```

44

```
ROM BIRL PADRE
IBO ODEA UBOATS
GITALONG RADIAL
  FULTONSFOLLY
GALAS OUT
LEAR CHASE ITCH
ART RHONE BARRE
ZIEGFELDFOLL ES
EARED DRONE POT
SLIM SUERS MOLE
  GAP FADER
SEWARDSFOLLY
TRADED LOUISXIV
SORREL AZAN ELI
  SPADE NEUT NIP
```

45

```
ABBA ACCA ASSET
HUES BAHN UTTER
ERST ACRO TURKS
ASTITCHINTIME
RAF OKES ESPANA
TROUT TENT KOL
  OLOR MON BORE
MATE ERASE RFDS
ALFS VIS RAAB
ILO GAFF FEAST
MORTEM LADE DAO
  WHIPPOORWILLS
CRAIG AWRY DUOS
BERNE RETE ACME
NADER ARAR SKED
```

46

```
STAD JABS STREW
WADI ULAR QUIVA
AXIS MOTSJUSTES
PINCENEZ EASES
  ALAS MEWL
SABRE WORKEDUP
ABODE HONEY IZE
MONS FARED BABA
ANG WINDY BONER
JEOPARDY LEAKY
  INKY EZIO
MUFTI CREPTOUT
ZINFANDELS ISLA
ACOLD ABET ALAR
GAPES BUSY NONO
```

47

```
PACT MASSE GOAD
LALO STAEL RILE
ARAN CARNIVALOF
COVET RIA ASSET
ANI HAMSTERS
CHETS OVI FLU
VSHAPE TREACLES
ATOLL HAS THESE
TOREADOR LIEDER
SAD NEP MOORE
TELEMANN RAT
ABOUT SER SAMMY
GOTTSCHALK PAPP
ISTO PODIA RULE
THOR OWENS ASES
```

48

```
LANA TAFFY MOAT
OXEN EXILE ANDA
FLAX NEXUS XYZS
TEPID SEX MIXES
EAR RELAX
ABETTED SEREAND
FOXY GEN XYSTER
ARE VESTRIS AVA
CARMEN HOC PLEW
EXTENTS BOTHERS
TUSKS NEO
DATES EHS XEBEC
ULAR STOOL NOLO
SAXE OCALA IXIA
ENID PHLOX XYST
```

49

```
BEAR BITES BREI
ELLE ACARE EARS
AMIS RAZORSEDGE
RENTIER SUNRISE
DREADFUL MAKO
REASON PECOS
TICTAC BAH GILA
OFA SETSAIL TEN
INTR DOT BUSYAS
TIBET REVERE
ASIN RERECORD
ILLUSED INSULAR
WALLAWALLA RITA
IGOT TWEET EVEN
NOUS SNIDE DESK
```

50

```
OVERSEE PALACES
RIVETER ANIMATE
BEEPERS STEPSON
STREPITOSO ANT
APE BENUMB
APPLE TOR GALAS
RAHS SWEETHEART
EYE FIE LES NEA
CINDERELLA SCAR
ANODE DIE CHASE
METTLE ARA
STE RENSSELAER
LUNATED OPALINE
ABALONE AETOLIA
BALLADE PRETEND
```

51

```
PESTS RAPID SMA
CHEAP ERASE CAN
TEMPUSFUGIT ROT
SHEARERS SECURE
GAYAS RABID
MAGNET HASP
ACRES WRIT SAVO
STOW CRAFT TRAM
CAGY AINT RAISE
EARS YONDER
PAPAS TARAS
HEARTS POLESTEP
ISR RESOLUTIONS
LIT UMORE TREVI
ORE TILTS ASSYS
```

52

```
NAP CAMAS MAAM
AGOG APART ALTA
SOSO MTIDA ITON
ANTAS LEGALIZE
ATEE ONEPM
POLESTAR DRAPED
INRE TADS INONU
ETA CUREALL SUB
RATIO ERNE ATRI
SPEDUP HOUSEMEN
ERATO RIGA
IWANTYOU PERDU
CAPT ONSET AKIN
41II LEERY NEAT
ALEC ARSIS DSO
```

53

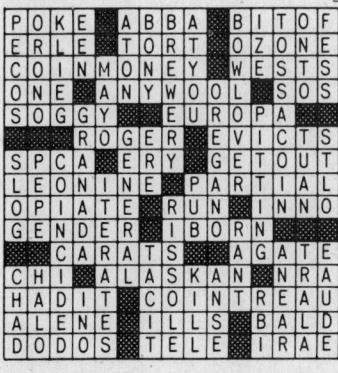

```
POKE ABBA BITOF
ERLE TORT OZONE
COINMONEY WESTS
ONE ANYWOOL SOS
SOGGY EUROPA
ROGER EVICTS
SPCA ERY GETOUT
LEONINE PARTIAL
OPIATE RUN INNO
GENDER IBORN
CARATS AGATE
CHI ALASKAN NRA
HADIT COINTREAU
ALENE ILLS BALD
DODOS TELE IRAE
```

54

```
FLIP LIB SURA
AURA BONES ENOS
SPIROAGNEWWATCH
TESTATE PARTAKE
IKE TENETS
ARLES BID ALSOP
DUOS WIN STEEVE
ENS HASHISH LEA
LEAFOF ALE MERC
ASNOT ATE WIDTH
GRAINS AWN
SEEMING SLIDERS
COLORTELEVISION
INES ORGIA ORSO
OSSA STS FEED
```

55

```
DEVIL BETS HASP
SCENE ALOE MCCI
CHANCELLOR SHAG
SOL TREE VIPERS
QUID MIDI
SCOURS LICENSED
THREE CANE ACME
RIDE JAPES FOCI
AMEN ORES CORES
PERSONAL GARNET
NEAT WORE
DEPART PEAR OSE
OLAV HARDLYEVER
ABLE AGOG OPERA
SAME NOME NINES
```

56

```
BARES AESOP
NUBILE BREWER
BAGASSE AGENDAS
OPA EIDOLON DCL
LABS EIKON ALII
ULOUS EEN ANENT
SMOTHER EMIGRES
TON EMU
OFFENDS AMELIAS
MOORE ISM EAGLE
EROS HAREM ROOT
GUT FEMORAL RHO
AMPOULE IDAHOAN
SAUCES GAMUTS
DIANE OMENS
```

57

```
CISCO MODEST
CENTIME SERENER
ANTARES TRAINEE
STILE TRACT AME
TIMES EERIER
ALIS TBAR ODER
DID ARAD CYBELE
ITA CONSOLE CAL
VETOED ONAN EBE
AREA EVEN CLOG
THAMES THERA
BAS OVERT HERAT
ALLOVER ELEVATE
BEANERY PIRATED
EXPERT DELED
```

58

```
CASCADE MISSED
APPARENT ELAINE
STONEAGE TABLAS
SIREN RAKE RAMI
ATT ABASED EGER
BUFF EVEN ADELE
ADULATE TELA
ELOPE TANTE
WELL THECOLD
ALDER ATRI ELEE
TEAR EROICA EVA
LISS MARC MORAN
ATHOME SEPARATE
SHINER OPERATOR
TANGLY SEALERY
```

59

```
BORN FOSSA LSTS
AREA ORATE OPAH
JACKKNIVES TORE
ASSERT EMOTIONS
    DISK PRON
PAPAS PAD INREM
ATIP ADDICT IRA
NOTE BULGE EVIL
ENC ESTEEM MEAL
LEHAR YRS BURNS
    FRAP TALL
SPOTLESS MESSES
PERI DISHABILLE
ARKS ARSIS VALE
TEST LETTS EBAN
```

60

```
LEFT ACTOR JAKE
ASOR SHUTE IBEX
STRUCTURED NOME
SHAMROCK MIXUPS
    PINK JAN
ACHE ISLAND ACC
QUAD STAB THRU
URDU HERBS YEAR
ALEP AVEC RAZE
SSS ANKARA ADES
    DOS WREN
JUNEAU COLONIZE
ANAX GRACENOTES
MIMI HUNKS UTES
STET TREYS SOSO
```

61

```
CAPA SELLS SCAT
ARAB PRIDE TOBY
TORN RINGA AMER
SWEETENS PIMPLE
   GREY MOREL
PUPAE SHOWINESS
ELATES EVES THI
ATLE OILER PIAL
CRI FUSE STROLL
HAMMERING BENTS
   PALLS ANAT
PESTIE ANOREXIA
ABET MANGO REND
POSE OMNES INNO
ANTS NOISE TOSS
```

62

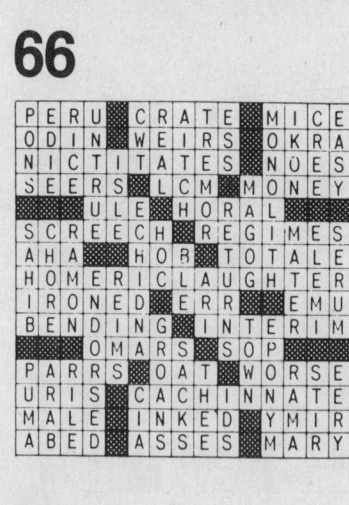

```
CCBB FONDA OCTO
AURA LANIN LOOM
SCAR ERECT YORE
THEBUMS KREMLIN
ASI BUMP
MARRONS UMPIRES
ANOA GOTT SCORN
HADA NWT CANE
AMEND JOOK HSIA
LEONORA NEGATED
SHAH EQM
CASCADE SNAPSAT
ALTO INURE IAGO
SALT SITAR OPEN
KNOT HEISS NOSY
```

63

```
SCHISM WASTES
STROPHE ALCESTE
ELATION SLANTED
DOT LATCHON RAG
AUER TOADY GAME
TIRED RIO CODER
ESSAYS DWELLERS
PLUM NAIF
STREAMED UMBERS
THORN XYZ BARAT
URBS LIKEA GAVE
CEE DOCENTS SEE
CARNERA IRACUND
OTTOMAN TENURES
SATINS HEATER
```

64

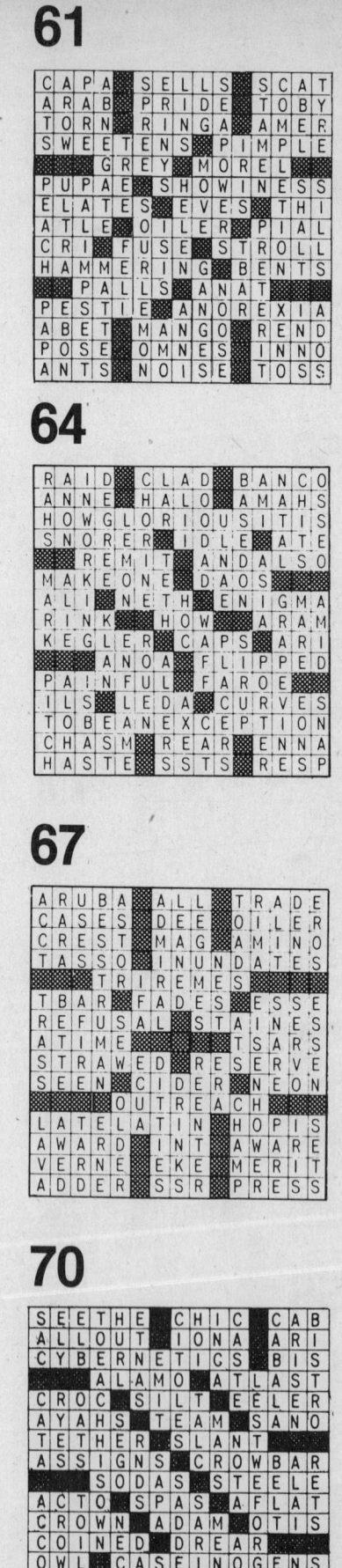

```
RAID CLAD BANCO
ANNE HALO AMAHS
HOWGLORIOUSITIS
SNORER IDLE ATE
REMIT ANDALSO
MAKEONE DAOS
ALI NETH ENIGMA
RINK HOW ARAM
KEGLER CAPS ARI
ANOA FLIPPED
PAINFUL FAROE
ILS LEDA CURVES
TOBEANEXCEPTION
CHASM REAR ENNA
HASTE SSTS RESP
```

65

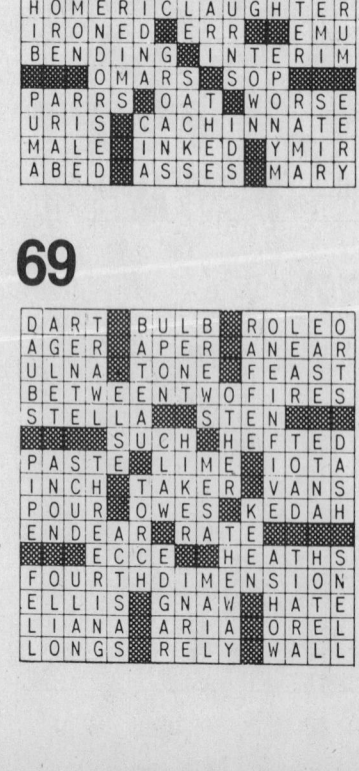

```
WHIT STAVE ALGA
AIDA EOSIN TULE
SKYJACKERS EMIR
HEL GUYS CRABBY
LORO SOUSE
JEJUNE WONDERED
ALARY DANCE JAR
BICE MERGE PAGE
OAK LACES SACRA
TSARINAS DARKER
NEEDY FONT
AMALFI BUNT OBI
TOPE BLUEJACKET
OVEN LINGO ALEC
PEST ENDON LATH
```

66

```
PERU CRATE MICE
ODIN WEIRS OKRA
NICTITATES NUES
SEERS LCM MONEY
ULE HORAL
SCREECH REGIMES
AHA HOR TOTALE
HOMERICLAUGHTER
IRONED ERR EMU
BENDING INTERIM
OMARS SOP
PARRS OAT WORSE
URIS CACHINNATE
MALE INKED YMIR
ABED ASSES MARY
```

67

```
ARUBA ALL TRADE
CASES DEE OILER
CREST MAG AMINO
TASSO INUNDATES
TRIREMES
TBAR FADES ESSE
REFUSAL STAINES
ATIME TSARS
STRAWED RESERVE
SEEN CIDER NEON
OUTREACH
LATELATIN HOPIS
AWARD INT AWARE
VERNE EKE MERIT
ADDER SSR PRESS
```

68

```
SALAD ATRI ARAB
PLATE URAL NOLO
ADROP DESERTION
DEVILFISH OILED
ERA EROS ROC
ATA EDOMITES
STALE ASEA PONE
PURISTS ARRANGE
ABUM ATEN ITERS
DEMENTIA ICE
NEA ROBE OPA
SORTS BLUNDERER
CREATURES ISLAM
ALAR LIST STOLE
RELY TESS HONED
```

69

```
DART BULB ROLEO
AGER APER ANEAR
ULNA TONE FEAST
BETWEENTWOFIRES
STELLA STEN
SUCH HEFTED
PASTE LIME IOTA
INCH TAKER VANS
POUR OWES KEDAH
ENDEAR RATE
ECCE HEATHS
FOURTHDIMENSION
ELLIS GNAW HATE
LIANA ARIA OREL
LONGS RELY WALL
```

70

```
SEETHE CHIC CAB
ALLOUT IONA ARI
CYBERNETICS BIS
ALAMO ATLAST
CROC SILT EELER
AYAHS TEAM SANO
TETHER SLANT
ASSIGNS CROWBAR
SODAS STEELE
ACTO SPAS AFLAT
CROWN ADAM OTIS
COINED DREAR
OWL CASEINOGENS
REE KLAN UNEASY
DDT SEWS SETTOS
```

71

```
TRAP    AMIC
CHALET ALAMOS
HESTER STRAMP
AMPERE PANTER
ORA RIMFIRE DES
KONG NOIRS POET
ANILE RTE HAWSE
NAV        OWN
METRE RUM BETEL
ASHE SONAR DONE
IKE ATBOXES ETO
EMPIRE ISOBAR
ROUSER MENARE
SONNET SAINTE
NYET    LASH
```

72

```
OPTS MACAO SMUT
ALSO ELUDE CARE
TEAL ALTER ERGS
HARDEN ESSENCES
    ELDER TOE
SPARKED CENSORS
TARE RIGID BIT
ENID BAR REVE
TIS FLICK USER
ICEFLOE LECTERN
    EAR LEECH
REVERSAL PILFER
ARAB ABATE ERIE
TAIL LEMUR SARI
ESNE ELANS SUED
```

73

```
SPED DAMS GLARE
HOWE OLIO REBEL
ALEF WALLTOWALL
MAROON DOW TIE
    ENTER ONSETS
PAL SOLES MOM
AMOS WISE ARENA
WASTENOTWANTNOT
STERN TANS STLO
NOS STUCK SAM
TROPHY EPEES
HUT ROB NYMPHS
ELIMINATED ORAL
DEMON SAGE KALE
ARETE TROD EYED
```

74

```
SHAD FEST SCANT
HONE OLEO CHOIR
OUTS OVERCHARGE
PRESIDED OERTHE
SIDECAR HURT
ARID TERZETTO
WATT DOORTODOOR
ALI BIGTOES MRG
RENDITIONS OBEY
NEGATIVE YOUS
NEVE SCUTTLE
SPECIE STARTOUT
WOMENSWEAR ANTA
INERT HAND KEEP
GESSO OLDS ESSE
```

75

```
BAAL LEPER BARD
EMMA ERASE USIA
EMIT GRIST DIAL
SORCERER REGALE
HEED EIRE
HECKLE AVENTINE
ALOES BREVE RAM
LILY LEONE LAVE
OHO LEAST LATEN
SURCEASE TOSEED
RAPT PAST
CELERY THISYEAR
ARIA ETHAN ELMO
POST AVAST ASEA
ESTE RATES REND
```

76

```
JAPANED JOCULAR
ULULATE EPICURE
REDBUCK JETAGED
IRE THETUNE STO
STR ONE OAHU
TSE JESTED PIUS
    GUSTO FALSE
JUJITSU FEELSAD
INANE VERAS
PERK SLIDER JPS
IDES ALE ULL
JUD SNOWJOB NEA
ACIDITY ALAMEIN
PETERED VARIANT
ADELIES AVENUES
```

77

```
TAPS ADAM CLASP
AMIE SOFA LENTO
CONQUEROR OGEES
KRAUT MONOGRAMS
EEL LEV ERSE
SPENSER ERE
CINC OEUVRE MOM
ONCEINALIFETIME
WEE LAREDO ONER
JAR INQUIRE
SHOO DIM DUC
NORTHSTAR IHATE
IRATE AQUITANIA
PATEN LUMS NCOS
SLEDS YIPS DYNE
```

78

```
MACE ELATE CRAM
ALAS XENON HOLE
ROTC CATERWAULS
STARTERS AORTAS
LOREN AGO SHY
CROWED CREDO
RUG KEYES YUCCA
ETUI DELOS TAAL
WHELP MINOS TWO
KOREA LIPASE
TAB IAN TONAL
ANOINT GOINGOUT
SCATTERERS INRE
TORE ROOST NIBS
ENDS SEGOS GAIT
```

79

```
ASKS FERA SOCKS
BLIP OXAL AMANA
LATINRITE TEREU
EYELETS FAULTED
LAITY BREW
LIFERS ACENTRIC
ODOR GRADI INA
FIRST MDS ARGON
TOT EDAMS OHIO
STHELENA BOTTLE
RALL NORMA
THISTLE FEATURE
HAGIA LEFTRIGHT
ETHEL OLEO OREO
METRE DARN NOON
```

80

```
JULEP SRS ACES
AMOLES TET MARE
MIRAGE ABALONES
EARNSINTEREST
SKED ZOUAVE IMA
DELETE SCAR
MADEIRAS SALLE
ABOMAS STREET
NOBEL DECLASSE
IVES TORERO
AER MANILA SAJO
MANIFESTATION
ONASOLID CRADLE
RENE ORU HEREIN
CASA REP ASRED
```

81

```
DODOS TAPA STAB
OVERT ICED ORDO
ZEBRA ECTO DADO
ENTICE RARAAVIS
STATURES EST
BOG ERRED SAL
AHEM TOD CANOVA
TONIGHT BRINGER
SHERRY MAA AURA
RYE DICTA EBB
ALA EARSHELL
CALENDAR SLALOM
AVIV AGER OPOLE
SIZE GOAL TINGE
TEEN ENDS SNEAK
```

82

```
ORTS SARAH RPI
PEEP ONESEATERS
ELMY BACKSPACER
NIE BECK OGIVE
BARBARELLI STIA
ONION EARL ENL
OCTO HUSTON
KEY LANSING RAJ
TITANS WINE
PTR SLAB LAPAZ
OREN EXASPERATE
TIMON NARY ROB
FLAPDOODLE FILE
UBIQUITOUS HAIL
LYN LENDS ANAS
```

83

```
FLAG PAAR ERNIE
LAVE ERLE RAISE
OVER WOODPECKER
PARADISE AMEER
     NOTE TRIM
TWAIN GRATEFUL
ROGUE PRIDE ANA
ITEM SLATE GRIN
CAN READE WAGON
ENTRANCE IRONY
     ESNE SAND
SPACE BESSEMER
ANIMATIONS NORA
LAPEL ROSE ERIN
APERS ABET REED
```

84

```
OLDS LISI RECAP
ROOT IRED EXUDE
BOXOFFICE STRIP
STYMIES SECRETE
    PATH TRUE
GIUSTI GEMARA
ARN SMART DELOS
MACK ELIHU SIPS
UNLIT TBONE BEE
TIESUP SADIST
    HERO PERI
CAMISES ATTRACT
AMEND ALLTHEWAY
MEDEA KILL CARP
PRIVY APSE TYRE
```

85

```
SHAD BASTE LTRS
WINY ADHOC AHOT
AFTERNOONS VEDA
PIE OGRE TEASER
    MOLE BAMBI
OFLATE HATBOXES
SLAG ERIE TAU
CARIBBEANCRUISE
ARG LENT SEED
RYEBEACH CLASSE
    MUSTY ROOF
AHORSE DOMO AFT
ROUT NOISEMAKER
ALTO UNDID GILA
BAHN PEONY ONLY
```

86

```
HEEL CHAPS OKRA
ELLE RIVAL BEER
EAST ENARE LEAK
PNEUMATICDRILLS
    PETAL DAG
GSA DET NOMADIC
LORIES LOG TARA
ETONS SAD METER
ATAT LIP RODENT
MORELOS SET SEE
    REO SATES
POTEMKINVILLAGE
ALAS SPEAR ULNA
RENT USAGE SLAV
ROKS POKES HATE
```

87

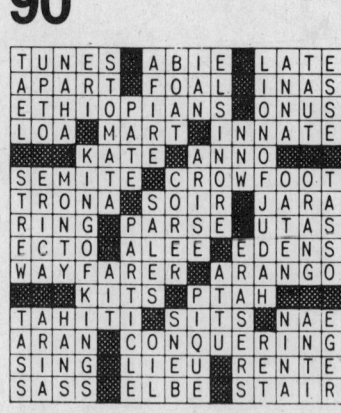

```
AJAR BREW GAGES
COMETOONE ABELE
THEBALLOT RATEL
ANN VEES ENDUES
    IER CREEP
ISSTRONGERTHAN
GETIN GORES NAB
OPUS HALED EDGE
TIM PALEA INGER
ABRAHAMLINCOLN
    LALAS SAE
ARETES TBAR ALA
NADIR THEBULLET
EMOTE RISETOTHE
WINED ENOL WARE
```

88

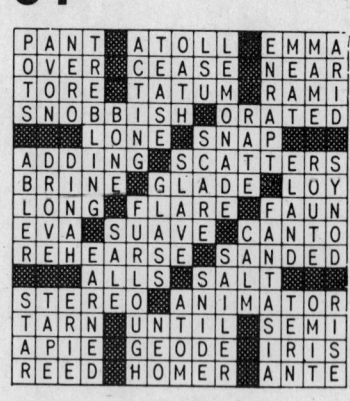

```
STEW ESTH SPARS
ARIA NERO ASCOT
MARX AGER YAQUI
EYEWITNESS LUGE
    OREO ENEMIES
INFRA SPARSE
NOOKS BALKY SBE
CARS DELAY SCAR
SHE JOLLY NEEDS
    REALLY CADET
EQUABLY FRAS
LUNT SANJOAQUIN
BINES COOL USNA
OPERA HURL AMOR
WURST ENDS BAND
```

89

```
ATTICA PCS SPAR
FEWMEN ROK TUBA
ONEACT IMITATOR
USER HAVEVIRTUE
LENES LATENS
    TOWITHSTAND
ARC LOGE NAIL
CARTOON WALDORF
KNEE IAGO SEC
GWASHINGTON
    CHANGE KEMAL
THEHIGHEST VASE
REVENGES APARTE
IBAR IRT BIDDER
PENS SES STAIRS
```

90

```
TUNES ABIE LATE
APART FOAL INAS
ETHIOPIANS ONUS
LOA MART INNATE
    KATE ANNO
SEMITE CROWFOOT
TRONA SOIR JARA
RING PARSE UTAS
ECTO ALEE EDENS
WAYFARER ARANGO
    KITS PTAH
TAHITI SITS NAE
ARAN CONQUERING
SING LIEU RENTE
SASS ELBE STAIR
```

91

```
PANT ATOLL EMMA
OVER CEASE NEAR
TORE TATUM RAMI
SNOBBISH ORATED
    LONE SNAP
ADDING SCATTERS
BRINE GLADE LOY
LONG FLARE FAUN
EVA SUAVE CANTO
REHEARSE SANDED
    ALLS SALT
STEREO ANIMATOR
TARN UNTIL SEMI
APIE GEODE IRIS
REED HOMER ANTE
```

92

```
MAJ BANTU AJAR
POLO AMOUR MOTO
ETAH BARRE AHEM
WHENJOHNNY DNA
    HOO LOA
ADAH JOHNBULLS
ADORN AVENS DEO
PLOT AMOLE DEAL
AIR ANELE PENNA
LBJOHNSON EAST
    ODA ARR
SHE LITTLEJOHN
WINS ADORE OBEY
INNS MOPER HOLE
GOYA BLEST NED
```

93

```
BOMB SABER JAMB
AGAR LLAMA ELIA
ARMA EASEL TALL
SEANCE ERETHISM
    COVE YIRR
EIGHTEEN GEORGE
MONEY RIGHT HIM
INAS BISES HOLE
TIR PAEAN BANTU
SALARY NEARNESS
    BIBS SVEN
GOURMETS EDITOR
ATTU ROPER BONE
STOP ROAST ARMS
PORT YPRES LEET
```

94

```
DAFT PALE BUELL
ORLY IVAN ENVOI
LIAR TAKECAREOF
COP CORE ETERNE
ENDMAN SARAS
    OATS BERTHAS
ASOKA CHOSE ONE
LODES HID TERNE
SOL TRICE RARER
ONEIRIC SERE
    NONOS CANNAS
CHOMPS PHOT DEN
HEXAHEDRON TOLE
ARETE DATE RULE
PANES EYES ISAR
```

95

```
FROSH ORALE CAB
LEPKE LILAC HER
ANTISEPTICS ARE
GAS SPEE TAROT
   TIOS SWAMI
TIARAS DIASPORA
ARMIN KELLY TIP
REAM CAROL TEMP
ING BARBS WHEEL
MEAGERLY HEARSE
  NEARS CAEN
LOSER CARP BAS
ABE INDEPENDENT
DOT SEIDE OVATE
SET HOMER TIMES
```

96

```
BAH STOP CARATS
USO HULA ANIMAL
RETAINER MOBILE
LATIN OFTEN GOD
 ARES OOO SONS
GEM STARTSUP
ARAB EFT MAILS
TALLINTHESADDLE
STEAL ENE ELBA
  DEPICTED EST
PALE ADO MECH
ENO CLOUD CLARO
CORRAL REMAINED
ODENSE SLAM DAD
SENSED EARP SDS
```

97

```
MOPS BANG WRAPS
ACUP ARAL RIVAL
CATECHIZE OPINE
ALICE DIAGNOSED
WANTAD SNAGS
  ESOS GETSTO
FERRETOUT DEPOT
ABO HARES ARI
CROPS PINPOINTS
TOTALS DOLL
  PIKES TALKAT
PRIEDINTO NURMI
OUTRE SOUNDSOUT
ESTER URSA ENSE
THORS EKES DEER
```

98

```
LUGER OGGI NASH
ASONE COON INCA
ZELDA ALOT EVEN
EDD GOLDFILLING
 SEALAB MILLE
DEMAND URANO
ASIS AGATE GAI
WATTAGE REDGOLD
SUH DOONE ALAE
 JALNA GOLDIE
 GOULD PRELAW
GOLDENSTATE AME
ERSE OFIT NATAL
ASEA TAME EDENS
LYNN EXES KOREA
```

99

```
ELMO DEMY SOLAR
BEAR EROO HAITI
RAINCLOUD OSMIC
ORMOLU SELF OME
  TEXASLEAGUER
RAM RENE ARES
ENAMI TSPS TIED
PANACHE OTRANTO
STIR ASIS ATETE
 PIED NIPS SES
EQUALJUSTICE
CUL MINI RAVAGE
HEAVE IDEALIZED
OUTER TEST CUTA
SEERS ERSE TRAM
```

100

```
PACO MOLAR SHEM
ILAY ABACA HERO
MISSTHEBUS OMIT
ASHTRAY IPSWICH
  EAR STAINS
FOURPARTY DUPED
INNS JAI ZEPHYR
LIL MANFRED ERA
MOOLAH FIB GRIM
SNOOD PEARTREES
 SCALAR ARE
CREAMER TWISTER
HINT AUDIOPHILE
ALEE CREDO AMAN
REDD HEWED MEND
```

101

```
GASP FATSO BARB
ARTE AXIOM EDIE
ELIA BORDELAISE
LORRAINE LITTER
  THAE MEME
CHARON CATERING
RILEY PANTS NOR
UNIE BONNE CASA
MGS TAKEA TOLET
BETTAKER TRALEE
 ICER FEES
ACADIA ROASTPIG
SPLITPSOUP ETAL
TATE IATRO RAMA
ASOR EXIST SHAD
```

102

```
AGILE SCADS
RENEGE BALLOT
PROGNOSTICATION
OILED COD WILLA
LEO SHOOS ION
ERG CHANNEL ENC
SEYMOUR EMBASSY
 INN IAN
GERMING STRANGE
ARE CERATES ERN
TRE DAVOS RET
TAXIS TEL LAVER
INEXPLICABILITY
TRIALS SALINE
STAND SATED
```

103

```
TOIL OWLS MOPAN
ALTO NEAT ALINE
LIES ELSA WEANS
COMETOTHINKOFIT
  REL DEI
CROSSING OSPREY
LOS SVELT HOUSE
ADIT ETUIS ASTA
SEEIT SEEPS SER
PORTAL DROOLERS
  NEE ONA
WHOSKIDDINGWHOM
HARTE GOOF YOKE
AMEER ANTE EMIT
MELTS READ REES
```

104

```
HAREMS BISHOPS
HABITUE ASTOLAT
ANIMALS SIAMESE
IDLE ETNAS EASE
LIE EEL TIP
SENT WRATH NEVE
REELECT ERASER
 TALE SMUT
GALOOT ALABAMA
EBON SIDON LANA
NAB DIV RIB
ELEC DETER TIME
SOLARIA NOMINAL
INITIAL EMULATE
SEASONS SEMELE
```

105

```
AMIS CREEP JAVA
RINK RENTE URAL
NERI OMAHA LIII
ONELANE ECHIDNA
 LIEN RHEA
PALED DEEPENING
AVATAR LAIDOVER
SIP EMILE IRE
TASSELED SLEEVE
ANECDOTES OLDEN
 RACE IBID
PATAMAR NINEPIN
ATOP TAUNT REDO
COME EGRET LAOS
AMES SENDS YULE
```

106

```
FOAM CUTE ATTAR
ANTIDOTES FIRMA
TESTAMENT ALIBI
SNEERS ARR BEN
ODAS AZURE CUR
 ATON APINGS
WAGER ONE REARM
EMOTE MAN ELLIE
ABOUT SMU POSSE
RIDDER ERIS
TEE HADES ALES
SIA SOL SONORA
TORSO CASUISTRY
OUTER ANTEDATES
ASHES NARD REDO
```

107

```
ICHOR  ARS  JEHU
TAUPE FLOW ODAS
ARETE ATMO ADZE
    FATHERSDAYS
SISTERHOODS
ENTIRE    MAPPED
ADES   MINE AARE
DOAK WOTAN WRAP
ORLE HOST  PASO
GESTAE    REAMER
    BROTHERWORT
MOTHERGOOSE
AGIO IRIS  NOTES
TEEN EELS  OVOLO
HERE SSS   WIELD
```

108

```
LAPP TACKS  SIFT
ARAR ENLAI IDEO
MIRO ADEEM MOLL
BARBEROFSEVILLE
   IRON   OIL
SPITES GENDARME
QUAY EGAD ERIES
ULM  SALEP  GUS
ASBEN MARE HOSE
DESTINES ADORES
   ALE   SCUP
LONGLIVETHEKING
AGEE SERAI ICON
SEAR SLAKE NANA
TETE ESTER SLOW
```

109

```
CAPO  HATCH JACK
HOAX ORALE ALAI
ANTI NAMER VAST
PERDIEM AMPERE
   OILY  TRILL
ZANZIBAR TAISHO
OKIE EROS INTER
NEZ LECTERN ALI
ANEMO STAY SILO
LEDOFF ELECTRON
   STEER BROW
FRAYED GROWERS
DREI TUILE ALOE
DISC OCREA GLUT
TOTS FETED ESTA
```

110

```
HAREM AMINO TMP
AVILA TONOF IAL
TALKSTURKEY ORE
SLEEKENS LOGGIA
   IDEES ROAST
MARINA  PLEB
ALONG TRIO BRAG
ROAD LATEX LETO
MENU OREL CEDED
   LAGO CARONS
TAEGU TALON
HONEST NOTARIES
AND TURKEYSHOOT
NEO RAILS TANNA
ERR ONDES APASS
```

111

```
CAPP CESS CRASS
OGLE LANE REMAP
REENTERED OVERT
SEATOFLEARNING
ESTHETE  TIES
   ESS VIM ELAH
ABOUT OVEN OLE
BLUSH ETE EMOTE
LES ERNE AESOP
EWER IDS ERA
   OBIT EDENTAL
HALLSOFJUSTICE
PARLE ELECTIVES
ARLES NICE MAIN
DIORS DPTS ETNA
```

112

```
SASA EPHAH OILS
ABUT FRORE XVII
XYST FINAL EYES
SQUEEZEPLAY
USU STE BLEACH
PEEWEE TOOK DUO
ASHY PROXY JET
AEF LIZ DHU
OWN ALATE ASTO
DON RENE RENTAL
SWATCH SOL MUD
BEACHCOMBER
GOGO VEERS ENID
OXEN RESET ATNO
BYRE ESTES USES
```

113

```
SPAT SCRAM FRAP
TOLA OLIVA PUCE
ALOG RATER ABCS
BOTTLENECKS BET
   AILS STEEL
HOLILY DEMURRER
AVILA BELA INRO
NET CRETANS EAU
ORTS EDEN PACTS
ISLANDER BECKET
   LETUP PANT
PIN NECKANDNECK
IDEA RUNIN IVAN
SECT CRONE NILE
ASKS HEXED ELKE
```

114

```
HOWL KENOS WHAT
ALOE IRADE IAGO
SINGINGTELEGRAM
HOTAND SUDS MRS
   TIES MOTTO
SWEETSUE MEANER
AHA STIRS SPIRA
NEST TRA AZOV
DRYAS SEUSS EDE
YESMEN DETERRED
   TOROS RIRE
ARR IDIO FURORS
THESOUNDOFMUSIC
LEEK LEILA NEMO
ITTY ESNES SLEW
```

115

```
CALIN  REGAL
PARADE ELEMIS
RANCHER SILIQUE
END RAE CTS UNA
MAYA LIBRE JOTS
AMISS DRU SURAT
PASSEE ABSTAINS
DEPRESSIONS
SPANIELS CAIQUE
PENTA DIS STURM
EADS POETS AISE
ANY PAR AIN CUR
RUBEOLA BLACKLY
TURNED ALTHEA
TASSO  TYLER
```

116

```
PEA SALON ARID
ANNS TIARA MULE
CONTRADICT ABEL
SORE CHASTISE
   ETAS ELLEN
GRAINY SIA SPA
THEMAINSTEM TEL
RAPS DAR CELL
ENE AMICABILITY
TAL LAC TENONS
   LIANA EYAS
TRANSITS NUDE
HENS PIONEERING
ANTE LORNA EAVE
NAST ENTER LYE
```

117

```
SLAB STOOP COPE
CADI HEDDA OVUM
ABERRATION MACE
PELEE SCRAMBLES
ELEMIS  MAI
   ENTERTAINER
SKIS ODER NEVER
AES SAGGARS IAL
BEANO ELIA ALMS
PREFERENCES
   GAS ENTRAP
MAELSTROM TRIGO
ACRE HELICOIDAL
CHIC EDEMA DEME
HEST RESIN ERAS
```

118

```
POTOMAC PALATAL
ALABAMA EPITOME
REMAGEN LAPALMA
TAPS BAALS SDAK
OTE VARNISH ANL
FERMI STS OLLIE
   OSSIE AWAITS
CHINCHERINCHEES
RONDOS ONEOR
ONCES LOC MSGRS
SOL EDOMITE AET
SRIS JUSTA AMAR
LANOLIN IPANEMA
ERELONG NEGATED
TYRANNY GROPERS
```

119

```
LUCI  ACME   LOIS
OPEN  TREES  IPSO
CONSEQUENT   PEEL
INSTRUCT   RAINED
    AGEE  MOLDS
ERATO  SPAL  PEEN
TENETS  AILS  SEP
ANIS  PRIDE  CAVE
SIM  ELAN  ROAMER
 GARMENTS  ALERT
  LOINS   TATE
AFFORD  NEPENTHE
BOAS  OVERANDOUT
BART  RIVER  ARNE
ALMS   PEST  REGS
```

120

```
HARUM  DAME  SLAP
ARENA  AVON  TICO
ENFIN  GOALPOSTS
COTTONGIN  ALLOT
   FEED  STEERS
 GABLER  GEE
DOLLAR  GUARDIAN
ALBUM  BAN  FANCY
MISTAKES  MADAME
    NET  NOMORE
LUNACY   SAKI
ENOCH   STROLLERS
ATTRACTOR  IONIA
SIRE  AERO  ALIVE
TEES  DREW  SAFER
```

121

```
APOLLO  ORGY  ABE
ARGUED  PEREGRIN
FERINE  OBERLAND
CESS   CREA  ARAS
EOS  IOTAS  DATO
COSMODROMES  TEN
CLEARED   SPCC
OSSIAN   ARABIC
  ALTA  DIALOGO
BIN  SINKINGFUND
ALOW  FEINT  LOS
LOLA  INST  POOR
LIEABEDS  BENGAL
ALACARTE  APENNY
DON  ASOR  BERETS
```

122

```
FESTAL   BAHAMAS
ASPECT  LAMEDUCK
SCORED  ITERANCY
HAIRY  ASTRO  ROW
ILLY  PETES  DORA
OLA  DOSED  NEEDY
NOG  ELON   SOL
 PENNYPINCHERS
 YIP  NOLO   EHP
LACES  AGNEW  VAR
ETAT  ASPER  BENI
THB  PECOS  MINGS
SEASIDES  GUNGHO
INNOCENT  ANDEAN
NEATEST   MISSIS
```

123

```
JOGS  EBBED  HEBE
URAL  QUIPU  EXIT
MAMA  URGED  MAZE
PLAYFALSE  TIMES
    SITE  SWAP
ARF  LESS  OUTFOX
PUREE  QUARTERLY
ANON  QUICK  RAIL
CONGRUENT  MAUVE
ENTREE  GENU  DEM
   OUST  DASH
CRISP  EQUITABLE
RODS  STUPA  ZOOM
ABLE  BROOD  EDOM
WEED  JAINS  DEMY
```

124

```
ATTAR  LAB  JAMES
LOUSE  ODE  ORATE
TURKEYRED  UTTER
ARK  VANE  PRIEST
  ELECAMPANE
BOYISH  ONE   GRS
LUCE  TURKEYTROT
AZOTE  ZOE  SHAVE
SECONDBEST  OVEN
ELK  DOE  HALERS
  TALKTURKEY
ARCANE  ETUI  ASE
DOING  SHIMMERED
EMOTE  EEL  BADGE
SENOR  WEE  ORSON
```

125

```
HECATE  RAM  CATO
AGATHA  ALA  ADAM
CATHER  III  TIRE
KNAR  SUNG  RATON
 FIB  SCHOOL
SMALL  CATACOMBS
POLLED  TET  GALA
ESQ  DRESDEN  GOB
NOUS  AMA  REGNAL
TREATMENT  ELITE
  GUARDS   RAF
BEGUN  IDES  SITS
ASEA  OTO  MUSCAT
SPAR  DUG  OLEARY
TYRO  ESS  GASTAX
```

126

```
ILLS  OOZE  SHIRR
REAP  UVEA  PADUA
INVENTING  AGLET
STEWARD  LINGERS
   IRE  SENNA
SLUNK  MASTERFUL
CONG  GAP  ORDURE
OUT  DORIANS  EGO
TRIBES  EDE  GLEN
TELEPHONE  HESSE
  ALEUT   PET
ALIMENT  PORTAGE
MERIT  SURPRISER
INANE  EVOE  NINA
DONGS  TAMS  GAUL
```

127

```
TAHOE  CHAS  LAMA
ADOBE  HALL  IBAR
NOMEN  ALLOTMENT
GREY  ALLEVIATES
SEL  COLORED
  ININI  GNASHED
IGNITES  YELLOWY
MIEN      ATEE
ABSENCE  SHAKERS
MESSIER  TOWEL
  CRUSADE  SIS
RETREADERS  BUNT
SPEARMINT  QUITE
VEIN  ITOL  ULTRA
PELT  CERE  ABEAM
```

128

```
BATH  LIAM  OBEY
ECHO  LIBRO  NAPE
STET  ASIAN  CREW
THEWORLD  STAKES
  ALEE  SIAL
CRATES  THEFLESH
HIDES  GROUT  AHU
EMIR  CRIER  STAG
SEE  PHOTS  SCENE
TRUELOVE  GARNER
  ROLE  ARNE
SECEDE  THEDEVIL
EXEC  RAREE  NASA
TINT  ILIAD  EDEN
ATTS  CLOD  DERE
```

129

```
COB   PSTS  KNOB
ONES  MOORE  KURE
CZECHOSLOVAKIAN
KARLOVYVARY  TNT
   EME  EDEMA
TAPROOM  SALAAM
ORRA  UELE  RINGO
PIA  ATLANTA  VIP
ETHER  TONO  FILE
DHARMA  SWELLED
  RAVEN  ASI
LUX  DEMOCRATIZE
ALEXANDERDUBCEK
MANY  GENUS  YOKE
BROZ  ENDS   NED
```

130

```
COIL  EARS  ELBOW
AGRA  WRAP  TIARA
BROTHERJONATHAN
SENHOR  PRISTINE
  SES  AUTO  LAGS
MAI  SORT   BYE
AIDS  WTS  RAFFLE
IDEATES  CAPORAL
LESION  CAR  XERO
  LEI  HEAT  EAN
PALO  THIN   OHM
ABERDEEN  ONEATA
THOMASJEFFERSON
TONAL  ASOF  BODE
IRANI  ZEUS  SNOW
```

131

```
TEALS  EARL   WITS
ANTAE  TREE   ATAT
GLASS  TACT   ISME
   ASSAYED   SNAP
 BELIE   DOCTOR
SALLOW  NEWEST
PREEN  DONNE  FAN
ORCS    ETC   FORE
TET  SPREE  MARTA
  REARED  DORMER
 PISTOL   EAMES
DICT   PISTONS
INCE  OCHA  EOSIN
STAR  STUM  RUPEE
HORS  ESNE  START
```

132

```
SPAT  TIARA   MSS
KEPI  ACRES  AETA
IRAN  MOATS  SLOT
DIRKSEN  RECTORY
 TEES   WARRENER
OCHRE   SECTOR
GOES  STATIONARY
POI  CLARION  NEE
UNDULATION  ATEN
 SATEEN   ARILS
ADMIRERS   FLIP
ORINOCO  PULSATE
RING  LOBOS  TSAR
TEDS  AMILE  ATTA
ADS   YSTAD  SOUL
```

133

```
CHOP  SALON  RAAD
HERA  CLARA  ENTR
IMAM  ROIST  ITEA
PINPOINT  INNING
  ELBE    ROAD
ZAGREB  CENTERED
ELL  OLSEN  SEINE
BLAS  EIDER  ROSE
REDAN  NEWEL  TUP
ANEMONES  SASSES
  PROW    STOA
MEDLAR  APOSTATE
ALOE  WAGER  URSA
DIOR  ALINE  RIAS
EARS  YESTS  NARY
```

134

```
ALBAS  ACTS  YALE
MIRTH  DHOW  URAL
MOIRE  AREA  LANE
ANGIE  MISTLETOE
 HARASS    HIT
ART  SLAT  EARTAG
BOSC   ELM  SEOUL
ANTA  PEACE  EYRA
SCANT  SOL  SAAR
HORDES  LIER  NEY
  YAP   INCUBI
STOCKINGS  MAMAN
LENA  KOHL  PRATO
ASON  ENTO  LILLE
GORE  DOST  EASEL
```

135

```
DESC  SPIN  TARA
AQUA  TODO  USERS
BURR  ANON  TIBIA
IMPART  CRO   USM
PIECE  CHEROKEE
WASTE  SEALANES
AGES   PILLAGE
YES  COLLATE  JAW
  CORVINE  TUNA
SHORTEST  DAVID
NIEUPORT  FIXES
ALA  OFF  MAXINE
PILAR  ISAR  CITE
SCENA  SIZE  ALTO
ARAL  HEED  BEEN
```

136

```
GATO  STRAP   CRI
ODOR  TRIPE  CHIS
YETI  RUMPUSROOM
ASHES  MEL  OUSTS
 ELLIPSE   USES
BURSAL    ISH
AVE  BITTEN  ECHO
NEAP  ARIES  DIOR
EARL  DARKEN  GAL
  ADS    ROTARY
CUTE   TWITTER
ARLEN  IAN  TABLE
FANNYBRICE  SUIT
ANAS  PETAL  ETNA
REE   EDENS  STET
```

137

```
LENS  DIVER  SINO
ERIC  ERASE  USOS
TACO  FASTIDIOUS
STERNE  SEND  BSA
 NECTAR    AAU
ATA  STOLL  SYSTEM
DAVIT  ASIS  SANO
AMASSED  DEPENDS
PART  OSLO  ATETE
TRILLS  ANCE  SOS
  CEE   ASTRAL
IFI  SEIS  ONAGER
CLOSEDDOOR  NATO
BOUT  GEESE  CLAP
MESS  EDDAS  ELLE
```

138

```
SLED   ALSO  EDAM
PESO  PRIER  NOPE
UNAU  LAVER  RUSE
DOUBLEBED  ROBED
 LABS    OFALL
BADEN   GURGLED
ALOUD  DOBIE  DOC
LOUP  POULT  RODE
DEB  SAUTE  LEMON
 SLIPSBY   IDEST
 EXCEL    SINO
COTTA  EATDOUBLY
AVAL  EDSEL  BROS
DELE  SAONE  LENE
INKS  TYPO  EWER
```

139

```
TOPOF  SWAP  SOFT
AMINO  WADI  CREE
WATERMELON  RATA
ARS  TALK  GRETEL
  BIRL   SPEWED
AMALFI   BLOND
DECAY  RAINDROPS
ALEC  BEING  IRAN
MARKCLARK  OVATE
  MOURN  AVENUE
 BRACES   BRER
POURON  NOIR  FPA
HUNK  OSCULATION
ALOE  SEAN  TILED
TENT  ECAD  ENEMY
```

140

```
BATE  BOLLS  JAVA
AARE  EPOXY  OVEN
HAIRRAISINGTALE
SAP  INNS  ATLAS
  SOIE    TARE
LOCATE  HOLIDAY
ATOM  MANES  NEO
COMMUNITYCHESTS
EEE  RILES  BETA
 STABLED  FARRAR
  NAES    MALO
PLAIN  SATE  HIT
SIMMERINTHECITY
TABU  ELITE  AVER
SROS  MOPER  DEME
```

141

```
LIMB  RATAN  IMAM
ABOU  ECOLE  NONE
MANS  CONCORDATS
BROTHERS  NOISES
 GLENN    SLAT
BEREFT  SPARERIB
APAST  SHEM  DONE
SIP  SATRAPS  USA
SCHL  LEEK  LAGER
OSSIFIED  DIGHTS
 BRED    LINER
EILEEN  DARKSIDE
STEREOBATE  ADIT
SEAT  RANIS  GENE
ERLE  SLANT  ORES
```

142

```
 CLODS    CAKED
 CHOPIN   OLIVER
TRIBUNE  GENESES
HAMES  EWE  DRIVE
AVES  PRINT  TREE
WAR  SAINTED  ERR
STARLING  NURSES
  HUNG    CAME
CAVORT  CANADIAN
ALA  SECANTS  DII
SLUG  RANTS  LEST
TILER  SEA  PEALE
SETSOUT  TAUNTER
 SETTLE   ARMIES
 DEEMS    SCANS
```

143

```
S P E W   J A M B A L A Y A
P A O L O   O R I E N T R E D
A S T A R   C A S S E R O L E
S H A N K B O N E S   S U L L
  U S I A   A R E S   S E I
O A F   N U B S   T H E R E
E P E R G N E   M I R E
S O U P P O T   A D O R I N G
    M O S S   M E G A T O N
T A S S O   N A S A   E M U
A L E   R A G E   O N E R
M L L E   F R E E F O R A L L
T O L L R O A D S   F I N I S
A R E A C O D E S   F A C E T
M A R M A L A D E   S N E D
```

144

```
N A S H U A   T I M T A M
D E S T I N E   U N A R M E D
R E S E L L S   M A N I P L E
O D A   L E T D O W N   L A E
S L U E   T H E R E   B E N D
S E L M A   E T S   B A S I E
E S T I V A T E   S O R T E D
    N E M E R T E A N
C I C E R O   M O N T R O S E
E V A N S   R I M   S A N T A
L A S T   G E N R E   T E R R
T N T   R U B E O L A   M I L
I H O P E T O   L O W T I D E
C O R O N E R   F I N A L E S
E S S E N E   E N S U E S
```

145

```
S A L A D   S L A B   N A S H
E R A S E   P O N E   I N T O
L I N E R   I O T A   G N A T
F L E A M A R K E T   H I L L
    I V E S   L A T E L Y
C H A S S E   I T E M S
L O G E   R E N E   A T H O S
A M A N I T A   A C H I E V E
P E R I L   R A K E   C R E W
    O L E N T   L A K E R S
B A R R E T   H A L T
A T O P   H E L I O T R O P E
S O U R   I R E D   I O N I A
I N S O   C I T E   C U L L S
S E E M   S E E D   S T Y L E
```

146

```
H O M E R   E T A L   A N N A
O R O N O   R H E A   M O A B
H A M A N   N E S S   E N V Y
O N E R   H E R I T A N C E S
    N E M O   E R L E   E L S
S E T   A B R I   E S E
O B O E S   A G R A   R O S S
F O U N T A I N O F Y O U T H
A N S A   C L I P   O S T I A
    M A C   N E A R   R R S
S S T   L E G S   R E M I
W H I T E P A P E R   A G R O
I A G O   T S A R   A L G E R
S M E W   E P I S   S I E V E
S E R S   D E N E   A C R E S
```

147

```
A R T I C L E   A L A M E D A
F E A T H E R   L I T E R A L
O N L E A V E   I G R A I N E
G E L   L E N G T H I N E S S
    A L L O Y   T A T
L A N C E   W R E N   F A D S
A D O R N S   E P I F O C A L
P I R O G U E   I N A R A G E
P E A C E F U L   G U Y R O D
S U S A   F R O M   L O I N S
    R P O   B A N T U
I N S P E C T O R A L   T I E
C O R O N A E   I C E C U B E
A M O U N T S   A R S E N A L
L A S S I E S   N E S T E R S
```

148

```
B I B B   A S P I C   B O N G
A M O I   P L A N A   E M E R
B I L L B O A R D S   S E R I
A D U L A   P R O B A T I O N
R E S O L E   A B O
    W I L L O T H E W I S P
C A R Y   M O R A   T S A N A
I B A   C O P A R T S   G O W
N O R G E   A C T A   D O W N
Q U E E N O T H E M A Y
    O T O   A V E S T A
B U S R I D E R S   E W A I N
A L E G   L O O K A R O U N D
H U G E   E A T E N   O R N E
T A O S   S N I P E   D A Y S
```

149

```
W H I M   T O S S   A B E N D
A I R E   W I L E   P I X I E
G R A N D I L O Q U I Z I N G
S E Q U I N   S U P S   L E A
    H E S   H E R   M E S S
A P H I D   F E L I N E
V A I N   W E D   G A L A X Y
E S E   J A W   S H Y   C I A
S T R E A K   L O T   S T I R
    G R E W U P   S T A I D
S M U G   S I S   D E R
T I L   A U N T   O R A N G E
E X T E M P O R I Z A T I O N
P U R E E   N U D E   U L A N
S P A R S   A M O N   M E T E
```

150

```
L O O M   M A R S H   P E O N
O G R E   E L I T E   A L T O
R E A D   A T L A S   R A I N
D E N I A L   E V I D E N C E
    T R I P   E T O N
P A R A K E E T   A T T E S T
E M I T S   C A S T E   T A R
R A V E   C A R T E   S A T E
I T E   C A N O E   S E P I A
L I T T E R   T E N E M E N T
    E N O S   P E R I
S P L A T T E R   T E N A N T
C O O P   E D I C T   O B O E
A L S O   N A T A L   L E S E
B E E T   E N A T E   E D E N
```

151

```
C A R D S   S O A P   P A C T
A B O U T   H O L A   I S L E
P E T E R P I P E R   C H A T
E T S   E A R S   T O K E N S
    F E T E   A I D E
S E M I T E   A C C E D E T O
A L O R S   G I R L   A L A R
M O U E   S A D I E   P I T A
O I L S   E G A D   P E D A L
A N D T A X E S   R A C E R S
    A C T S   M U R K
S T A T E U   D A L I   K E N
M A G I   P R E H E N S I L E
O L E O   L O C A   G E E S E
G L E N   E B A N   S E V E R
```

152

```
S H E   M I D A S   S T U D
L A X   I S O M E R   A E R O
A L I   S L O A N E   I N G E
V E T E R A N S   B E N D E R
    M E N   S P A R T
T H R E A D S   S T I P P L E
H E A R D   A M A H   A L A S
R A M A   A N E L E   T A N S
O V A L   B E A M   P R I C E
W E L D E R S   S A L I N E S
    G N A T S   L A C
S H A R E D   T R I C K L E S
P O L E   E L A I N E   O D E
A N T E   S O R T E R   S I X
N E O N   W E E D S   S T Y
```

153

```
A L I S T   A N T E D   P E D
S O T T O   L A U R A   R Y E
H U C K L E B E R R Y   O R A
E T H   T R E S   B I P E D
    L E S E   A B E L E
I M P A C T   C O N D E N S E
N O O N S   T A R A S   S E A
S N R S   M U F T I   S I N G
E D T   M E D E A   M A T T E
T O R N A D O S   M A G Y A R
    A B N E R   T A T E
A R I C A   O O N A   D A P
B O T   C O C K A N D B U L L
L O O   L U R I D   O W E T O
E F F   E R I E S   R I L E Y
```

154

```
U P P E R   O P U S   H A N D
G O O N E   D O N E   A R I A
H A N D M E D O W N   N E E R
    G A D S D E N   D A C E
S C R A P S   D E V I S E D
P R I M   E S S   T I N
R A C E   L O C A T E   R E D
A V I S O   A R R   S H O V E
T E N   S P R A G S   A S I A
    A T A   M O W   S I L L
P A S T E L S   A T T E S T
I N C H   M A N A T E E
N O R A   O P E N H A N D E D
E D E N   F O R E   S E I N E
D E E D   F R O W   E R A S E
```

155

```
SCAR  SERVE  PRAY
PONE  CLOAK  EASE
AMEN  ALONE  RIEN
SATELLITE  ATLAS
    WEEPS  ERI
REA  ART  STINGER
ELLA  SIXTHSENSE
BOIRE  CAR  ENATE
AGGRAVATES  TREK
GENERAL  ATT  SSS
    STE  SMEAR
TENTH  TELEPATHY
OGEE  TAPIR  PIES
LIAR  INANE  INRE
ASPS  OGLED  DEER
```

156

```
ENOL  SAUCE  TURF
DADA  ASSAY  EVIL
EVERYWHERE  RENE
METRO  ESPLANADE
ASSURE  EVA
   PERIPATETIC
MIBS  GNAR  REDAN
ADA  BOTREES  LIE
PELEE  ELAN  SENT
OMNIPRESENT
    DNA  SUREST
DENIGRATE  DACCA
OLAV  UBIQUITOUS
DUPE  RECUR  ALMS
OLES  ELSIE  LESE
```

157

```
SLIPSHOD  CALLAS
MEDICARE  ORIOLE
OVERONES  NELLIE
GYM  OGLE  TAILOR
   GPS  RTE  SSS
HOBOS  AVENGE
AHIT  TENDOLLAR
INDOUBT  ESPOUSE
RESILIENT  PFCS
   TERNES  BEFIT
SHE  EDS  COD
TOLAST  TWAS  PIT
AMORET  LANTERNS
REGINA  ELEONORA
TREATS  STANDFOR
```

158

```
ANTI  ALIBI  PLEA
TERM  BACON  HORN
TRIP  SPORT  ADIT
AVERSE  NEATNESS
RESOUND  SCAT
   BETAS  TRAUMA
BILATERAL  ASNEW
ARAB  RELIC  MIRE
BOILS  DESOLATED
ANDEAN  SPRIG
   STET  SOLOMON
PESTERED  NARINE
ALTO  ERODE  IDIO
LIAR  ISLET  AGON
MARY  DELLS  LENS
```

159

```
BORIS  GUSH  TOBY
EXACT  URAO  ALIA
ALBEE  PIGGYBACK
RIB  RAPS  SERVES
SPINNEY  THAI
   TOUT  PRETZELS
CREAM  ELIAS  AIT
AYAH  BLOND  AGRA
PER  QUITE  MILER
ASSAULTS  FARE
   GALE  DEJECTS
STRESS  OOZE  LEI
LIONHEART  SCARB
ORAD  YULE  TAWNY
BEMA  EKES  EDSEL
```

160

```
HITS  GORKI  SAKI
OMIT  AMAIN  CLIP
DATA  MARTS  IONS
   MOLIERE  TOLEDO
WOTS  BIRL
STALE  VOLTAIRE
TERRE  RILLS  NID
INIT  CITES  GAGE
PAP  IOTAS  LENIN
STENDHAL  MINED
   OLES  DONT
PRATES  HOUDINI
LAIR  ITALS  LIDO
OGLE  VOLES  ELUL
TESS  EPODE  SEND
```

161

```
DISAVOWALS  CAKE
IMPRESARIO  OBIS
SPRINTRACE  RUTS
EAU  DEN  IVANTHE
NICK  STERE
GREW  SAC  REARED
AMTS  AIRS  ALENE
GER  UMLAUTS  SAP
ENEAS  STER  ATMO
STFPUP  CRY  PREP
   PARCH  AALU
STEALER  ALI  ILL
WEAR  MAURITANIA
INRE  IMPALEMENT
GENL  APARTRIDGE
```

162

```
MAILER  CES  TAE
IGNITE  ORAN  ERN
MARTHASVINEYARD
ILE  CIE  DRAPES
SIRRAHS  ADIPOSE
TUAN  GNU  ATTA
EMIT  POINT  SST
   LOVERLESS
RBI  NORSE  AHME
ARME  LIE  REAM
TOPSOIL  VISAGES
ATLAST  IAN  ENA
THOUSANDISLANDS
AER  ANOA  TANTES
TRE  TBS  STEADY
```

163

```
WISP  GILS  MEDIA
ANNO  EBON  AMEND
RAID  NEVE  LIVRE
ENDO  EXALTATION
SEEFOR  BLAT
   SNARL  RESUME
EXPEL  AERO  PROA
DELAYER  OCTAVOS
ENOL  NEMO  ENATE
NOTSAD  ADANO
   BOOK  SOFTER
HIVEOFBEES  OATH
ADEAR  ESTE  XRAY
YEAST  ADAR  EDAM
SALTS  HOLT  NICE
```

164

```
HEATHEN  BRACE
RANCHERO  ROLAND
ONTHERUN  AVENGE
AGREE  DANCE  TIP
SEED  BIGOT  GINA
TRE  RATED  DICER
PERE  STARLET
   WHELK  ENTER
THERISE  SETH
REACT  SAONE  SAP
ANTE  AMPLY  MERE
DEW  STELA  BASRA
EVADES  ORIENTAL
DEVICE  MINDSEYE
REATA  BASSETS
```

165

```
FOOL  ANENT  HOED
AGRA  FOLIO  UPTO
TEEM  OUSTS  MARC
HELICON  ETOILES
NIL  RECD
PARADISE  MEONCE
AMIE  SEMS  ARIAS
GIS  SHAMEON  CPT
ANEST  TERN  THEE
NOROOM  TEETHERS
   FOOL  MAE
ALCALDE  METWICE
MOOR  ITSIT  OMAN
OTIS  SHAME  ONME
KILO  HEXER  LOPS
```

166

```
GARB  BERRY  BALD
AMOR  AROAR  ARIA
OBOE  RIOTS  REDS
LIMERICKS  TRASH
   DEUS  NIKE
STREAM  ACONITE
HEARD  FAKE  SLOP
EAT  ERASERS  IDE
ASEA  ELKS  EVADE
FEDERAL  BRADYS
   RADA  CAVU
BATON  PRETENDER
OLES  DAYAT  TOTO
AGIO  AROSE  ESTA
TALL  OTTER  DEAD
```

167

```
DIGIN   CPA    NADA
IRADE  ILL   CIVIL
BATES  TAL   OPERA
QUOTATIONMARKS
  ING  MADCAPS
   RUB   AMA  TEA
JAPAN  GUTENBERG
ATOMS  ORE   ILEDE
CONSCIOUS    OASES
KIT   AND    INC
   BRITAIN   KEA
INVERTEDCOMMAS
NOONE  RIA   EARNS
NOTED  MEM   SITES
ONES   SUE   SLOWS
```

168

```
BAAL    COKE   RAPT
ASSAI  HAIL   IRAE
KOHINOORDIAMOND
URE   VIR    BASED
      ASE  SSE  ELY
ASPADEASPADE
SHAPE  HEM    EGAD
KIWI   CRUDE  RAGA
ANNS   RAN    TIGER
   HEARTTOHEART
SPA   AWE    AAR
LUXOR  RHO    FLA
UNIONLEAGUECLUB
STOP   AXLE   SHADE
HAMS   POST   EXIT
```

169

```
FOLIO  RAJA   SHAM
EVANS  OREL   TULE
WASNT  OCRA   OLLA
   HOLYTHURSDAY
   VERY   SMOG
ALTARS  HAIRYAPE
SORTS  BALSA  GEM
SOIE   TOLET  SATI
ANA    BROOM  VOTER
MYDREAMS   LEPERS
    EAVE   MARR
  EASTERSUNDAY
STLO   RAPS   ANIMI
STAR   SNEE   NOMAD
WENT   EGER   TSARS
```

170

```
NABE   SET    SEN
ORAL   TAR    ORURO
DELAWARE   RAPOSA
SALTER  ARISTATE
   ESTATE   EIDER
HEART   NEVADA
INK   ELIDES  LIMP
LVI  RAM  RIT  DIE
TYNE   VASSAR  END
  TOATEE   USAGE
SABER   ELDEST
OVERRIDE   STRESS
LEANED  COSSACKS
SNARL  TIA    TRIG
LYE    SLY    HUNT
```

171

```
FABLE  MYTH   BARS
IDEAL  ISEE   URIS
LOAMY  NEAR   RAGE
MRSASTOR   COY
    IER   PUMMELS
MISCUE  PALAEMON
UNARM  SOWER  POE
STLO   SILLS  NITA
SOT    AIRES  ONRED
ETEOCLES   BLEEDS
LONGRUN   CRY
   LER   MYRMIDON
RABI   IVOR   POOKA
AMON   AINU   UNLIT
PING   NAYS   SATES
```

172

```
ARCA   MADAM  CRAB
VIOL   AROMA  YOGA
EVIL   DEGAS  CLUB
CELEBES    SHELLEY
   GOG    SERA
ROSEBOWL   DODGER
AAL    SOILS  SERGE
ITIS   DRAMA  SORA
LECHE  EMITS  OER
SNEEZE  ATLASMTS
   TRAP    ARE
COLLAGE    SNICKER
ASEA   RABAT  TARO
PLAN   ELEMI  OLIO
POND   SEEPS  REEF
```

173

```
BIGNAME    CALDERA
ACAUDAL    OVERRAN
SIGNORA    PENANCE
ALEC   LINER  MIEN
LYDIA  SASSY  EDT
   OLD    BEECH
CAT    GUEST  LAMIA
ALAMEDA    ICELAND
MINOR  RECAP  PAD
   PITON    WET
ACC   ASFIT  DAMEN
DLIV   WADES  HEMO
HAVANAS    PERIDOT
OREGANO    IMITATE
CATSPAW    DEVILED
```

174

```
CHAP   METRO  TIFF
HULL   OTHER  ARAL
ISLA   URALS  NONO
CHICANERY  AGNEW
   ART    SOMME
PONTIAC    NOBLEST
IRAE   ION    NOONTO
NIC    UNLUCKY  FED
GERUND  TOE   MIRA
SLENDER    TYRANNY
   NEWER    SAT
LATER  HIGHJINKS
AMOR   HANOI  SOLO
MIRV   ESSEN  SIAM
PETE   WHERE  ERNE
```

175

```
SWAM    SATI   PISH
KALE   ATTIC  UNAU
URSA   NAOMI  EGGS
ATONETIME  BROOK
   TSAR   TEUTO
ADIT    LABRADOR
GNOME  GABBY  TIO
AGUE   SAILS  PILL
REB    SPIRE  CAMEL
ALLROUND    USED
   EARNS   SALT
PETIT  TIMELIMIT
AXIS   TIMER  MARE
TIME   EMILY  ELAN
ATES   LETT   SONS
```

176

```
MAGI   PEALE  ABCS
ICON   ATRAS  PEAT
GOLDILOCKS   HARD
SUDANI  LEOTARDS
   ENT    BARREN
CINE   LAMS   RIGGS
ALB    WARP   RETOOL
RIOTACT    PATELLA
VOYAGE  RIPE  DDT
ENSUE  HEST   ODAS
   TRAUMA   ARI
REINSURE   OMEGAS
ALOE   GOLDFINGER
MENS   INDIA  SERO
PEAS   ESSEN  EROS
```

177

```
MIGS   ABLY   ESTER
ALEC   CLOE   SHAVE
GETACROSS  RAKED
OFAPIECE   OPENS
OTTER   OSAGES
   CUTUPS   DOCK
ACK    UNITES UVEA
HAIRSET    COPPERS
OSLO   ATTIRE ROE
YELL   SLEETY
   SLAYER   TORTE
MATSU   RUNOVERS
UNION   NAMENAMES
GAMUT  ACES   TIME
STETS  BEAT   ETAS
```

178

```
  BABA   TAM    BEAD
SOILS  EMU    AARON
TORAH  SOS    STERE
ALEC    STRIPTEASE
GASKETS    CAEN
   ODE   PHIS   TAT
ALOUD  PAAR   HERO
SEXTYGIRLSSEXTY
IVES   ANIL   HATES
AYN    ELKS   LAD
   AXEL    NEGLECT
TOPBANANAS   IDLE
AVAIL  MET    ONION
BENET  PAT    RECTS
NESS   STY    ORTS
```

179

```
GENIAL  AMAZED
A AMILNE CORONET
BRILLIG TRIESTE
ANTE SAMOAS NRA
CIT LETONS BAAS
USEDITEM SCARCE
SHRIFTS ODETS
ATE DNA
STADE DEVIANT
OWNERS DECEMBER
BEAM ASAFOX APE
REN PRUNER STHN
ADIPOSE NOTATED
SLAPPED SUNDEWS
ESSENE ESTERS
```

180

```
GOOF SAFE AFAR
OMNI FELIS BILO
LEER ITERS SRAS
FIREPLACE POESY
ALEE SPIRE
AFRIT FIREBALL
SLIME FADES TIA
CARS EINES HEED
AMI ACRES BARGE
BONFIRES SENSE
GAMUT SANG
SOLES RAPIDFIRE
EMIR SALON IDOL
RANI APART REDS
FREE ESNE ESSE
```

181

```
FISHING ASPALE
INCITES ARCADIA
DEAREST BEAROUT
START MISTS
MALONE HIST
SAC TETE TEMPER
KNUTE AMAS ORNE
AGRA ERODE NIDE
TOLL RYND DYNES
SLEEPS ILIA TRE
AWOL SCENTS
FALAS NIPAS
SHOWIER LEVANTS
REHONED ERECTED
INSETS ASSERTS
```

182

```
CARTA PLUS AFTS
OLEAN RANT PRAY
DAILYNEWSPAPERS
INK OSS ELLES
ARRS STIES
SUNLAMP TENSPOT
ALOOF AMORE ERE
UNIT TSARS LEAN
CAN PASTY PICTO
ESTOILE TURKHEN
ENOLS ERSE
FREUD ALB IWO
VIEWSANDLISTENS
ANSA RODE MISTY
COTY KNAR ASTOR
```

183

```
METS DREAM SAKI
OMRI RIATA TRIN
LIEN APRILFOOLS
DRAGOMEN ARRANT
SUDAN EPEE
MOULES ARRESTED
ARRAS SCROD HAO
FAIR STROP HERS
INN HIRER PEALE
AGGRADES GESTES
HELP CHOIR
CATICE NOONTIME
PRANKSTERS ACID
AULAE ARAT TARE
SMELL GALS ELAN
```

184

```
AFAR JEST DOFF
LURE OFTEN IDEA
BLACKSTONE RIND
ALBERT PORTENDS
SALE REOS
MOSLEMS INTEND
BASES MUDDY NOR
EGAD DANES ATTA
GIG PISUM SCREW
SCENES PANTHER
EARN LIRA
BLACKOUT COEVAL
RENT BLACKMARIA
IOTA ELOPE NANS
TSAR OSAR SITS
```

185

```
LALA WAAFS DOLT
ABOU ATRIA EMER
MATTERHORN MENO
HORSEANDBUGGY
CSA RAN AERATE
AURA WAFERS SHS
BRIMS ELATH
FOOTBALLCOACH
IRANI FRAYS
AHU ATAXIC ENDS
CASSIA SHE TEE
QUEENVICTORIA
UNDE INARTISTIC
ITUP ADMIT LALO
TSPS NIPAS ASIS
```

186

```
SPLAT WOOL EDAM
LEASH ALAE ARNO
ONTHEALERT GUNS
ONE ALLA TARGET
PIRATES SERES
TEE OKRA TAN
SPOOR FREESTONE
PAUN SONAR IRIS
ENTERTAIN SMELT
EGO EELS BEE
FATES REEDING
SADDER JATI NEE
EGAD ADAMANDEVE
RATE GOBI TAPES
FRED ERSE OUTRE
```

187

```
ALOOF SMUT NEON
BAKER MENU OTOE
ENERO ANAX MAZE
DAH ZEST ELATED
REDHANDED
STRAND LOOKINTO
IRAN ALTOS CORR
XYZ AES VAG
ESOP IDLER MEGA
STRADDLE ETAMIN
NAYEPAISE
AMATOL ARNE NEW
JOSH LATE TRAVE
ANTE ISHA SIZED
ROAR CAYS EMIRS
```

188

```
AROW PANDA DRUB
RAMI AVERS RARE
EPIS DEMOS ESSE
ATTHEDROPOFAHAT
FRET PRIM
ACCORD GETGOING
GOERS MADE FROE
HUD RABID AWN
ARAB IKON GETIT
STRIPPER DURESS
THEA PERE
DROPINTHEBUCKET
RASA ERIKA TIRO
AJAR REFIT OLIO
MART SEINE ROCK
```

189

```
SLOGS BUTCH
SPEWING HIGHHAT
THANMEETSTHEEYE
REV PARRIES RWS
EREB DEANS SCOT
WEIRD NMS ATHOS
SNARLUP SPEED
THICK PEREZ
AHMED GORILLA
SWEAR POI LEANS
HALS BURSA DFDT
AKU PUTSONE ERA
PERSISTENTRUMOR
ENCORES SALAMIS
SHOOS SEWED
```

190

```
SCONE STH FUAD
PHLOX ACRE ONME
LODGE PRIMERIBS
AIM CAPELIN CIE
SCAT DEAL SHOER
HENRYJAMES ORNE
AMOR DEFUNCT
FICHU MASSE
TANTARA LIRE
ALSO NIPANDTUCK
ULTRA ROTA ORAN
TAA GASSERS ATE
OWNERLESS IMETA
GATS TAUT GOULD
SYST ELM HOSES
```

191

```
PAJAMA   OUTCAST
LEADON   ASHANTI
ARILED   ARMENIAN
NOLI  SIN  BASTE
    BLOCKHEAD
BAMBI  ELONGATE
ALIEN DEED  AVA
LORDED   OFPREY
ENE  ASST  IRONS
DESECRATE LOTTO
   GOTWITHIT
REIGN CEE  RAZE
AARDVARK XRATED
GRAYEST  ENCORE
ANNEXES  RATION
```

192

```
SLAW BASK  BIPED
LARA UPTO  ENLAI
OTIS REAP  ALORS
THEHUNDREDDAYS
SELENE  KILN
      IDES REDDER
AMIDO BANG  SITE
SEVENCOMEELEVEN
IGOR ONOR  LASSO
NARROW  SODA
     INES ONSALE
NINEDAYSWONDER
CONGO NUTS  ALAN
FONDU TRUE  RAPS
SNOOT AIDS  LIST
```

193

```
CLAMS  SCUT  BOLE
HORAE  COME  RUIN
ASANA  URBANIZED
TENDS  BOO  EDENS
      ROMAN CULLS
PATINA  ELATE
ORAL NATURE  BUD
MCMLXXI MERCURY
ESE  ECTYPE HYDE
     ABASE RHESUS
BERET  AHSIN
AURIC WRY  NIMBI
BRASSBAND GLAIR
ELSE  AVER ELITE
TYES  REDO DELES
```

194

```
TACO SPAD  SCAUP
ARAP HERE  HANSA
BARE APES  ORDER
HANGBYATHREAD
BOOBS  ROTS
SHINDY LONESOME
WANES MAYOR  VAN
EVE  MAKER  ENT
DEE PANED  PARTE
EARRINGS DOLLAR
ONOR  BIOTA
ENDOFONESROPE
AROMA VINH  OPUS
GREEK ENNE  NERO
ASSNS SAYS  ADES
```

195

```
BOSC TARR  HOSES
LENO AGIO  ASIDE
ENOW SEACAPTAIN
BOWLES  ARSENES
BICEPS  IBA
TALLULAH SULFAS
AMOY LOPER  RIT
TAW SEATING OME
UNE KRUPP  KNEE
MARTYR UPSTATER
ELA  TAKEUP
EARNING ARROWS
GROUNDLING IRAE
LIVRE ISEE  ECCE
IDEES BORN  SHOP
```

196

```
CAFE ARABS  MEDE
IRON POILU  EARL
TART PORKBARREL
EMERALD  SLINGS
SEXES  LIEN
BAHAIS BESPOKEN
ETATS DEATH  OLE
VID MEANS  ODE
AMO NEARS  LIKED
NEWWORLD SITARS
OBIT  DENEB
BABOON OVERUSE
SILLYGOOSE ARUT
FREE UNDER  TREE
SEWN ERASE  EATS
```

197

```
AMOK BEE  UPKEEP
MIMI OAT  SIENNA
EDEN ORTHOPEDIC
SING KNEE  EPODE
SAKE  IPSO
GLACIER GRINGOS
REMOTE THENERVE
ARAN PIETA  SOAR
MOISTENS CAPOTE
PINCERS SHIRTED
INST  AMMO
ATTEA AIME  MOST
COUNCILMAN INTO
TRACES ART  SCAB
HONEST MAS  EERY
```

198

```
PAW FAILS  CHUAR
ANI INTERCHANGE
RID RESTORATION
ITER LOO  INTONE
SARACEN  ESNE
ZED INTERCOM
PELEE ENTAL  HUE
EVAS MELEE  MAST
RES TILER  CARTE
INTERSET  COY
LAUD TROOPED
OREADS SEE  RAVE
PUTTEESTRAP PAT
INTERSPERSE ADE
STARS AMEER  SER
```

199

```
EPIC FLAG  ASSET
SODA RENO  TETRA
POINTOFNORETURN
HONESTABE  SMOG
MEET EDT  PRY
CHASM  CIRCUS
LIT URN  ANITRA
ORIGINOFSPECIES
DECOCT EOS  MAI
POETRY THEMA
MOM NAY  DUET
APIN CREDITMAN
TELEPHONENUMBER
CREEL NONE  ELBA
HARDY EWER  REST
```

200

```
CACHE STAG  CRIB
AFOUL ERIA  HIRE
SINGLEWINGBACKS
URGE SEPT  ROOST
SEA KARL  MASC
LEU EVEN  HIT
THEIR MAIN  SEGO
HOMERICLAUGHTER
ALPS RILL  NASTY
IDO TAXI  CAM
ROOK ANAT  MAN
AGIRL KNOT  SACO
DOUBLEACROSTICS
DEMI TRET  SANTE
ASST CASH  TRESS
```

201

```
MEAD TABS  CRONE
ALSO HOOK  HAVES
JOHNHENRY INERT
OPENEYED NORIA
RENAN  ENSOUL
BARRET  TODO
TAJ INESSE  OREM
SCOUTED TRUNDLE
PHEN MAILER  SIN
SEDA INNESS
OBLATE  URALS
TRALA DOLLEDUP
BAKED RINGABELL
ARETE ETTE  ELLA
RESOD SAOR  LAST
```

202

```
ITERATE  ACETA
MUTILATE BALUN
INCLEMENT AYANK
TIEL PRAISS  TIL
ACT CONMAN  LESE
TAE ANAEROBE
ETRES  LLARETA
EASTS  TRUMP
SHOOTER  ASPER
INDIRECT  UNE
TOWN AROGUE  TIP
OPE PRETAP  GATO
WILLA DELICATES
INLET  SIDETONE
TESTE  ASSERTS
```